Albert C. Ellithorpe, the First Indian Home Guards, and the Civil War on the Trans-Mississippi Frontier

ALBERT C. ELLITHORPE

THE FIRST INDIAN HOME GUARDS AND THE CIVIL WAR ON THE TRANS-MISSISSIPPI FRONTIER

Edited by M. JANE JOHANSSON

LOUISIANA STATE UNIVERSITY PRESS
BATON ROUGE

Published with the assistance of the V. Ray Cardozier Fund

Published by Louisiana State University Press

Manufactured in the United States of America
First printing

DESIGNER: Mandy McDonald Scallan
TYPEFACE: Whitman
PRINTER AND BINDER: McNaughton and Gunn, Inc.

Library of Congress Cataloging-in-Publication Data

Names: Ellithorpe, A. C. (Albert Chapman), 1824–1907, author. | Johansson, M. Jane, 1963– editor.
Title: Albert C. Ellithorpe, the First Indian Home Guards, and the Civil War on the Trans-Mississippi Frontier / edited by M. Jane Johansson.
Description: Baton Rouge : Louisiana State University Press, [2016] | Includes bibliographical references and index.
Identifiers: LCCN 2016005787| ISBN 978-0-8071-6358-0 (cloth : alk. paper) | ISBN 978-0-8071-6359-7 (pdf) | ISBN 978-0-8071-6360-3 (epub) | ISBN 978-0-8071-6361-0 (mobi)
Subjects: LCSH: Ellithorpe, A. C. (Albert Chapman), 1824–1907—Diaries. | United States. Army. Indian Home Guards. | United States—History—Civil War, 1861–1865—Participation, Indian. | United States. Army—Officers—Diaries. | West (U.S.) —History—Civil War, 1861–1865—Regimental histories. | West (U.S.)—History—Civil War, 1861–1865—Personal narratives. | West (U.S.)—History—Civil War, 1861–1865—Campaigns. | United States—History—Civil War, 1861–1865—Regimental histories. | United States—History—Civil War, 1861–1865—Personal narratives. | United States—History—Civil War, 1861–1865—Campaigns.
Classification: LCC E540.I3 E44 2016 | DDC 973.7089/97—dc23 LC record available at https://lccn.loc.gov/2016005787

The paper in this book meets the guidelines for permanence and durability of the Committee on Production Guidelines for Book Longevity of the Council on Library Resources. ♾

To my biggest supporter, my mom,
Belle Standifer Harris
(1925–2015)

While upon one of our daily scouts the other day we encountered the enemy's pickets. One of their number, more daring than the rest, made a charge upon one of our cavalry, crying out, as he charged forward, "here goes, boys for a *Fed, a pair of boots and a navy.*" He missed fire, and the next instant he went reeling from his horse, with a *navy* bullet through his head. These little encounters are of daily occurrence and keep up a constant school of excitement, a little dangerous but very instructive and beneficial to the soldier.

—ALBERT C. ELLITHORPE, *Chicago Evening Journal,* December 26, 1862

CONTENTS

MAPS AND FIGURES

PREFACE

Every few years a historian calls for a "new" approach or a "new" emphasis in their field of study. Some of these ideas fall on fertile ground and wield great influence. In 1976 John Keegan, a British historian tired of the traditional battle piece, examined combat from the common soldiers' perspective in *The Face of Battle: A Study of Agincourt, Waterloo, and the Somme.* His work led to a renewal of interest in common Civil War soldiers and their battle experiences. In 1990 Maris A. Vinkovskis influenced nearly an entire generation of historians when he called for a new social history of the Civil War. Both Keegan and Vinkovskis affected me as a graduate student as I studied the lives of common soldiers in the Twenty-Eighth Texas Cavalry and, with a nod to Vinkovskis, utilized census and tax records to develop a socioeconomic profile of the regiment. The latest summons is a call to "weird" the war.

Stephen Berry, the lead editor in *Weirding the War,* discouraged historians from revisiting the "tired questions" about the war and invited a focus on "new social types." Looters, war profiteers, prostitutes, and African American deserters were examples of these new social types. Emphasizing the diverse groups that inhabited the war years is a laudable goal and so is shining a light on probably the weirdest part of the war: the geographical area west of the Mississippi River.[1]

More than 150 years after the conflict, there is still a regrettable level of ignorance about the war west of the Mississippi River (labeled by historians as the "trans-Mississippi"). Many myths surround the war in the trans-Mississippi, a notable one being that "not much happened there." Yet the lead compiler and tabulator of Civil War actions, Union veteran Frederick H. Dyer, counted 3,101 military actions west of the Mississippi. That number, comparable to the 3,616 actions that occurred in Tennessee and Virginia combined, indicates that the western region obviously saw much military activity. Many, too, have the misguided notion that the trans-Mississippi was a convenient dumping ground for generals who had failed in other theaters. But historians are systematically demolishing this misconception, most notably in a recent book of essays entitled *Confederate Generals in the Trans-Mississippi.* A persistent rumor claims, further, that there are few surviving records that document the war in the trans-Mississippi. How many researchers have believed that assertion and gone on to create yet another study about the eastern campaigns? And yet, if historians dare to explore, they will find rich and, yes, "weird" resources about the trans-Mississippi.[2]

The writings of Albert Chapman Ellithorpe, a Federal soldier, are but one example. A Chicago businessman and inventor, Ellithorpe was a commissioned officer in the First Indian Home Guards, a triracial unit made up of white commissioned officers, loyal refugee Creek and Seminole Indians, and African Americans. The regiment served solely in Arkansas, the Indian Territory, and Missouri. Even here in my Oklahoma home, the very place where most of the regiment's soldiers came from, friends and acquaintances have expressed amazement that such a unit existed. And yet there was not just one but three Indian Home Guards units as well as several Confederate Indian units. Ellithorpe's writings are the most detailed account known of service in an Indian Home Guards unit. This is not to say that his writings are entirely satisfactory to a modern historian. One wishes that he had written of his interactions with Indian soldiers, but these men are rarely mentioned directly by Ellithorpe. His motivations are unexplained as well. Why did he accept a commission in an Indian Home Guards unit when he no doubt could have been accepted into a "typical" white regiment? But as his writings make clear, Ellithorpe was an unusual man, and going a different way may have appealed to him.

He never directly wrote of his attitudes toward Indians, but he certainly felt that the more "civilized" among them were much like white men, an attitude rather unusual for a white man to hold at that time. True, he admired the bravery of his Indian soldiers and wrote sincerely about their skills as counterinsurgents. As he explained to a Chicago audience, his own regiment was composed mostly of full-blood Indians, "yet they are educated, and when in their own country pursue the civilized avocations of life. Many are large farmers and heavy stock raisers. They are educated in their own language; they have books printed in the Creek tongue and in a very neat style; their schools are conducted in good order." The Cherokees, he wrote "have been undergoing a gradual change from barbarism to a civilized condition for over forty years. Nearly one half are as white as our own race, and speak the English language fluently. They are probably the most enlightened race of Indians upon the continent. The uninitiated would hardly think that he was conversing with an Indian, unless the fact was made known." He concluded with a statement that some Chicagoans may have found unbelievable: "From these facts you will readily see that, although we have an Indian brigade, yet its appearance of order, discipline, and soldierly bearing will compare favorably with white brigades."[3]

It is time that the story of these soldiers is told, along with other weird topics in Ellithorpe's writings. His journal, his twenty-three newspaper articles written for the *Chicago Evening Journal,* and his surviving correspondence do not reveal a glorious, grand war of Good versus Evil but instead a messy, complex situation peopled by real (i.e., imperfect) human beings. At times Ellithorpe tried to convey an image of a glorious war in his newspaper articles that were for popular consumption, but even there his basic honesty could not keep out uncomfortable, intruding topics. Political maneuverings for prized positions, corruption, and fraud were documented by Ellithorpe's pen. Masses of refugees fleeing the armies were regarded with both compassion and occasional distaste (depending on their loyalties) by him. Set-piece battles such as Prairie Grove are the subject of Ellithorpe's writings, but more frequent are accounts of the nasty and brutal guerrilla warfare of the border region. Rather than being repelled by this type of warfare, which would seem like a more proper attitude for a gentleman of his time, Ellithorpe participated with some gusto.

It is only fair for a reader to wonder about the editor's opinion of Ellithorpe. There is ample evidence of Ellithorpe's intelligence in his writings, his immense loyalty to certain individuals, his compassion for refugees, and his paternalistic desire to protect his soldiers from those who tried to exploit the vulnerable. He could also be self-righteous, egotistical, prickly, combative, and opinionated. In short, he was anything but boring. Take some time and journey into the weird world of Ellithorpe's life and his Civil War career.

Editorial note: Ellithorpe's writings were transcribed as faithfully as possible. His handwritten documents were relatively easy to transcribe, thanks to his clear handwriting and the good condition of his journal and most of his letters. Like many Americans of his day, Ellithorpe misspelled many words, but most of them have been left uncorrected to preserve the flavor of his writings. In some instances correctly spelled words have been placed in brackets to ensure that readers understand his meaning. Superscript numbers and letters appear occasionally in Ellithorpe's journal and in his correspondence; superscript letters have been changed to regular type to aid in readability. Standard editorial markings have been used throughout. Occasionally, lengthy paragraphs in his diary and letters have been divided to aid understanding, but many of the short paragraphs that appear in his journal have been allowed to stand. His newspaper articles have been transcribed as published. Because Ellithorpe broaches a number of themes pertinent to the trans-Mississippi that may be unfamiliar to readers, the editor has chosen to write lengthier chapter introductions rather than to consign complicated material to endnotes. Also, much biographical information about Ellithorpe has been included to place him in the context of his times.

ACKNOWLEDGMENTS

I first saw Albert C. Ellithorpe's journal in the late 1990s during a visit to General Sweeny's Museum of Civil War History in Republic, Missouri. It was opened to the entry about the Locust Grove skirmish, and my attention was immediately caught by the bold handwriting and the description of a fight just a few miles from my home. A number of years later, I found that the journal had been digitized as part of the excellent *Community & Conflict: The Impact of the Civil War in the Ozarks* website. While reading through the journal online, I made an impulsive decision to edit the document. Learning that the Wilson's Creek National Battlefield had purchased the journal as part of Dr. Thomas P. Sweeney's collection, I received permission from Deborah Wood at the park to edit the journal. The staff at Wilson's Creek has been unfailingly helpful, kind, and professional. On an early visit Alan Chilton presented me with numerous files of background materials and the surprising information that Ellithorpe had also written articles for the *Chicago Evening Journal* during the conflict. Deborah Wood also allowed me to examine the original journal and provided me with a number of visuals for use in this book. It is not an overstatement when I say that this book could not have been written without the assistance of the staff at the Wilson's Creek National Battlefield.

My employer, Rogers State University, gave me the precious gift of time by awarding me a sabbatical during the fall 2014 semester. Being allowed to concentrate full time on this project greatly accelerated my progress. Special thanks to Dr. Frank Elwell, the dean of the School of Liberal Arts, for encouraging me to apply for the sabbatical; Dr. Kenneth Hicks, my department chairman; Dr. Richard Beck, vice president of academic affairs; Dr. Larry Rice, president of Rogers State University; and the University of Oklahoma Board of Regents for awarding the sabbatical. Crucial assistance was also provided by Kelly Ewing and George Gottschalk at Roger State University's Stratton Taylor Library. From the "easy" requests for articles and books to the challenging reels of microfilm and one extremely rare pamphlet, Kelly and George processed my numerous interlibrary loan requests with promptness and total success.

The staff of the Kansas State Historical Society was helpful during a research visit and gave me permission to publish valuable materials as well as a wartime photograph of Albert from the Ellithorpe Family Papers.

Thanks to a grant from the Oklahoma Humanities Council: "This research was supported in part by a grant from the Oklahoma Humanities Council (OHC) and the National Endowment for the Humanities (NEH). Findings, opinions, and conclusions do not necessarily represent the views of the OHC or the NEH." The grant funded a crucial research trip to the Bizzell Memorial Library at the University of Oklahoma to examine papers of the Office of Indian Affairs.

The Charles Koch Foundation provided funding for the employment of Jason Riggs, a research assistant and now a Rogers State University graduate. Jason was given the mind-numbing task of scrolling through microfilm reels of the *Chicago Evening Journal* and the *Leavenworth Daily Conservative* newspapers and searching out newspaper articles in online databases. He cheerfully took on these tasks and discovered several previously unknown articles penned by Ellithorpe as well as much background data. Jason also accurately transcribed all of the Ellithorpe articles that he located.

Dr. Gary Zellar, University of Saskatchewan, proved to be extremely generous with his time. His articles about African Creeks in the First Indian Home Guards and his broader writings helped immeasurably. He assisted me by deciphering some of the cryptic citations in Annie H. Abel's books, exchanged viewpoints on Col. Stephen H. Wattles and Ellithorpe, emailed transcriptions of pertinent *New York Times* articles, and sent digital images of pages from the First Indian Home Guard Regimental Order Book.

Other people also provided aid: Sara H. Huber and Janet B. Croft at Bizzell Memorial Library; Mary Francis Ronan at the National Archives; Carley Robison at the Knox College Archives; Tom Mooney, curator of manuscripts, at the Nebraska Historical Society; Terry Zinn of the Oklahoma Historical Society; Crispien Van Aelst of the Illinois Regional Archives Depository; and Leigh Armstrong, for photographing the two surviving issues of the *Chicago Evening Star* at the Chicago Historical Society. John Emond served as my "legs" by making photocopies of various courts-martial and compiled service and pension records at the National Archives. Mrs. Jean Simons Zito, a direct descendant of Stephen Ellithorpe, an older brother of Albert, answered questions about the family's background and sent me an Ellithorpe genealogy book. Mrs. Sally S. Hutchinson of Pryor, Oklahoma, visited and documented Ellithorpe's gravesite at Chicago's Rosehill Cemetery.

Unfortunately, Albert's biggest fan, my mom, passed away soon after the completion of this manuscript. My mom, Belle Standifer Harris, was also my most important supporter. Over the years she spent countless hours accompanying me to battlefields and archives in spite of the fact that she was uninterested in the Civil War. Thanks to her support and encouragement, I became a professor and a Civil War historian.

Albert C. Ellithorpe, the First Indian Home Guards, and the Civil War on the Trans-Mississippi Frontier

CHAPTER 1

LIFE BEFORE MILITARY SERVICE, 1824-1862

[He is] a young man of superior ability.
—JOHN CARBUTT, *Biographical Sketches of the Leading Men of Chicago*, 1876

In Chicago's Rosehill Cemetery a government issued grave marker inscribed "Maj. Alb't Ellithorpe 1 IND H. G. Inf" stands modestly. Cemetery visitors probably assume that *IND* stands for "Indiana," but in reality it stands for *Indian*. How Albert Ellithorpe, an "Old Settler" in Chicago, a businessman, inventor, and adventurer, found a place in a regiment made up of refugee Creek and Seminole Indians is a compelling and fascinating tale. Although he was proud of his wartime service, it was just one of many colorful phases of his life, rather than the ultimate part, as it was for many veterans. His postwar life was nearly as exciting as the wartime years. From involvement in a sex scandal to the creation of elevator safety devises, Ellithorpe regularly made the postwar news in Chicago.

The cocks crowed, and "Old Towser" barked for the first time in six months when Albert Chapman Ellithorpe was born at 1:00 a.m. on July 9, 1824. His father, John W. Ellithorpe, a Massachusetts native whose first wife had died in 1809 after bearing four children, married Elizabeth Betsey Chapman one year later in Vermont. Born into a blended family in St. Albans, Vermont, Albert was the youngest of seven brothers and four sisters. In some ways treated as a pet, his sisters once dressed him in a colonial style suit and then with hilarity nicknamed him "The Old Man."[1]

Young Albert grew up on a three hundred–acre farm with a third of the property devoted to a thousand-tree sugar maple grove. Tapped by the family, the sap was used to produce the tasty maple sugar that provided most of the family's income. The industrious Ellithorpes also grew an impressive variety of food crops: beans, corn, potatoes, pumpkins, squash, and various fruits. Additionally, the women wove most of the family's cloth on a large loom, built by John and given to his second wife as a wedding gift, and made most of their clothing. As an elderly gentleman, Albert recalled with pride the nearly self-sufficient nature of his family, its abhorrence of laziness, and its expectation that all would fulfill their daily tasks. Pride developed in other ways too. Albert boasted of his maternal grandfather's service in George Washington's army and his father's military service during the War of 1812 at the battle of Plattsburgh.[2]

When Albert was seven, the family moved a few miles across the border to Caldwell Manor in the Lower Canada province, where an uncle already resided. Except for the loss of the splendid sugar maple trees, the Ellithorpes found the new farm an improvement over the old one. As the years of his youth went by, Albert attended school and exhibited mechanical skills. He recalled later, "I could do many things with tools that I noticed was talked about, and to me, in a flattering way." At about age eleven he accompanied his father to Belleville in the Upper Canada province, where his father superintended "the construction of some bridges" and answered his son's questions about the projects.[3]

At a young age, however, Albert became involved in a political issue. Although many of his contemporaries served in the Mexican War, Albert participated in the Canadian Rebellions of 1837 and 1838. Individuals desiring better government in the provinces of Upper and Lower Canada sparked the rebellions, which were particularly pronounced in Lower Canada, where the Ellithorpes resided. Albert made his loyalties known early by shouting "Damn the Queen" in a crowd while other boys cheered for the monarch. Even at this age, he showed a key feature of his personality: a willingness to express his opinion even if it was unpopular. Authorities confined Albert to a guardhouse, but they released him after a reprimand and a lecture on proper respect for the queen. In the fall of 1838 a number of Americans organized a secret society called the Hunters Lodge, and armed forays were made into Lower Canada. Three Ellithorpe brothers—John, Jed, and Albert—joined in the excitement as part of the Windsor Rifles. Fourteen-year-old Albert carried dispatches and participated in several military actions. At the battle of Odelltown, British soldiers captured Jed and Albert and imprisoned them. For about nineteen days the two sat it out in a fortress situated on an island in the Sorell River, but on an early November night several of the guards got drunk and left the guardhouse door unlocked. The brothers stealthily slipped past them and made their way back home. Albert "was a crippled, used up boy" but proud of his efforts to fight for a cause that in his opinion espoused liberty.[4]

Even during the rebellions, Albert planned to go westward and practice his skills as a carpenter and joiner. He would be similar to "a small minority of young men—ambitious, innovative, and self-directed—who pursued self-improvement with single-minded zeal"; the most famous of them would be Albert's later (and older) acquaintance, Abraham Lincoln. Many of these young men cut family ties, but Albert relied a great deal on his relatives in these early years. His older brother, Timothy, worked as a compositor at the *Chicago Democrat*, the town's first newspaper, and Albert decided to move to that village. Only chartered since 1837, Chicago reached a population of about four thousand by the time he decided to migrate there. Although a town of that size does not seem large to many Americans today, it was bigger than any place Albert had lived. The opening of the Erie Canal, with its New York City connections, in 1825 had helped increase investment in the Great Lakes region. Interest in the area was given a huge boost when New York City investors Arthur Bronson and Charles Butler speculated in land there, and further enthusiasm ensued when the state legislature again took up consideration of a bill to construct a canal. Completed in 1848, the Illinois and Michigan Canal linked the Chicago area to LaSalle on the Illinois River. From that point there were connections to the lucrative Mississippi River. Albert could hardly have selected a more promising area for growth. With later railroad connections, Chicago grew to 109,260 by 1860 and then swelled to 503,185 by 1880. The population continued to skyrocket, reaching 1,099,850 in 1890. When Albert died, in 1907, Chicago had surpassed two million in population, quite a contrast to the small town he had migrated to almost seven decades earlier.[5]

Albert packed his belongings and left Lower Canada in late February 1839. He offset the cost of his passage by working as a steersman on an Eric Canal boat. Fourteen-year-old Albert arrived at the *Chicago Democrat* offices on April 1, 1839. Bemused newspaper employees watched as the boy walked into the office in "a long, sheeps-gray overcoat of home manufacture in its entirety, except the buttons, which were of bone, black, and about the size of a silver half dollar. The coat was of the extreme Holland cut, the waist came in contact with the skirt behind, about the middle of the back and adorned with two of the great buttons. The skirt reached up behind within four inches of the buttons, a stiff collar, that barely missed contact with my small, English cloth cap, mounted on the back was a capacious 'Canuck Chappeau' or what we call a hood, about sixteen inches in length terminating at a sharp point with a red tassel about the size of a goose egg."

Settling in his brother's household, Albert "had a spirited conflict with myself as to the course I should pursue; whether to apply my energies to accumulation of wealth, or to acquiring a liberal education." Albert decided to pursue both but focused first on the practical matter of accumulating wealth. Initially, he performed odd jobs as a carpenter and gathered lumber to construct fanning mills. In the meantime he had shipped his tools to himself along with a fanning mill that he used as a construction model. Farmers used fanning mills to remove unwanted matter such as stones and dirt from wheat, oats, and other grains. Timothy noticed the lumber piling up in the yard, the construction of a workbench and a little workshop, and worriedly asked, "Albert, what are you going to do with that lumber?" Having been assured by his brother that the boy had a viable business plan, Timothy supported Albert as much as possible. Albert manufactured twenty fanning mills and made a profit of $360 from the venture.[6]

Agricultural work and odd carpentry jobs filled the warmer months, but Albert, Timothy, his wife, Emily, and her sister Kate set up a logging camp during the winter of 1839. Squatting on land that is now in the Bowmanville neighborhood of Chicago, they set up the "Vermont Camp." That winter the men cut cordwood for sale and received a lucrative government contract to supply wood to post offices and land offices. Beginning in 1839, Chicago dealers started to supply lumber across a wide radius. Although the Ellithorpes were local suppliers, some dealers developed ties to timber markets in Wisconsin and Michigan and developed profitable businesses. In the spring of 1840 the group moved to land claims obtained by Timothy and other family members in Kane County, west of Chicago. The tough job of plowing up the prairie commenced on the springtime days. Farming and logging were the work cycles for young Albert for the next three years, along with his odd jobs.[7]

Not all was work, however. Chicago experienced a growth spurt reflected by a construction boom. Wood frame buildings were mostly built, but some brick plants started operating too. Cultural and social avenues opened. Albert joined a temperance group and lectured regularly on the evils of drink. One of the great reform movements of the age, the temperance movement became quite prominent in Chicago from the early to mid-1840s. The American Temperance Society, the Young Men's Temperance Society, the Washington Temperance Society, and the Independent Order of Rechabites were all established by 1846. Albert started boarding in the spring of 1843 with the Brown family, who were, in his opinion, "cultured" people. Here, back in Chicago, he found employment in a shop where wagons were manufactured and repaired. Sales were challenging because poor roads made it difficult for farmers to travel to Chicago to purchase wagons. Also, the shop's owner, Mr. Perkins, experienced financial problems. At age twenty Albert used all of his personal assets to take out a loan and purchased the shop, leaving only $2.50 in his pocket. He got the business on a good footing, however, and sold it a year later in 1845. Clearly, Albert Ellithorpe was a young man on the make, and although he never ascended to the top tier of leadership in Chicago, he fit the elite's profile, which consisted "mostly of young, self-made men from New England and New York State, this elite dominated business, politics, and the professions and assumed leadership of the city's intellectual and philanthropic activities."[8]

Albert had long desired a more substantial education and took mathematics and language classes from Rev. William E. Manly, a universalist and a temperance supporter. Cutting his business ties, Albert stayed with a former customer in Iroquois County, Illinois, and taught thirty to forty students in a log school. Meanwhile, he decided to attend Knox College in Galesburg. He attended the Preparatory Department of Knox College with other "Young Gentlemen" in the 1845 and 1846 terms. Many young men present in the 1845 term chose not to return in the 1846 term, but Albert diligently persisted. He also continued teaching, this time at a Chicago school, where "he brought the ungovernable and refractory children to a state of obedience and discipline hitherto unknown, by his prompt and vigorous treatment of two or three of the rebellious ringleaders of the school."[9]

On June 19, 1848, at age twenty-three, Albert married sixteen-year-old Maria Louise Sammons. Like her husband, Maria was an early settler in Chicago. Born in New York in 1832, she immigrated with her family to Chicago at age six, but tragedy occurred fifteen years later when her father, Frederick, froze "to death on the Calumet River." The Ellithorpes' first child, Laura Maria, was born almost a year after the marriage, on May 13, 1849. Although Albert never attended school again, he made "use of every opportunity that presented itself, to betake himself to his books." He also returned to business by starting another wagon and carriage business and left it in charge of a foreman when he embarked on his next adventure.[10]

The news that gold had been discovered in California electrified the nation. Young, adventurous men interested in making money, such as Albert, were particularly susceptible, and like many, "he fell a victim to the gold fever." Albert traveled with an overland group that probably left in the spring of 1850. His young wife and baby daughter moved in with a wagonmaker (possibly Albert's foreman) and his family. "After a year of varying fortune in the gold region," Albert traveled home via Mexico to check on moneymaking possibilities and to seek more adventure. Sailing from Vera Cruz on the *Faustina*, Albert arrived home sometime in March 1851. After reuniting with his family, the young couple's second child, Mary, was born ten months later.[11]

Although his year in California and Mexico may not have been a great financial success, Albert made enough money to expand his business. Setting up at the corner of Randolph and Morgan, he partnered with Mr. Kline and manufactured "carriages ranging through all the styles, from the light open buggy to the heavy family and livery carriages." The company racked up sales of fifteen thousand dollars in 1853 and won a number of prizes and awards for their products.[12]

The carriage business, however, was not Albert's only venture. Sometime in 1851 he purchased rights to a limestone deposit "near Western Avenue." The limestone was first marketed as a building material and used in 1852 to construct the Second Presbyterian Church at the corner of Washington and Wabash. Not only did the stone assume an antiqued appearance after several months, but the material had "irregular streaks of inky blackness," giving it a singular appearance. Some in Chicago called it the "Church of the Holy Zebra." The distinctive building burned during the Great Chicago Fire in 1871, unmourned and unmissed by many. Because the stone was an unsuitable construction material, Albert advocated the idea of using it for street paving. In the early 1850s there were no paved roads on the west side of Chicago and only a couple of paved streets in other areas. Partly to advance the idea of street paving, Albert decided to enter city politics. Chicago was an ugly city when he embarked on his street paving idea: "Everything was covered with mud after soaking spring rains, and there were no paved streets or sidewalks and no sewers. Nor was there any drainage . . . Roads in and around the city remained impassable for weeks in the spring, bringing business to a virtual standstill . . . In the summer, when prairie winds dried the roadways, Chicago's air turned into swirling clouds of dust." Clearly, improvements needed to be made if Chicago was to compete with other cities.[13]

In the early 1850s Chicago was divided into nine wards, with two aldermen representing each ward. Albert Ellithorpe ran successfully against T. B. Dwyer in 1852 for a Sixth Ward alderman seat. The victory was short-lived because Dwyer contested the election results, leading to a decision by the common council to have a new election. Ellithorpe served for a month on the council and then was replaced by Dwyer following the second election. In the next cycle Ellithorpe ran unsuccessfully for election, but then he won a seat in 1855 and again in 1856. As part of his alderman duties, Ellithorpe served on the police board with Thomas Allen and William L. Church. His influence on the council in regard to street paving is unclear, but he, along with Ives Scoville, invented a pulverizer to crush the limestone into a gravel that was suitable for a paving material; for their efforts the men were awarded patent 22113 on November 23, 1858.[14]

That year Albert and William Colby, an alderman, created the Colby and Ellithorpe Company. The pulverizer crushed the limestone, and then it was "spread a foot thick on the streets." Regular use compressed the gravel, and as Ellithorpe explained many years later, it then became as "smooth as the modern asphatum roadway." Several city streets, such as Western Avenue, were paved in this way. Ellithorpe's improvements came at a time when Chicago developed a sewage system and a city water supply. Chicago's level terrain and lack of altitude above Lake Michigan meant that the city's elevation had to be raised "by as much as ten feet in places" to accommodate the piping. Throughout the 1850s and over the subsequent twenty years, buildings and street heights were raised to cover the new pipes.[15]

The late 1850s was not only a time of national political turmoil but also marked the start of another gold rush, this time in the Colorado Territory. Ellithorpe, with his previous experience as a miner, knew there was a need for a quartz pulverizer that would simplify the extraction of gold, so he modified his machine and then marketed it as the Ellithorpe Quartz Pulverizer. As described in a news article at the time, the Pulverizer was "simply constructed and portable . . . Its weight is only 210 pounds; and by the application of three horses or mule power, it can be made to pulverize to the finest powder, one ton per hour of the hardest description of quartz rock, or ten tons per diem." Perhaps because he was more familiar with California, Ellithorpe chose to market his machine there first and traveled again to California in 1859.[16]

The business environment there, however, proved to be difficult for Ellithorpe. Many of the miners he encountered had southern sentiments, and he was not shy about expressing his antislavery opinions. So little headway was made in marketing his machine that Ellithorpe decamped and traveled to Colorado, where the environment was more conducive to his business success. He installed pulverizers in about twenty "different localities," with the first one in the Nevada Gulch, near Central City. On December 13, 1860, a tragedy occurred nearby, at Nevada City, when the boiler exploded in one of the pulverizers and killed Robert Tilney, a miner from Iowa. According to a newspaper account, "The accident was the result of gross and culpable carelessness; the engineer was a German unacquainted with machinery, and hired by Ellithorpe on economical principles." Whether Ellithorpe actually bore some blame for the incident is not discernible.

Ellithorpe also had several mining claims and entered into a contract with W. C. Jewett. Each man had several claims as well as machinery for crushing and otherwise processing the quartz. The men agreed to "unite these several individual interests for the purpose of further and more fully developing the resources of these several quartz claims." They concurred that each would own half and each would receive half of the profits. If a claim was "unprofitable," then machinery could be moved and the claim abandoned. In the fall of 1860 the two men had a contract dispute, with Ellithorpe apparently attempting to sell some equipment from the claims and accusing Jewett of violating the terms of the agreement. Jewett hotly disputed this charge and took to the pages of the *Rocky Mountain News*, writing: "Mr. Ellithorpe's insinuations are unjust, as untrue. He is indebted to me for heavy damages, for violation of contract, which I, the community will soon put characteristic of the man."[17]

Ellithorpe, always searching for new business ventures, purchased, or at least acquired part ownership of, the *Rocky Mountain Herald*. A postwar biographical piece claimed that he "vigorously, ably and earnestly wielded his power in its columns in the cause of loyalty and freedom and against slavery and secession." Here Ellithorpe made public his support for Abraham Lincoln in the 1860 presidential contest and arranged for riders to travel from a stagecoach stop in Julesburg, Colorado, to Denver with news of the outcome of the election. Riders were to carry white flags to denote a Lincoln victory; otherwise, red flags would be flown. A cannon was fired, and a "mass meeting" took place soon after riders carrying white flags arrived with the news of Lincoln's election.[18]

Ellithorpe returned to Chicago sometime in late 1860 or early 1861. He continued his journalistic career by establishing the *Chicago Evening Star* in August 1861, just four months after the war started. An afternoon newspaper, its "remarkable and unprecedented success" led to its expansion from six to seven columns in late September. It is in the pages of the only two surviving issues of his newspaper that one gets a clearer sense of its owner's political attitudes. The antislavery spectrum encompassed a diverse group of people, ranging from racists who wanted to bar African Americans from the territories to abolitionists who called for equality for African Americans. Ellithorpe probably fell somewhere in the middle of the spectrum. His readers were informed that the war was one "of Freedom against Slavery . . . One or the other must fall, which shall it be?" Slavery, he wrote, was a "hideous deformity . . . Its sole reliance is in its own power to corrupt and pander to the profligate, vicious and inhuman of the age." Ellithorpe blamed white southerners for destroying the old compromises crafted by Henry Clay and Daniel Webster and "thrust[ing] their abominable, revolting system of slavery extension upon us." Maj. Gen. John C. Fremont, commander of the Western Department, declared on August 30, 1861, that Missouri's slaves were free. President Lincoln squashed Fremont's proclamation because of political necessity, but Ellithorpe wrote of his support for the measure. His newspaper ceased publication, probably in early 1862, as Ellithorpe became increasingly engaged in recruiting for the military. Ironically, he could have been writing of himself in an article he penned about a slowdown in recruiting in Chicago: "There are plenty of men who are quite willing to join the army as officers. A regiment of Brigadier Generals could be formed in Chicago in a week."[19]

By late 1861 Ellithorpe had contributed money and time to the creation of a regiment of cavalry that would be designated the Thirteenth Illinois. He expected to receive a commission as lieutenant colonel or as major in the new regiment because of his recruitment efforts. When the unit was organized, however, Joseph W. Bell was awarded the colonelcy, and Theobald Hartmann, who had been raising a separate cavalry unit, became lieutenant colonel after his recruits were added to the Thirteenth Illinois. The top positions were completed when Charles A. Bell, the colonel's son, became major. Ellithorpe was left out. Never one to passively accept a situation, he confronted Colonel Bell on the evening of January 15, 1862, in the main hall of the Tremont House. Normally a peaceful venue for grain buyers at that time of day, its serenity was shattered when the two men exchanged angry words. Next, "the Colonel using some epithet rather more forcible than elegant slapped the Major [Ellithorpe] in the face. The Major, his soul in arms, retorted by dealing the Colonel a blow in the face, and knocking him down. The bystanders rushed in, and peace was restored." Now decidedly divorced from playing any role in the new regiment, Albert Ellithorpe looked for other opportunities.[20]

CHAPTER 2

THE INDIAN EXPEDITION, JULY 1862

The tables turned—We will open the journal on the other side of the *question.*
—ALBERT C. ELLITHORPE, July 3, 1862

Albert Ellithorpe's search for a military role led to his appointment as a commissioned officer in the First Indian Home Guards, composed primarily of refugee Muscogee Creek and Seminole Indians. While Ellithorpe worked to recruit the Illinois regiment, a number of complex political events occurred in the Indian Territory, events that led to the creation of two regiments made up of "Loyal Indians."

During the secession crisis and well into 1861, the Confederacy quickly saw the "strategic importance" of the Indian Territory and worked diligently to create alliances with the Five Civilized Tribes (Cherokee, Chickasaw, Choctaw, Muscogee Creek, and Seminole) as well as alliances with several smaller tribes within the territory. Albert Pike, the Confederate commissioner to these tribes, rendered his finest work for the Confederacy in negotiating the treaties. Pike worked before the war for the Chickasaw, the Choctaw, and the Muscogee Creeks, aiding them "with their claims against the federal government." Not only was he a familiar partner, but Pike also possessed several other advantages. Lingering Indian resentment over their removal from their southeastern homelands, a fear of losing their slaves, a failure by the federal government "to fulfill treaty obligations," and an apprehension of federal invasion made Pike's task easier. Geographical proximity to and pressure from the Confederate states of Texas and Arkansas also influenced decisions by tribal leaders. Although treated poorly by southern states during removal, the Indians had close cultural, family, and economic ties to the South. Significantly, too, the Lincoln administration failed to counter Confederate overtures to the Indians, pulled Federal troops out of the Indian Territory, and abandoned all of the territory's military posts by mid-May 1861. The precarious state of the Southern Superintendency of the Office of Indian Affairs played a role too. Based in Fort

Smith, Arkansas, the Southern Superintendency oversaw the Indian Territory and southern Kansas. Southerners held all of the key positions in the superintendency, and when they resigned, there was a leadership vacuum. Some of those who left even helped Pike negotiate treaties of alliance with the Confederacy.[1]

The secession crisis and the outbreak of war subjected the tribes in the Indian Territory to incredible internal pressures that in some cases reopened old divisions. The three tribes that suffered the most from internal strife were the Cherokee, the Muscogee Creeks, and the Seminoles. The Chickasaw and the Choctaw were more unified and allied with the Confederacy in May and June 1861, respectively. Chief John Ross of the Cherokee Nation struggled to keep his nation neutral, but after a contentious and tumultuous few months, the Cherokee agreed to an alliance that October. Ellithorpe's military career took him into close contact not only with Muscogee Creeks and Seminoles but also with African Creeks and African Seminoles. The groups were tied together by the Muscogee language and their participation in the pre-removal Creek Confederacy.[2]

The Muscogee Creeks consisted of two parts or divisions in the Creek Confederacy before removal: the Lower Creeks and the Upper Creeks. The Lower Creeks were associated with the McIntosh faction. The leader of the group, William McIntosh, a signer of "a land cession treaty," had been assassinated in 1825, and his sons, Chilly and Daniel, supported the Confederacy. Upper Creek Opothele Yahola, a longtime opponent of the McIntosh faction, eventually saw removal "as inevitable" and negotiated the removal treaty of 1832. The Lower Creeks "settled in the Arkansas-Verdigris river valley" in the Indian Territory, and the Upper Creeks settled about forty miles away, "farther south, primarily along the branches of the Canadian River." Born about 1780, Opothele Yahola, large physically, was viewed as powerful and venerable. He insisted that treaties made with the United States be honored, but the Muscogee Creeks allied with the Confederacy on July 10, 1861. The Seminoles also had their share of rivalries. Chief Billy Bowlegs and another prominent leader, John Chupco, opposed a Confederate alliance, but a rival, John Jumper, "met secretly and unofficially with Pike." By late summer the tribe was split, with half desiring a Confederate alliance and half desiring to be loyal, yet neutral, in the war. The Seminoles allied with the Confederacy on August 1, 1861.[3]

The Lincoln administration offered little assistance to Loyal Indians and simply advised Opothele Yahola and his followers to be neutral. In effect the Loyal Indians were left to fend for themselves, and Indians opposed to the Confederate alliance collected at Opothele Yahola's Upper Creek villages, located near present-day Boley. Although Opothele Yahola's relationship with the African Creeks had been poor in earlier times, he now worked to ally with both them and the African Seminoles by promising their freedom if they joined his camp. About five hundred of them, many who were slaves, went to his camp from the late summer into the early winter of 1861. The outbreak of war had not only shaken the Indians out of their settled way of life but had also disrupted the lives of blacks living in the Indian Territory. Some slaveholding families in the territory took their slaves to Texas, but other blacks ran away, sometimes with the assistance of sympathetic Muscogee Creeks, to Opothele Yahola.[4]

Ellithorpe would interact not only with Muscogee Creek and Seminole Indians but also with African Creeks in his regiment. Muscogee Creek oral tradition maintains that the first contact between the groups occurred when an African ship wrecked along the Alabama coast in pre-Columbian times. There were, however, also Africans in Hernando de Soto's expedition, which began in 1539. Several Africans from the De Soto expedition escaped or deserted and joined Indian villages in what later became the southeastern United States. In the 1860 census there were "1,651 black slaves and 277 free blacks living among the Creeks. Altogether, African Creeks made up 14.3 percent of the tribe." Slavery in the Muscogee Creek Nation was unlike slavery in other parts of the South. There was a slave code, but the slaves possessed more freedom of movement and less supervision than slaves in southern states or even in other Indian nations. Living in similar housing as that of their masters, African Creeks had their own gardens and could earn money, and some even possessed firearms. African Creek slaves not only played a vital role with their physical labor but also served as translators and trade negotiators, providing a valuable linguistic connection between non-English-speaking Muscogee Creeks and the English world.[5]

The free African Creeks worked at a variety of occupations. Many were engaged in business, but others were "small farmers, ranchers, or laborers." The increasing debate about slavery in the 1850s led to a tightening of slave codes in southern states as well as in the Muscogee Creek Nation, with the Creek Council placing greater restrictions on slaves and free blacks in the mid-1850s. Ominously, on March 10, 1861, just four months before their alliance with the Confederacy, the Creek Council ordered free blacks to choose an owner and get rid of their personal property or "be sold for twelve months to the highest bidder." In the face of these changes, it is no wonder that African Creeks and Seminoles found Opothele Yahola's offer appealing.[6]

Initially, Opothele Yahola's stance was viewed with little concern by Indians that sided with the Confederacy. Most outsiders viewed it as a Muscogee Creek internal situation that could be safely ignored. Concern spread, however, as increasing numbers of runaway slaves made their way to Opothele Yahola's villages and as he reached out to another group, the Quapaw Indians. Rumors circulated in November 1861 that the old warrior planned an attack on Confederate colonel Douglas H. Cooper's encampment of Texas cavalry and Indian troops. According to some, as many as seven to eight thousand people were in Opothele Yahola's villages. If his warriors were added to a federal force, then Cooper's command of about two thousand soldiers might have trouble defending the Indian Territory.[7]

Cooper decided on a preemptive strike, and on November 15, 1861, he and his men marched on Opothele Yahola's camp but discovered that the group had decamped several days earlier. A series of four skirmishes ensued, with the first taking place on November 19 and the last, Chustenahlah, occurring on December 26. The Loyal Indians and their African allies were decisively defeated at the last encounter and fled in a winter storm along with noncombatants to Kansas. Administrators in the Office of Indian Affairs were unprepared for the influx of thousands of refugees entering camps "along the Cottonwood, Fall, and Walnut Rivers" in the southern part of the state. Conditions were terrible, and authorities struggled to organize aid for perhaps the largest refugee group the federal government had ever dealt with up to that point. Indian agents and military personnel stepped in, but the refugees had lost essentially everything and needed supplies. Adding to the exodus over the next few months were refugees from other tribes in the Indian Territory. By the spring of 1862 large numbers of horse carcasses littered the ground around the camps, adding to the health threat. These conditions necessitated a removal of the refugees to a new site, this time to near LeRoy, Kansas, a town situated near the Neosho River. By early October 1862, 5,487 refugee Indians were in southern Kansas, with 3,619, or 66 percent, being Muscogee Creek and 919, or nearly 17 percent, being refugee Seminoles. Later that month William G. Coffin, in charge of the Southern Superintendency, estimated that 10 percent of the refugees had died.[8]

The organization of the First Indian Home Guards began at LeRoy in the spring of 1862. A year earlier Confederate officials organized several Indian units, marking the first time in American history that regimental sized units of Indian soldiers had been created (map 1). Since colonial times Indian soldiers had served as valuable auxiliary soldiers; now the exigencies of war led to the creation of larger units. The organization of Indian units by the federal government, however, necessitated some attitude shifts. In May 1861 Simon Cameron, Lincoln's secretary of war, had written, "The nature of our present national troubles forbids the use

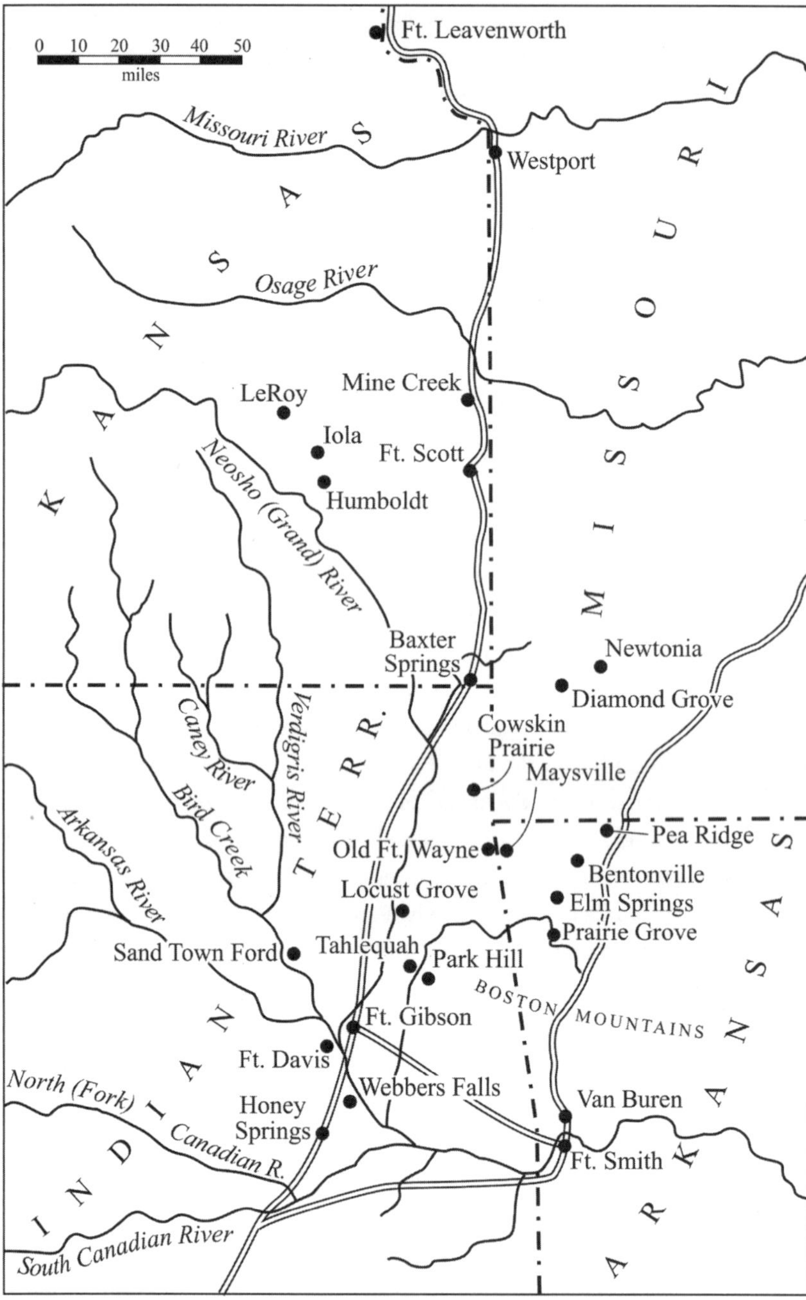

MAP 1. The Border Region. Map by Mary Lee Eggart.

of savages," but the situation had now changed. On January 2, 1862, Secretary Cameron explained the administration's intention to enlist four thousand Indians.

Such a dramatic shift in official attitudes was driven in part by Senator James H. Lane of Kansas (fig. 2). Even while Opothele Yahola and his followers were being driven from the Indian Territory, Jim Lane met in November 1861 with President Lincoln to advocate for an expedition through the Indian Territory and into Texas, where he hoped to free slaves. In January 1862 Lane traveled to Kansas with the expectation that he would lead the expedition; journalists in Kansas dubbed it the "Lane Expedition" and enthusiastically promoted it. Gen. David Hunter, the commander of the Department of Kansas, refused to authorize Lane as the leader and instead stated that he would take personal command and ordered its organization to begin in February 1862. Plans expanded on March 2, 1862, when Commissioner William P. Dole asked Interior Secretary Caleb B. Smith to get War Department authorization to order two white regiments to accompany two thousand armed Indians into the Indian Territory to resettle the refugees. The plan quickly stalled out due to allegations that Confederate Indians had scalped Federal soldiers during the battle of Pea Ridge in early March. This led to reconsideration of the plans by officials in regard to enlisting Indians; moreover, the general public had never been too enthused about the arrangement. The administration quickly, but briefly, scaled back enlistment efforts until Lincoln ordered the expedition to go forward.[9]

The next few weeks brought a flurry of command changes, contradictory orders, and finally the enlistment of Indian soldiers and the creation of the Indian Expedition. In mid-March 1862 Hunter was reassigned to the command of the Department of the South, and Gen. Henry Halleck took command of the new Department of Missouri, which included Hunter's old command. He soon placed Brig. Gen. John W. Denver in charge of the District of Kansas on April 1, 1862, but five days later Brig. Gen. Samuel D. Sturgis replaced Denver. Sturgis, however, did not remain long in command. The newly instituted Department of Kansas led to the appointment of one of Lane's favorites, Brig. Gen. James G. Blunt, on May 5, 1862. Lane would not command the expedition, but securing Blunt's appointment had far-reaching effects in the border region of the trans-Mississippi. Blunt soon tapped Col. Charles Doubleday, the commander of the Second Ohio Cavalry, as the leader of what would now be styled as the Indian Expedition. Senator Lane, who "more than anyone else . . . was responsible for persuading Abraham Lincoln to use Indian troops," hovered in the background, hoping to obtain command of the expedition. The Muscogee Creeks and the Seminoles themselves wanted "the great war chief, General Lane . . . [whose] heart is big for the Indian," to lead.

Ultimately, however, Blunt replaced Colonel Doubleday with the commander of the Tenth Kansas Infantry, Col. William Weer, a Kansan, who turned out to be a disastrous choice.[10]

The Indian Expedition "required a rare, if not unprecedented, level of interracial understanding, trust, and cooperation" as well as a willingness to risk white lives in an effort to restore the Indian refugees to their homes. There were several goals for such a venture: restoring the refugees to the Indian Territory would resolve the problem of caring for them; plus, the refugees wanted to return. Commissioner Dole accordingly promised them they would return as soon as possible. Another desire was to combat enemy troops in the Indian Territory, and once that threat was removed, Kansas and parts of Missouri and Arkansas would be more secure. Although the battle of Pea Ridge had raised questions about using Indian troops, the battle had also severely damaged Confederate strength and made an attempt to return the refugees more viable. Halleck was unenthused and refused initially to order white troops to accompany the Indian Expedition, but on April 5 he capitulated. White officers bearing new commissions provided by President Lincoln arrived in Kansas to organize what became the First Indian Home Guards and the Second Indian Home Guards.[11]

Ellithorpe had worked for several weeks to secure a military commission. Prominent Chicagoan Joseph Medill endorsed Ellithorpe to Illinois's adjutant general, Allen C. Fuller, before the fistfight with Col. Joseph W. Bell by stating Ellithorpe "possesses just the stuff" to deal with the rebellion. Ellithorpe had valuable connections with Senator Lane and Maj. Gen. Samuel R. Curtis also. Additionally, Lincoln had advised him on prewar legal matters, and in a postwar biographical piece Ellithorpe claimed that Lincoln had stayed overnight at his Morgan Street house on one or two occasions. Officers were needed for the new Indian regiments, and besides his connections, Ellithorpe had important expertise; he had language skills that would be valuable in a regiment that mostly consisted of non-English-speaking soldiers. Ellithorpe had learned French as a boy living in Canada and later studied languages in Chicago with Rev. William E. Manly. His knowledge may also have included an Indian language. In 1897 Ellithorpe told a Chicago reporter "that Lincoln knew that he [Ellithorpe] could both speak and write the Cherokee language—he had learned it of a missionary to those Indians." Ellithorpe's regiment would consist of Muscogee Creeks and Seminoles, but his adeptness at picking up languages made him unusually well qualified to serve in an Indian regiment. He traveled to Washington, D.C., where he received a commission as first lieutenant. Commissioner Dole then ordered him to Fort Leavenworth, Kansas, where he arrived on April 19 and dropped by the *Daily Conservative*'s offices to provide the latest news about the Indian regiments. Officials mustered him two days later at Fort Leavenworth.[12]

Ellithorpe and other officers now rapidly organized the First Indian Home Guards, and other men partially organized the Second Indian Home Guards for service in the Indian Expedition. The newly designated commander of the First Indian Home Guards, Col. Robert W. Furnas, was mustered in on April 18, 1862. Furnas, originally from Ohio, was a newspaperman in Brownsville, Nebraska Territory, and left behind his wife and their seven children when he traveled to Fort Leavenworth to report for duty. Traveling from Nebraska with the colonel was his aide, thirty-eight-year-old Stephen H. Wattles from Bellevue, Nebraska Territory. Wattles was commissioned as lieutenant colonel on May 22, 1862.[13]

Like Ellithorpe, some of these white officers held viewpoints that marked them as somewhat radical for their time. Colonel Furnas was a Free-Soil advocate. The opinions of Lieutenant Colonel Wattles are uncertain; given that he was Furnas's aide initially, perhaps he shared similar Free-Soil attitudes. His distant cousin Augustus Wattles helped advise the Lincoln administration on Indian policy and advocated for the creation of an Indian state whose residents would have citizenship and congressional representation. Scottish-born Maj. William A. Phillips, a newspaperman like Furnas and Ellithorpe, moved to Kansas in the 1850s and held antislavery viewpoints. Many antislavery advocates were concerned by the plight of Indians and felt that their lives were similar to that of the slaves. Many did not recognize the importance of tribes, however, nor seemed to have any understanding of how they functioned. The fact that some of their soldiers had probably been slaveholders and that former slaves were in the ranks must have posed an intellectual challenge. Or perhaps, like other abolitionists, they simply ignored the inconvenient reality that some Indians were slaveholders.[14]

The *Leavenworth Daily Conservative* assured its readers that Furnas, Wattles, and Ellithorpe "have labored with untiring energy in organizing the first regiment, and the Indians have promptly seconded all their efforts." Unlike the later enlisted African Americans, soldiers in the Indian Home Guards units received the same pay and benefits as white soldiers, and their company commanders as well as most other company officers were Indian. Opothele Yahola was too old to serve, but several of the Indian officers in the First were prominent men. Tuckabatchee Harjo, Opothele Yahola's nephew, was a company commander. Tulsy-Fixico, a prominent Upper Creek leader, also received a commission. Halleck Tustenugee, a veteran of the Seminole Wars, received a commission as a captain. John Chupco, assistant principal chief of the Seminoles, also was commissioned as an officer. Many sources also state that Billy Bowlegs, a Seminole warrior, received a commission in the First Indian Home Guards. This Billy Bowlegs is not to be confused with the older man, a principal chief, who died sometime between 1859 and 1864. Sonaki Mikko, also known as Billy Bowlegs, served faithfully as a company commander in the First Indian Home Guards (figs. 3–6).[15]

Muscogee Creeks constituted eight of the ten companies, one of which included a group of Yuchis that were "affiliated" with the Muscogee Creeks. The remaining two companies consisted of Seminoles. The Muscogee Creeks and Seminoles, as Ellithorpe explained, "speak one language nearly & are thus naturally drawn together & they are not willing to be divided." Scattered through the regiment were men described as "Yellow," "African," or "Black" on the muster rolls. These twenty-five to thirty African Creeks and Seminoles "were the first African American soldiers officially mustered into the federal army and to participate in combat during the Civil War." Many of them had already experienced combat during Opothele Yahola's retreat from the Indian Territory several months earlier. They served as soldiers, but they also continued their role as liaisons, or "linksters," between Indians that "spoke little or no English" and white officers. Even with these African Creek interpreters, challenges remained. As Lt. Edwin C. Manning explained: "If I had no negro at hand I could give no orders. Any old soldier will recognize how embarrassing this might be at times." The men had to negotiate not only racial barriers but also language ones.[16]

As the organization of the two new regiments proceeded, there was turmoil at the top. On April 25 Brig. Gen. Samuel D. Sturgis issued Order No. 8, halting the enlistment of Indian soldiers, and ordered the arrest of violators. Lieutenant Ellithorpe, now serving as his regiment's adjutant, had already signed up a number of soldiers and would, by the end of April, enlist 58.6 percent of the soldiers in Company A, 74.6 percent of those in Company C, 53.2 percent of the men in Company G, and 39 percent of those in Company I. Furnas informed officials at Fort Leavenworth that the regiment was organized, so Sturgis's order threw everything into confusion. A resolution was soon reached. When Brigadier General Blunt became the commander of the Department of Kansas on May 2, he quickly countermanded Sturgis's order, and the organization of the Indian Home Guards resumed, with the unit mustered on May 22, 1862. Meanwhile, Confederate Indian troops had returned to the Indian Territory, and Col. Douglas H. Cooper and Col. Stand Watie actively employed them in hit-and-run attacks. The Indian Territory, however, was vulnerable to a determined Union offensive.[17]

To Commissioner of Indian Affairs, William P. Dole, June 9, 1862

[Ellithorpe commented on the situation while the expedition was being organized.]

Leroy Kansas
June 9th 1862

Hon. Wm P. Dole
Com. Ind. Affairs

Sir

It has been some time since I wrote you & to fill my promise I again drop you a line.[18] I presume you feel a lively interest in whatever relates to the Indians. The 1st Regt is now mustered into the service & will probably today number something over a minimum Regt. It is composed entirely of Creeks & Seminoles. Eight companys of the former & two of the latter.

I have understood that the report of the Creek Agent gave the number of Creek men at 1990—if this is a fact, it is far from a correct statement—The actual number of Creek men over 14 years of age (refugees) will not number over 900 some of these are unable to be soldiers. The actual number of Seminoles (men) will not exceed 300, over 14 years of age, many of them are old & disabled as soldiers. Thus you will see that but one Regt could be raised from that quarter. You are aware that the Creeks & Seminoles speak one language mostly & are thus naturaly drawn together & they were not willing to be divided. The second Regt is now forming from the various other tribes & I have no doubt will be filled[.] it would have been filled long ago, but Col Ritchie did not repair here for a long time in fact not till after our Regt was raised[19]—Adjutant Dole came here promptly to do his duty[20]—but in the absence of his Col could not facilitate his regt without assuming a responsibility that would have been unwise. I regret that he could not have been placed in our regt for he will prove a faithful & reliable officer & should I be transfered to any other position which I am strongly in hopes I may be, I hope you will exercise your influence to transfer him to my place, this will be agreeable to all the officers of the 1st regiment & desirable on his part.

The condition of the Indians here at the present writing is very favorable. sickness is abating, & their spirits are rising. I think I have fully settled the fact of the Indian capability & sussiptibility to arrive at a good state of military discipline. You would be surprised to see our Regt move. They accomplish the feat of regular-time step equal to any white soldier. They form in line with dispatch & with great precission, & what is more they now manifest a great desire to learn the entire white mans discipline in military matters. That they will make brave & ambitious sholdiers [*sic*] I have no doubt. Our country may well feel proud that these red men have at last fell into the ranks to fight for our flag, & aid in crushing treason[.] much honor is due them.

I am sorry that Dr. Kile did not accept the appointment of Q. M. but owing to some misunderstanding with Col. Ritchie he declined.[21]

You will please remember me to Genl Lane & say that I have not herd from him since I left Washington.

Very Respectfully your
Obt servant
A. C Ellithorpe

[*Source:* National Archives, Record Group 75, Office of Indian Affairs, Letters Received by the Office of Indian Affairs, 1824–81, M234, roll 834, frames 1436–38.]

More soldiers were needed in the two Indian regiments, and William G. Coffin, the director of the Southern Superintendency, devised a novel recruiting technique based on the Indians fascination with artillery. Near the end of May a group of fifty to sixty Seminoles, including the man known as Billy Bowlegs, traveled to Iola, Kansas, where they witnessed a cannon fire two or three rounds. Robert T. McMahan of the Second Ohio Cavalry wrote in his diary that the Indians were "well pleased with what they saw." Several days later Rabb's Indiana Battery fired their cannon for a group of Indians at the Osage Mission near St. Paul, Kansas, causing some to run away, while "others laid hands over their mouths (Indian sign of fear)." Perhaps hearing of these encounters, Coffin persuaded Allen's Kansas Battery to travel to LeRoy. He hoped "to make considerable addition to the Army from the loyal Reffugee Indians here, as they have great confidence in '*them waggons that shoot*,' this has been a point with them all the time." On June 13 Allen's Battery arrived and gave a demonstration before "nearly Two thousand Indians." Coffin reported that it "was received by the Indians with entire satisfaction and applause, it has made a grand impression upon them and has also strengthened their confidence in the success of the expedition . . . I doubt very much whether those Indians could have been induced to go at all had it not been for that Battery going along with them." That night Colonel Weer ordered a war dance, and soldiers such as Jacob Haas of the Ninth Wisconsin Infantry carried wood for a massive bonfire.[22]

The next day, with Allen's Battery leading the way, the First Indian Home Guards and the Second Indian Home Guards started for Humboldt, about thirty-five miles to the southeast. Sources vary on how many Indian soldiers left LeRoy. Coffin estimated a total of 1,000, but another source stated that the First Indian comprised "over 1,000 men," with the Second Indian, incompletely organized, numbering between 500 and 600 soldiers. Although about 360 men of the First were mounted, many were not, and they, along with men from the Second, "strugg[led] along under a broiling sun with heavy knapsacks, as they had not sufficient transportation." The M1817—or Indian rifle, as it was called—was carried by many, although some other older firearms were also utilized. This .54 caliber smoothbore weapon without a bayonet was serviceable but hardly modern. Because it was expected that more Indians would join once the force entered the Indian Territory, extra guns were transported.[23]

First marches were particularly hard, and it took two days to cover the distance to Humboldt. Considering the rawness of the troops and the heat, this pace was respectable. Coffin reported to Commissioner Dole that the officers had worked hard "and the improvement the Indians have made in drilling is much greater than I supposed them capabell of." Colonel Weer reported that many of the Indian soldiers, weakened from a harsh winter spent in refugee camps, were ill and that they had no medicines or a physician of their own yet. Fortunately, a surgeon from the Tenth Kansas stepped in and treated the sick. Indian agent Edwin H. Carruth, a former missionary and teacher in the Indian Territory, accompanied the expedition "to watch carefully over the two Indian Regiments," to assist its officers, meet with Loyal Indians in the Territory, and give them assurances that the federal government stood behind its treaty obligations, and to aid "Indians in a suffering condition whose Loyalty is *beyond doubt*." On June 16 the force left Humboldt for Baxter Springs, about ninety-five miles away, in the southeastern corner of Kansas.[24]

The expedition consisted of two brigades under the overall command of Colonel Weer. The First Brigade consisted of the First Indian Home Guards, Allen's Battery, the Second Kansas Cavalry, and the Tenth Kansas Infantry. The Second Indian Home Guards served in the Second Brigade along with Rabb's Indiana Battery, the Second Ohio Cavalry, and the Sixth Kansas Cavalry. The reporter traveling with the Indian troops marching from Humboldt was fascinated by "a portly 'medicine man,' who marches in the front rank at the head of the column.

He carries a somewhat weighty bag of 'medicine' round his neck." Coffin wrote to Dole that the "Indian Regiments left for the Indian Territory in good Stile and in fine Sprits the Indians with their new uniforms and Small Military Caps on their High Heads of Hair made rather a Comecal Ludisrous but Still a gay and rather a prepossessing apperance they marched off in columns of 4 a breast Singing the war Song all joining in the chourse and a more animated Scene is not often witnessed." The men arrived in Baxter Springs on June 25. Now united, both brigades were reviewed two days later before their march across the Kansas border and into the Indian Territory.[25]

Challenging environmental conditions helped lead to a tumultuous expedition. Drought and hot weather, burned-up grassland, and limited water supplies plagued the soldiers. Meanwhile, the Confederates experienced command problems, which hindered their ability to oppose the Federal advance. After the battle of Pea Ridge, Brigadier General Pike and his Indian troops returned to the Indian Territory and retreated to within thirty miles of Texas. Later in March, Pike received reinforcements in the form of an Arkansas battery and two Texas cavalry regiments. Col. James J. Clarkson of Missouri was also given authority to raise a battalion of "displaced" Missourians and other men. Pike was a poor and passive military leader in contrast to his subordinate Col. Stand Watie, a Cherokee Indian and opponent to Chief John Ross, who actively ranged through the northeastern part of the Indian Territory and into southwestern Missouri. Maj. Gen. Thomas C. Hindman replaced Gen. Earl Van Dorn as commander of the Trans-Mississippi Department on May 31, 1862, ordered Pike to move north, and gave Colonel Clarkson command of all of the forces in the northern part of the Indian Territory. In late June, Colonel Watie and his men were camped along Spavinaw Creek; Clarkson and his soldiers were farther south on top of a hill at Locust Grove.[26]

Union troops broke camp at Baxter Springs and marched for the Indian Territory on June 28. To escape the intense heat, the men left at three in the morning. The First Indian Home Guards pulled out with Col. Frederick Salomon's brigade and on June 29, after a tiring march, arrived at Round Grove on the east side of the Grand River. The men continued searching for Confederate opposition, with the brigades separating and moving down opposite banks of the Grand. On July 2 Col. William R. Judson, the commander of the Second Brigade, learned that Watie's wagon train was at Locust Grove. Clarkson later claimed that he had ordered Watie to scout for the enemy on the west side of the Grand River but that "this order was not obeyed," thus allowing the disaster at Locust Grove. Ellithorpe was included in the strike force chosen by Judson, which consisted of one section of Allen's Kansas Battery and detachments from the Tenth Kansas Infantry, the Ninth Kansas Cavalry, and the First Indian Home Guards. Because the troops were to travel quickly, members of the Tenth Kansas rode in wagons, and all of the men traveled as lightly as possible. They left near sunset on July 2 and rode twenty miles down the west side of the Grand River on a warm night. Civilians were taken from each cabin that was passed and detained until the raid was completed. At 4:00 a.m. the force crossed the Grand at Landrum Ford, only three miles from Locust Grove. The attack commenced at dawn, when "some of the brightest stars were still shining." Confederate soldiers were unaware that an enemy force was nearby and slept without "their trousers on" on that warm night. The surprise was complete.[27]

Eighteen-year-old George Falconer was one of the men in Clarkson's battalion. He was a farmer from Sebastion County, Arkansas, and had enlisted on April 1, 1862. At some point he acquired a small, brown, hardbound journal and documented his journey into the Indian Territory.[28]

JOURNAL ENTRIES, GEORGE C. FALCONER, JUNE 18–JUNE 27 1862

Fort Smith June 18.th /62.

George C. Falconer left for Col Clarksons regiment June 18.th /62 and crosed the arkansas river at wilsons ferry 12 miles above Ft Smith and s[t]opped at shotes 9 miles from fort smith.[29] days ride 27 miles. Thursday June 19th 30 miles. Friday the 20 35 miles. encamped near Park hill.[30] Saturday 21t days travel 30 miles. stopped 8 miles south of grand Saline.[31] 22 days travel 30 miles. encamped 10 miles west of Col Stanwaties mills.[32] 23 overtaken they comand. day's march 17 miles. 24th layed up 5 miles from Cow Skin Prairie. 25th days march of 20 miles encamped 1 mile from grand river. 26th moved days travel 8 miles & encamped 4 miles from grand river on ~~grand~~ Finches prairie where found abundance of good grass and water. federals reported to be at Bentonville & near Cow Skin Prairie. 27th Moved 7 miles farther south on grand prairie where we encamped on wolf Creek. grass is very plentifuly but water very scarce. nothing interesting from todays march. cooking and attending to our horses is all the amusement that we can find. we see today a federal who was taken prisoner at Bentonville. he had been left there on a spree he was taken by a man that lived at Bentonville he was turned over to Col. Stanwatie[.]

Although the number of Confederates captured at Locust Grove varies according to the source, Clarkson reported that forty-nine of his men, including Falconer, were captured during the fight. The skirmish at Locust Grove led to modest casualties but is a fine example of how even small military actions can have outsized results. The Federal victory at Locust Grove sent a wave of consternation through the Cherokee Nation. The loyalty of Confederate colonel John Drew's Mounted Rifles was so undermined after Locust Grove that six hundred of his men defected to the Federals; it was the only time during the war that virtually an entire regiment shifted to the opposing side. These former Confederates filled out the vacancies in the Second Indian Home Guards and were used to start the organization of the Third Indian Home Guards. The collateral damage from the skirmish continued. Federal forces entered Tahlequah, the capital of the Cherokee Nation, and then traveled the short distance to Park Hill, where Chief John Ross resided. Ross had never been enthused about the alliance with the Confederacy, and Union troops arrested and then paroled him. Ross and several family members left the Cherokee Nation—all escorted by a detachment of the Sixth Kansas Cavalry. Ross then went into virtual exile in Philadelphia. Another outcome of the skirmish was that Falconer lost his diary to Lieutenant Ellithorpe. Ellithorpe began the diary with a statement that it had been "captured." The remainder of this chapter consists of correspondence and Ellithorpe's journal account of the Indian Expedition.[33]

JOURNAL ENTRIES, JULY 3–JULY 14, 1862

[*Ellithorpe wrote the following statements on the first two pages of Falconer's journal.*]

This Book was captured at the Battle of Locust Grove—I make a Journal of it for present use—The Battle was fought on the 3d of July 1862 at Sun rise A.M.

This Book was captured at the *Battle of Locust Grove July 3d 1862.*

[*Immediately following Falconer's entries, Ellithorpe penned his own journal entry.*]

THE TABLES TURNED—

We will open the journal on the other side of the *question*
A C Ellithorps
Maj 1st Ind Regt

Private Journal
July 3, 1862

Grand Saline—or—Locust Grove Battle Ground—This book is one of the trophies taken this morning.

With a force of 200 Creek Indians from the 1st Indian Regt under command of Lieut Col S H Wattles & Adjutant A.C Ellithorpe about one hundred men from the Kansas 9th & a small detachment of Infantry from the Kansas 10th together with 3 guns well maned from Captain Allens Kansas Battery, we made a forced march of 35 miles from 10½ Oclock on the evening of July 2d & surprised the enemy, about two miles across Grand River upon the top of a high hill called Locust Grove hill.[34] The detachment of Indians were in the advance & [commanded] by Lieut Col. Wattles & Adjutant Ellithorpe. Wattles upon the left & Ellithorpe on the right. The charge was made up a steep hill some 50 rods, the enemy commenced fire as soon as ~~the~~ we rose over the brow of the hill, the fire was rapid but their range was to high, the balls passing over our heads some two feet. Upon our rapid approach at a cavalry charge the enemy broke ranks & ~~soon~~ fled in terrible confusion, leaving every thing pertaining to their command [fig. 7][.]

So hasty was the flight that the cooking vesels were left upon the fires & their whiskey, todys ready prepared & untouched.

The sun was just rising & a more beautiful morning never dawned over that country.

The Rebel command consisted of a portion of Clarksons& Stand Waities commands both of which were much superior to our force.[35] The whole amount of property taken would probably amount [to] one hundred thousand dollars[.]

But owing to ~~both~~ the inefficient & loose manner in taking care of the property but little will be saved to the government[.] The great mishap of this expedition so far is the inefficient & unreliable character of the officer in command (Col Wm Weere)[.][36]

No dependence can be placed upon him, as was fully demonstrated in this battle, for while he well knew during the whole nights march that we were approaching the enemy, he made frequent visits to his bottle & the nearer we approached the enemy the greater his excess, & by the time the attack was made he was in no condition to give an order, in fact he did not approach the battle ground untill some time after the battle was over & then in a state of intoxication. While we were yet encompassed with enemys on three sides, he threw himself into his ambulance and became entirely unconscious, & past being aroused.

Our position was a critical one & the command, either must push the battle farther or draw from the field.

Efforts were mad[e] to arouse the Colonel to no purpose[.] a consultation was held by the subordinate officers & finaly resulted in taking what we could of the enemys outfit & falling back some 10 miles through the excessive heat of a scorching day.

This is a terible state of affairs, when the lines of any army are placed in the hands of a worthless drunken officer[.]

July 4, 1862

This is a glorious morning & our troops are all in fine spirits.

The greatest lattitude is given to the men, & a general jolification is being arranged—Our Drunken Col. is again sober, only to get drunk again. Every countenance beams with delight today, & there is nothing to mar the general glee, except the few suffering sick, that cannot participate in the general festivities—The balance of the Brigade came up last night in command of Col Judson.[37] The ground we are camped upon is finely located & called *Hudsons crossing.*[38]

The day is past & the glorious 4th of July has seemed far more dear to all in the command than ever before. It has furnished an occasion for reflection, & every one seemes to more fully realize the sacredness of the day. It brings to the mind, most forcibly the spirit which prompts the real patriot to reverence the day which historically markes the birth of our national existence. Our reverence for this day is no idle reverence, it is a short but holy period in every passing year that gives new life to the fire of real liberty. Although a long succession of years of peace & prosperity have aparently dimmed our ardour—yet now that our Liberties are endangered, the presence of this Annual birthday of Freedom, rekindles the smoldering embers to a furious flame, each heart seems to be inspired with a new love & firme resolve, to hand down to future generations the same old day of Liberty regenerated & purified by the blood of a mirrod [myriad] of Patriots[.]

Holy day! May God bless & sanctify it to the nations honor & long prosperity[.]

July 5, 1862

We this morning took up our line of march down the west side of Grand River.

All the prisoners taken at the Battle of Locust Grove were forwarded to Fort Scott under convoy[39]—Col Clarkson seemed much down cast & from his appearance deeply regrets ever conspiring to destroy the Govt—The rest of the prisoners are of that ignorant class, who neither think or reflect beyond the present wants & necessities of day by day life. The days march has been hard & excessively hot. we have made 20 miles, no incidents of particular not[e] has occurred, some few scattering rebels have been taken, & a few men claiming to be union have come to our lines.

July 12, 1862

Since the 5th I have had no spare moments to even write a line. Every hour has been ocupied & most of the time I have been at the head of a scouting party—reconnoitering the country between Grand River & the Verdiquis River.

I have been in the saddle nearly 20 hours out of every twenty four, the fatigue has been so great into camp. Many nights we have sat up all night, watching the enemy who have been very near us, without tents & but little to eat, for I did not take more than two days scanty rations upon my scouting parties—

In the morning I started again to assertain the location of MacIntoshes forces above the mouth of the VerdiGris River.[40]

And from all the indications I expect a very lively time. We shall see what it will result in[.]

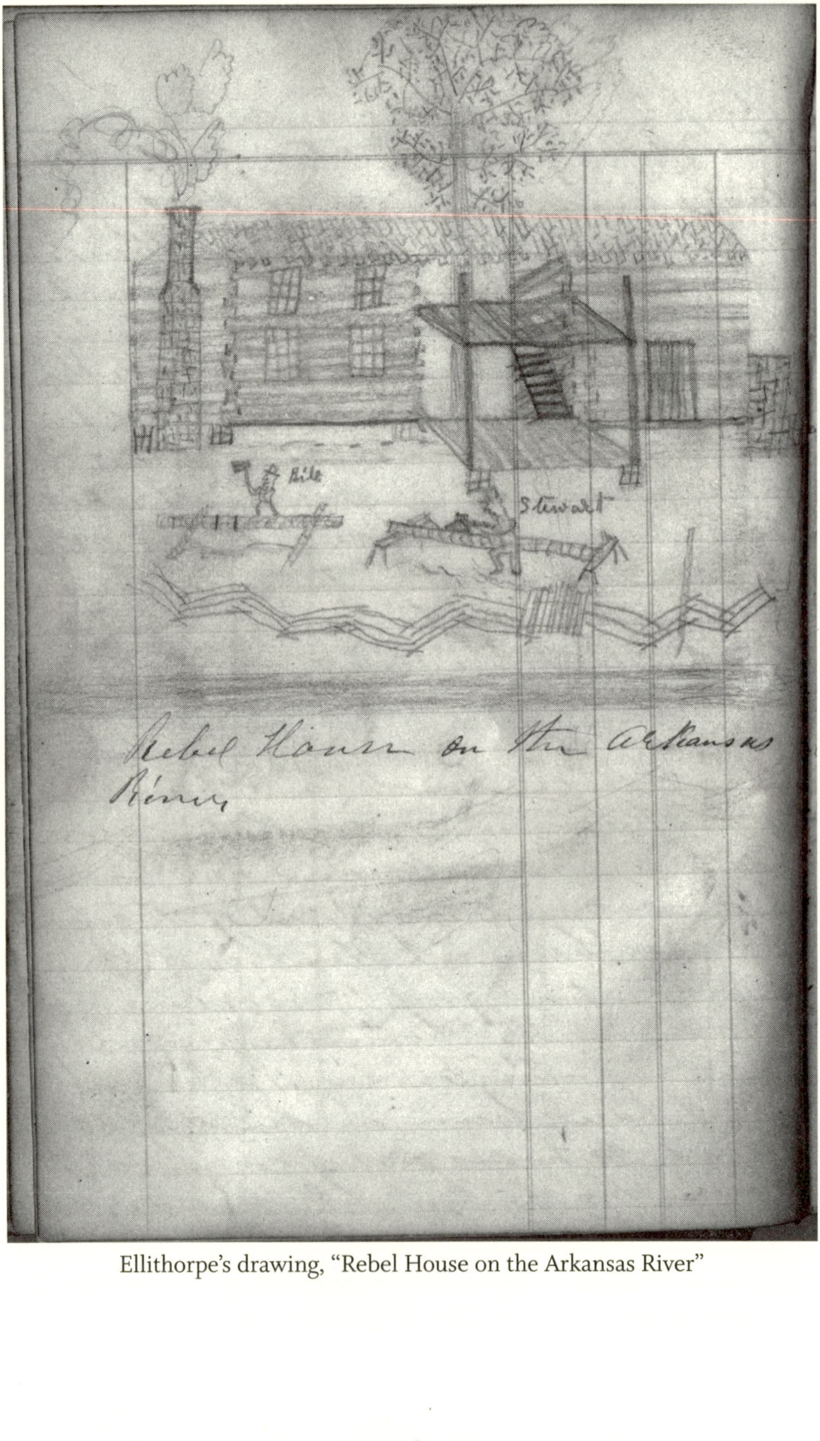

Ellithorpe's drawing, "Rebel House on the Arkansas River"

July 14, 1862

Yesterday morning as arranged I started with a scout of two hundred & fifty men & arived at Sand Town a small Indian village, on the East bank of the VerdiGris River at 4 Oclock P.M.[41] Upon close examination I found signs of the enemy in a thickly timbered bottom on the west bank of the river. the brush was so thick that I dare not undertake to penetrate without first learning the strength of the enemy, & to do this was a dificult task, not having any canon to shell the woods, I finally resolved upon the following plan, I detailed 30 men of the most daring to approach as follows—Placing themselves one hundred yards apart & on a line with the river they advanced to the bank cautiously, with instructions to remain there untill dark as pickets so disposing of themselves as not to be observed ~~by~~ from the oposite side—after dark I advanced my whole force cautiously, leaving a rear picket & guard to the center of the advance line of pickets, then pushed the pickets across the river to the oposite bank, with instructions not to fire the first gun, that I might know positively of the ~~ap~~ presence of the enemy. The advance was cautiously made & for over half an hour not a sound was herd, here I saw the value of the Indian as a daring scout. Soon two of my pickets returned with inteligence that the enemy were posted in force about one mile distant from the bank of the river with pickets extending some ½ a mile from their camp. I withdrew from the woods to the river bank & ordered the men to rest as best the[y] could untill day light, resolving to attack them at that time.

During the night a heavy rain fell, & not having any shelter, the guns were exposed, to remedy this I made the men wrap their blanket around the guns & take the storm themselves. This precaution was in most cases effective[.]

At daybreak I commenced a cautious advance through the woods in battle line, with pickets extended two hundred yards. half an hour brought us ~~to~~ within sight of the enemys camp[.]

The pickets fell back to the main line & then I ordered a charge with instructions not to fire untill the enemy were fully aroused (their camp was asleep) the men moved at a double-quick. The woods were dense & the alarm soon run through the camp. A deep bayou of some 40 feet wide divided us with a thick skirt of brush on the side oposite me which covered the enemy mostly from sight. I ordered to fire, upon the first voly the[y] fled in great consternation leaving every thing behind, with 10 killed & some 30 wounded.

The Camp consisted of only some 300 Indians & Texas rangers most of the guns were left on the ground with all the inferior camp fixtures. We pursued but to no purpose the[y] made their way to their mane command[.]

This proved to be only an advance guard or scout, with which they intended to surprise us—but the surprise was turned upon them—I now am ocupying the ford[,] both sides of the river & awaiting the approach of reinforcements to make a general attack. I am fearful they will succeed in crossing the Arkansas before we can overtake them.

I have dispatched messengers to hurry up my reinforcements—My men behaved nobly & not one was injured.

To President Abraham Lincoln from Colonel Robert W. Furnas and Lieutenant-Colonel Stephen H. Wattles, July 14, 1862

Head Qts 1st Regt Indian
Home Guards Camp on Grand
River, Cherokee Nation 15 miles
North of Fort Gibson July 14th 1862

His Excellency the President
of the United States and
The Secretary of War

Sirs

Permit us to respectfully represent that Major William A. Phillips of this Regiment has been detailed from my command to act as colonel of the new Cherokee Regt.[42] The remaining officers now ask that Adjt. A. C. Ellithorpe of this command be promoted to the rank of major, to fill the vacancy occasioned.

We further ask that the promotion be made for gallant and noble conduct at the battle near "Grand Saline" or the routing and taking of Col. Clarkson's command. Adjt Ellithorpe at the head of his Command personally taking the Rebel Col prisoner.

Adjt. Ellithorpe has been with this Regiment from its commencement and has showed himself fully competent possessing great energy, and is very successful in managing the Indian Soldier. His thorough acquaintance [wi]th their customs and habits [ma]kes him an indispensable officer.

We trust you will be pleased to grant our request, as we can assure your excellency that it will promote the interests of the Government and especially of our Regiment.

Very Respectfully
Your obt. Servt.
Robert. W. Furnas
Col. Comdg.
S. H. Wattles Lieut. Col.

[*Source:* Kansas Historical Society, Ellithorpe Family Papers. *Note:* The letter is torn at the places indicated by brackets.]

To Colonel William Weer, July 15, 1862

Head Quarters 1st Indian
Regiment Camp on Grand River
July 15th 1862

Col. Wm Weere
Com In Expd

Sir

From a copy of the Division Q M report upon the contraband goods taken at the battle of Locust Grove I notice several palpable er[r]ors. ~~which~~ I would most respectfuly call your attention to those most flagrant & injurious to my Regiment. Viz—the report sets forth that 500 horses were taken at the Battle. The Division Quarter Master should certainly know with regard to that fact & I have no doubt of the correctness of that portion of the report. I find that in the closing remarks of his report he says: "The horses & several other articles were taken possession of by 1st Indian Regt Home Guards from which no report has been obtained." You will see by the following state of facts that this statement is untrue.

	No of horses brot from Leroy	No obtained from the Eny
Co. A	38 horses	31 horses
" B	51 "	18 "
" C	37 "	14 "
" D	33 "	10 "
" E	~~22~~ 23 "	20 "
" F	~~42~~ 42 "	25 "
" G	28 "	22 "
" H	24 "	21 "
" I	44 "	20 "
" K	39 "	24 "
	359 "	205 "

Herewith please find a full & as I believe a correct account & statement of all horses in my command, how & when obtained & by what authority. Under your verbal instructions to mount the remainder of my Regiment as soon as possible from the stock of the enemy, my men to some extent, as you will see, have availed themselves of your instructions. *[See chart.]*

Thus you will see that our total increas of horses will not exced 205 from the time we have entered the enemys country, & over 100 of these were obtained prior to the battle of Locust Grove many of them being ponys identified by our men as those stolen from them before, & during their flight to Kansas. What the Division Quartermaster may mean by the "*several other articles* taken" is best known to himself, if he desires to make an official record against my Regiment & to the entire exclusion of all the other detachments engaged in the packing up of Col Clarksons camp, he [illegible word] merits the severest sensore. That many articles from the rebel camp may be in the possession of the men of my Regiment may be true, & that I am not only willing, but anxious, that every article should be accounted for is also true, But that my regiment, after galantly meeting & conquering the enemy should be discredited for that which they are not guilty of will not be tamely submited to at the hands of a Quartermaster who seems to see but one side of the picture.

As his report forms a portion of the official record to Department head Quarters I would respectfully ask that this document be also forwarded to that Department ~~Head Quarters~~

I have the honor sir to be
Your Most Obt Servant
[A. C. Ellithorpe]

[*Source:* Robert W. Furnas Papers, Archives and Manuscripts Division (Lincoln: Nebraska Historical Society Microfilm Publication, 1951), reel 1, frames 371–73. *Note:* Although the letter is not signed, the handwriting is definitely Ellithorpe's.]

JOURNAL ENTRIES, JULY 15–JULY 19, 1862

July 15, 1862

This morning my reinforcements arived giving me over two thousand men. we immediately set out to attack the enemy upon the upper crossing of the Arkansas our scouts report them in force what the result will be I canot tell now (12 M) late

July 16, 1862

As I anticipated the Rebels fled upon our approach the[y] will not fight unless the[y] are sure of having greatly the advantage, or unless they are forced to it. we return again to day to our old camp at Vanns Crossing[.]

This evening strange & unusual news reaches us.

When I left the camp of the main army on Grand River A Councill of War had been called & was in session. Called by Col Weere, Com Expedition[.]

The decission of the Councill was to fall back with the entire force, untill we should come within supporting distance of Fort Scott, & alsoe for the protection of our comissary trains from which we have herd nothing for over 9 days. Neither have we had any communication with Fort Scott for the same time. Great fears are entertained that our trains &

messengers are cut off—if this be the case & the rebel forces are making a flank moovement upon us from Missouri, & if Curtis has been compelled to fall back from Helena,[43] we are undoubtedly in great danger of being cut off at leas[t] of suffering for commissary stores.

Col Weere it seems has refused to coincide with the decission of the councill of war, to fall back, & ordered the troops on half rations.

This created great dissatisfaction throughout the entire command[.]

Col Salomon of the Wisconsin 9th last night assumed command & enforced that assumption by putting Col Weere under arrest & ordering all the white troops back by slow marches in the direction of Fort Scott[.][44]

Great excitement prevails for Were has many friends, & is a Kansas man, while Salomon is a foreigner & from another state. The Kansas men think it is an assumption of power that will discredit the Kansas troops. What the termination will be, & who is right I will not now pretend to say, but when facts are more fully developed the right will be justified.

July 17, 1862

We are now on the road to Baxters springs again no enemy, except small scouting parties are to be herd from—The weather is hot dusty & the country suffering with a great drought, our stock is failing fast, & many of the men are falling sick with disentary & fever[?][.]

July 19, 1862

We shall reach Baxters springs in the forenoon tomorow where we shall lay for some days & recruit.

General Orders, No. 1, July 19, 1862

HDQRS. FIRST INDIAN BRIGADE,
Camp Corwin,[45] on the Verdigris, July 19, 1862

GENERAL ORDERS, No. 1.

I. In consequence of the retreat of all white troops from the command of the Indian Expedition I hereby assume command of the Indian regiments in the field.

II. The commanders of the First, Second, and Third Indian Regiments will be present at these headquarters at precisely 8 o'clock p.m. for council of war.

By order of Col. R. W. Furnas commanding First Indian Brigade.

A. C. ELLITHORPE
Lieutenant and Acting Assistant Adjutant-General

[*Source:* U.S. War Department, *War of the Rebellion: A Compilation of the Official Records of the Union and Confederate Armies*, 128 vols. (1880–1901; repr., Harrisburg, Pa.: National Historical Society, 1971), ser. 1, 13:481.]

JOURNAL ENTRIES, JULY 20–JULY 21, 1862

July 20, 1862

We are in camp with good water & good grazing for stock. The men enjoy the rest & the health of the camp is fast improving, the pure spring water is almost magical to restore health, the weather is also cooler[.]

July 21, 1862

I am today ordered to Fort Leavenworth as bearer of dispatches & take with me the surgeon of our Regt[46]—The Indian Regts are all here in camp, & formed into a separate brigade under the Command of Col Furnas[.] I am appointed A A A Genl[.][47]

I leave this afternoon & shall not meet with many incidents worthy of recording hence I close this journal for a general entry at some future time[.]

To Colonel Robert W. Furnas, July 25, 1862

Indian Brigade
Camp Wattles
July 25th 1862

R W Furnas
Com Indian Brigade

Sir

Permit me to inform you that on the 22nd instant a scout & foraging party detailed from the 1st Indian Regt went out into the Enemys country, returning with quite a large amount of property contraband of War. To-Wit Seven horses, four mules, two double wagons, & many other smaller articles. The horses were taken from known secessionists, I am informed that this property is about being taken from the camp without accounting to the Government, or even having been turned over to the proper authoritys according to explicit regulations. I ask your attention to an investigation of all the facts connected with this affair.

Respectfully yours
A C Ellithorpe 1st Lieut
& A. A. A. G.

[*Source:* Kansas Historical Society, Ellithorpe Family Papers.]

To Colonel Robert W. Furnas, July 27, 1862

Hudsons Crossing
July 27th 1862

Col. R. W. Furnas
Com Ind Brig.

Sir

I have the honor to rept my interviews with the several commands as follows, Viz. My interview with Maj Williams was satisfactory.[48] he desires to remain in the country & will cooperate with any movement to facilitate the entire expulsion of the enemy from the country. Col Jewel will act strictly under the orders of *Genl* Salomon, (who has been confirmed a Brigadier).[49]

In my interview with the Genl I can but think that his plan of operations is in the main *good.* The cherokee country will be held firmly & Genl Salomon will give you timely information of his movements, You will find it the best of policy to *adhere strictly* to his orders. You will be in reach of the main army all the time & you need not imagine that the country is going to be abandoned—The Genl approves your plans of possessing Fort Gibson,[50] Park Hill, Taliqua,[51] the ford [?]

across the Verdigris &c. But hold your present position as gen'l Head Quarters. The Genl wants two companys stationed between this point & your camp—Select some good point & place a company at each post for the purpose of transmitting safely dispatches & protecting [illegible word] messages &c, & further to facilitate speedy communication with the Fort,

Col Jewel will send you white men to assist you, communicate further with him on that part. Every thing is tinder footed & you must tread cautiously but above all things *obey orders strictly*—Capt Brooks was killed two days ago while scouting East of the [illegible word] & oposite from this point—The Doctor is improving slowly[.] I find some of our *stray* Indians on the road which I send back with passage[.]

Now Col act in conjunction with Salomon it is safe for you at least, I leave here immediately—I send the mail belonging to the Indian Regts—

I get letters from home informing me of the serious & dangerous illness of my Wife.

Will you forward me leave for absence, for a few days & I will not use it if possible to avoid it.

Yours truly
A C Ellithorpe

P.S. The balance of Allens Battery will always be within assisting distance, as well as the force to support it. The plans of the Genl will be mad[e] known to you from time to time[.]
ACE

[*Source:* Robert W. Furnas Papers, Archives and Manuscripts Division (Lincoln: Nebraska Historical Society Microfilm Publication, 1951), reel 1.]

CHAPTER 3

BUSHWHACKING IN ARKANSAS, AUGUST–NOVEMBER 1862

The women do nothing, apparently, but lick their snuff, chew and smoke, eat hog and hominy, and raise an inferior quality of stupid, sallow babies.
—ALBERT C. ELLITHORPE, *Chicago Evening Journal,* December 1, 1862

From the end of the failed Indian Expedition in late July 1862 until early 1863, military officials and the Office of Indian Affairs staff sparred over the Indian refugee issue. Southern Superintendent William G. Coffin opposed the return of the refugees until the situation in the Indian Territory stabilized. Coincidentally, Maj. Albert C. Ellithorpe and Coffin were both in Washington, D.C., in mid-September 1862, and while there, Coffin asked for Ellithorpe's opinion on the controversy. Ellithorpe's letter, in which he sided with Coffin and Indian agents H. W. Martin and E. H. Carruth, is one of the documents presented in this chapter.[1]

Brig. Gen. James G. Blunt advocated energetically for the return of the refugees as soon as possible and insisted that the Indian Home Guards were sufficient protection for the Indian Territory (fig. 8). In spite of their disagreement on this issue, Ellithorpe and Blunt became friends, and it is clear from his writings that throughout his life Ellithorpe admired Blunt. A physician in civilian life and two years younger than Ellithorpe, Blunt was a New England native, like Ellithorpe. In 1856 Blunt moved to Kansas from Ohio and soon immersed himself in politics. Both men were antislavery advocates, but Blunt became involved in the war earlier than Ellithorpe, when he served in a Kansas brigade created by Senator James Lane in 1861. The two men had much in common and maintained contact through much of the war.[2]

When Blunt pushed for the return of the refugees, he irritated Indian officials, who saw the decision as their responsibility, but Blunt had powerful allies, including many of the refugees themselves, the Indian Home Guards soldiers, and an Interior Department that was weary of bearing the expense of the Kansas refugee camps. Although providing no evidence, Blunt warned Caleb B. Smith, the interior secretary, that "a clique of mercenary and unscrupulous speculators" that included some "Agents and Superintendents, have had their pockets well lined with the profits from contracts." Furthermore, Blunt explained, the refugee question was "intimately blended with the military affairs of the Indian Territory." Ultimately, the return of the refugees was delayed until early 1863, when relations improved between Blunt and Indian officials.[3]

Ellithorpe's involvement with this policy issue occurred while he traveled and engaged in a variety of activities from late July to the end of October; unfortunately, he documented none of them in his journal. Near the close of the Indian Expedition, Col. Robert W. Furnas ordered him first to Humboldt, Kansas, to forward supplies and then on to Fort Leavenworth to deliver dispatches. Additionally, Col. Frederick Salomon ordered Ellithorpe to accompany Dr. Andrew Holladay, who had been wounded at Locust Grove, to Fort Scott. Ellithorpe stayed at Leavenworth awaiting orders from Furnas and met with Blunt there. On September 2 Blunt extended Ellithorpe's travels, ordering him to Washington, D.C., "as a bearer of dispatches." On his way eastward Ellithorpe met with Illinois governor Richard Yates in an effort to obtain arms, stopped in Chicago for a short visit with his family, and by September 8 had delivered the dispatches to Secretary of War Edwin M. Stanton. While in Washington, Ellithorpe visited with Superintendent Coffin and wrote his letter about the refugee situation. Ellithorpe "got an interview personaly [*sic*] on my own account" with President Abraham Lincoln and had no need to use a note from Senator Lane requesting that Lincoln meet with Ellithorpe. What the president and Ellithorpe discussed at the meeting is unrecorded.[4]

Following his return to Kansas, Ellithorpe was on detached service with Col. Norton P. Chipman from late September to mid-October. Chipman had been "severely wounded" at Fort Donelson, Tennessee, while serving with the Second Iowa Infantry. Now Gen. Samuel R. Curtis, the commander of the Department of Missouri, utilized him as his chief of staff. Ellithorpe accompanied Chipman and Furnas on a fact-finding and inspection tour in mid-October. According to a *Leavenworth Daily Conservative* reporter, the men visited the Indian encampments near LeRoy, with Furnas serving as interpreter. Colonel Furnas estimated that after the expedition, half of the soldiers from his regiment absented themselves without leave and returned to their families near LeRoy. Perhaps it was at this time that Ellithorpe met with the Creek leader Opothele Yahola in an effort to secure his assistance in persuading soldiers to return to the First Indian Home Guards. As an added lure, unlike soldiers in white units, soldiers absent without leave from the Indian Home Guards were often punished with only the loss of their pay. After the visit to LeRoy, the men rode to Fort Lincoln, a few miles north of Fort Scott, to see the recruits that would become part of the First Kansas Colored Infantry, the first African American regiment to experience combat during the war. Ellithorpe then rejoined his unit and, according to postwar statements, participated in the skirmish near Old Fort Wayne in the Indian Territory on October 22.[5]

Ellithorpe started keeping his journal again on October 28 and faithfully wrote in it until his last entry on March 17, 1863. A handful of letters written to and from Ellithorpe are included in this chapter, along with his first *Chicago Evening Journal* articles. Eventually constituting twenty-three articles, these documents amplify many of the themes in his diary. Signed with pseudonyms such as "Booneville," "Creek," "Cherokee," and "Seminole," Ellithorpe definitely penned the articles. The events described mirror the journal, and at times Ellithorpe employed similar wording in both the journal and the articles. Also, he mentioned writing to the *Chicago Evening Journal* in his November 19 and December 21, 1862, diary entries. As further support, an 1876 biographical piece informed its readers that "Col. Ellithorpe, in a few graphic letters to the *Chicago Evening Journal* over the *nom de plume* of 'Creek' and 'Cherokee,' described some of the battles and chronicled some of the incidents of the exciting campaigns of the Army of the Frontier. The *Rebellion Record*, published after the War, incorporated portions of these letters bodily in its historical pages, without knowing their source or their writer." His motivations for writing the articles are unclear. The newspaper's editor may have solicited them, but Ellithorpe enjoyed writing and no doubt suspected that a Chicago audience would be curious about the war on the exotic "frontier."[6]

Guerrilla warfare is one of the major themes documented not only in this chapter but in most of the subsequent chapters. Guerrilla warfare in Missouri was a continuation of the border war with Kansas that started in the late 1850s. The passage of the Partisan Ranger Act by the Confederate Congress in April 1862 accelerated guerrilla warfare; this law provided for the recruitment of partisans, a process that started in Arkansas in May, just two months after the battle of Pea Ridge. The rugged and heavily forested northwestern part of Arkansas where Ellithorpe campaigned was well suited for guerrillas. Guerrilla warfare quickly became the main form of combat in Arkansas, so much so that historian Daniel Sutherland emphatically declared that it was "not a war within a war, as some historians have suggested, not even a second war, but *the* war."[7]

Besides writing about the challenges of this type of warfare, Ellithorpe wrote of the incredible destruction wrought by the armies and the plight of refugees and runaway slaves. Access to supplies in this frontier region was critical, and Ellithorpe chronicled the arrival of supply trains from Fort Scott, Kansas, and the use of gristmills in the area. Army demands and throngs of refugees outstripped supplies sent from Fort Scott, and the army had to obtain supplies locally, which Blunt solved by "thrashing out and grinding wheat; a game we can play at as well as the rebels." On the eve of the war there were thirty-five gristmills in northwestern Arkansas. Besides processing grain, some of them also "carded wool, ginned cotton, and wove cloth." During the Pea Ridge campaign, Confederate troops had destroyed some of the mills in the region in an effort to keep these valuable resources from Union troops. In the fall of 1862 the Kansas Division, which included the First Indian Home Guards, camped near Bentonville, Arkansas, where Lt. Edwin C. Manning of Company C reported that his company "was detailed . . . to run a gristmill about three miles north of Bentonville. We collected wheat from the bins of the little farms in the vicinity and made flour for the brigade."[8]

Ellithorpe also focused his attention on events within his regiment. He worked hard to rebuild his unit's strength, discipline, and morale while positioning himself to secure the colonelcy of the regiment. Colonel Furnas submitted his letter of resignation on September 17 and in it confessed, "I have always doubted the propriety and policy of arming and placing in the field Indians." In this remarkably forthright letter to Secretary of War Stanton, Furnas stated that his opinion had been confirmed, for "full blood Indians cannot be made soldiers and that to attempt it is a useless waste of both time and money," a position that Ellithorpe disagreed with. Furnas wrote that the language barrier between Indians and whites was a major barrier because only a handful of the Indian soldiers could speak English: "*All* communication has been through Interpreters, all of whom are *ignorant un-educated Negroes*, who have been raised among the Indians and possess to a great degree their peculiar characteristics. The commander has but little assurance that orders are correctly given, and none that they are understood or appreciated." Furnas wanted to return to the Nebraska Territory, where he hoped to reenter the service and be "more useful." Furnas's resignation was granted, and when he returned to Nebraska, he recruited and then commanded the Second Nebraska Cavalry for the remainder of the war.[9]

Lt. Col. Stephen Wattles assumed command following Furnas's resignation, but Ellithorpe had charge of the regiment during Wattles's periodic absences. Ellithorpe discovered that Lt. George Dobler had defrauded the government and uncovered a scheme in which Wattles had appropriated the pay of some of the African Creek interpreters. This was not the first time, nor would it be the last time, that Wattles engaged in wrongdoing. After the Indian Expedition, Wattles had allegedly sold a pair of horses and tried to sell a wagon that were government property. Many assumed that Wattles's troubles would lead to his cashier or resignation. Ellithorpe, along with others, hastened to seize the colonelcy plum, although he acknowledged the possibility that Kansas politics would ensure his defeat.[10] He determined to command a regiment whether it was his or another one and suggested in the late summer the creation of a sharpshooter battalion armed with Henry rifles.[11]

To President Abraham Lincoln, from Brigadier General James G. Blunt, September 2, 1862

Head Quarters Dept of Kansas
Fort. Leavenworth Sept 2d 1862

To his Exelency [*sic*]
Abraham Lincoln

This will be presented to you by Major A. C. Elithorpe whom I dispatch to Washington, on business connected with the interest of this dept. Major Elithorpe also desires authority to raise in the North Western States a battalion of Sharp Shooters to be armed with Henry's Repeating Rifle. Such a force would be of incalculable value to the service in this Dept. And I trust he may have Success in obtaining the authority to put them in the field fully Equiped with as little delay as possible. He is instructed to confer with you fully upon all matters connected with the Military Service in this Dept.
I have the honor to be your

most obedient Servant
Jas. G. Blunt Brig. Genl.
Commanding

I fully concur in the above recommendation & deem such a course indispensable or at least highly important.

J. H. Lane

[*Source:* Kansas Historical Society, Ellithorpe Family Papers.]

To Albert C. Ellithorpe, from William C. Coffin, September 11, 1862

Washington DC Sept 11th 1862

Major Ellithorpe
of the 1st Indian Regiment
Home guards

Dear Sir

As you have been presently connected with the late Military Expedition from Kansas South into the Indian Territory I Respectfully request you to State for the information of the Indian Department your opinion upon the following points.

first would it be Safe in the present Condition of the Country to restore the Southern Refugee Indians now in Southern Kansas the women & children, the old feeble & infirm to there [*sic*] homes in the Indian Country

What is your Opinion from what you Saw and herd from reliable Sources as to the amount of Subsistence in that country crops, the present [illegible word] forage &c.

What amount of Military force if any will it require to restore and protect them there and where is that force to come from and have subsist in the Indian Country if those Indians are restored to their homes this fall and the Confederate invasion of Kansas occurs how would they be affected by it

An early and explicit answer to the above interrogatories will I have no doubt be of public Utility and aid the Government in regard to the best and most Economical course to pursue with those unfortunate People that have already Suffered more for their loyalty than any People in America[.]

Very Respectfully your obedient Servant
W G Coffin
Supt of Indian Affairs
Southern Supt [illegible word]

[*Source:* Kansas Historical Society, Ellithorpe Family Papers. *Note:* Added to the letter is an undated comment: "This letter was answered in extensio—and the Govt acted in conformity to the suggestions therein[.] A.C.E."]

To William C. Coffin, September 12, 1862

Washington D.C.
Sep. 12th 1862

Col. W G Coffin
Supt of Indian Affairs
Southern Superintendancy

Sir

In replying to the several interrogations contained in your letter of the 11th inst, I shall base my answers entirely upon my own observations & experience, obtained during a six months campaign, with the Indians, & in the Creek & Cherokee countries. Feeling a deep interest in the welfare of these loyal refugee Indians, who have sacrificed *all*, rather than fight against our Flag, I shall be cautious, & advise no policy, but that which will insure their safe restoration to their homes.

The important question in your letter, & that which embodies the whole subject matter, is the following—"Would it be safe in the present condition of the country to restore the Southern refugee Indians now in Southern Kansas, the women & children, the old, feeble & infirm to their homes in the Indian country"

I answer—It would not be safe to take the women & children to the Creek or Cherokee countries this fall for the following reasons. 1st The corn & vegetable crop north of the Arkansas River will not afford them subsistence for a single month. The excessive drouth has almost completely destroyed it, & what little would have matured is laid waste by the frequent foraging parties of our own army, or those of the Rebels[.]

The amount of military force necessary to restore & safely protect this people in their homes, would far exceed what is at present, at the disposal of the Department of Kansas, And should they be removed to the Indian country, & our forces again be compelled to fall back for the protection of Missouri or Kansas, it would again involve their precipitate flight, or insure their total destruction.

Again—the effectiveness of our troops would be materialy embarassed by the presence of such a vast number of timid & helpless creatures—I base my judgment upon the following facts—viz—

The Expedition which I have been with during the summer, exploring this country, consisted of three Brigades, but containing actualy only about 6 thousand men.[12] We routed, captured, & pursued the fragments of several Rebel commands, driving them south of the Arkansas River, oposite to & in the vicinity of Fort Gibson. This done, we found the whole of Western Arkansas alive, & the numerous rebel squads were at once reinforced from the gu[e]rrila parties of Missouri[,] Arkansas, Texas, & the various rebel Indian tribes until they now number a force of from 30 to 40 thousand strong, under the command of Pike, Drew,[13] McIntosh, Rains,[14] Stand Waitie, & others, ready to contest the passage of the Arkansas River at any point, & in fact capable of crossing to the north side of the River & possessing the country we have twice passed over. Why did our command fall back? simply because we had not force sufficient to cross the Arkansas River & maintain our position & because we were to [*sic*] remote from our depo[t] of supplies. The Creek Country West of the Verdigris River is almost destitute of forage for man or beast, owing to the drouth—Hence to remove these families would [illegible word] to the Govt great additional expense, not only to subsist but to protect them—Where they are they need no military protection & food is abundant[.]

You will bear in mind that a large portion of the Indian country is south of the Arkansas River & is at present the strong hold of the Rebels. Many portions of it [are] mountainous & rug[g]ed affording secure retreats, that will require a powerful army to dislodge[.]

I have the honor Sir
to be yours most
Respectfully
A. C. Ellithorpe Maj
1st Ind Regt

[*Source:* National Archives, Record Group 75, Office of Indian Affairs, Letters Received by the Office of Indian Affairs, 1824–81, M234, roll 834, frames 1324–26.]

From Colonel Robert W. Furnas, October 17, 1862

Hd. Qr. 1st Ind. Regt.
Fort Scot Kansas Oct. 17/1862

To whom it may concern

I take great pleasure in saying that Major A C Ellithorpe has been attached to my command during the past summer, both in the organization of my Regt and in the field. I have found him as a business man one of the most efficient, active, earnest and energetic I have ever had to do with. He is a thorough military man, brave and dashing as could be desired: Always at his post and ready for any emergency; and his social qualities are unsurpassed. I can cheerfully recommend him for any position he may hereafter desire in the Army or elsewhere.

Very Respectfully
R. W. Furnas
Col. 1st Ind. Regt.

[*Source:* Kansas Historical Society, Ellithorpe Family Papers.]

JOURNAL ENTRIES, OCTOBER 28, 1862–NOVEMBER 5, 1862

October 28, 1862

We encamped this evening in the town of Bentonville Arkansas. The village formerly contained about fifteen hundred inhabitants[.] But now the dissolution is almost complete—not over 300 women & children remain, but very few men are here, & those mostly old & decriped. Most of the Town was burned by the forces under *Sigle* [Sigel] in consequence of some outrage committed by some of the citizens upon our soldiers[.][15]

The Town was burned some time in February[.]

The county of Benton gave a large majority for the Old Union[.][16] That question was submitted to the people.

Yet the Southern pressure forced the people to submit to the division policy—

Camp Bowen,[17] Benton County, November 3, 1862

This day I assumed com of the 1st Indian Regt all the other field officers having resigned or being absent. Yesterday, Genl Blunt issued an order detailing me to duty upon his staff. But my Regiment having no commanding officer, I shall remain in command untill some other arraingment can be made[.]

This evening after getting into camp & while at supper, our picket guard was fired upon by the scouts of the enemy—I had my regiment in line of battle in less than five minutts—The firing was close to camp. My men were anxious for a fight & showed no fears. Our camp is in a rich portion of country & forage is plenty[.]

Bushwhackers are also plenty, & our men are fired upon several times daily. I shall go on a hunt after them probably tomorow. The country is covered with thick brush & admirably adapted to this cowardly mode of warfare—Yesterday we killed one & took one prisoner, he will probably be shot[.]

November 4, 1862

This day little has been done except attending to camp duties. The whole of the Kansas division of the army is now in camp at this place—Consisting of three Brigades viz Salomons, Clouds & Weer's.[18] The day is fair but windy[.]

November 5, 1862

We marched this morning at day light, making a feigned retreat a distance of 15 miles. The object I think is to draw the enemy after us. we are now in the vicinity of Bentonville. Contiguous to us are 4 Grist Mills. we intend to put them all in operation making flour & meal for the army—forage is plenty & water of the best quality in abundance. We learn that a large force of the enemy are East of us under Rains. Genl Schofield has fell back to Elk Horne tavern[19]—the old Pea Ridge battle ground. This movement is to draw Rains farther north & at the same time prevent him from getting into our rear[.]

To Colonel William F. Cloud, November 5, 1862

Head Quarters 1st Ind Reg H. G.
Camp Bowen Nov 5th 1862

Col. W. F. Cloud
Comd 3rd Brig

Sir

Two Companies of "Creek Indians" belonging to this Regiment are now at Leroy Kansas. While there a few days ago, in an interview with "Opothleoholo" the "Old Chief," I became convinced that with the proper efforts, I could again induce these Indians to join their regiment—I also find by conference with the Indians here that they desire that these soldiers shall again join the command.

To this end I have consulted that they may transmit a message to Opothleoholo and have agreed to communicate with him myself through Col Coffin the "Superintendent" of "Indian Affairs"—Being convinced that this course will tend to place the regiment in a much more useful condition, I now only await your approval.

Your Most Obedient Servt
A. C. Ellithorpe
Maj Comdg Regt

[*Source:* Kansas Historical Society, Ellithorpe Family Papers. *Note:* Many parts of the letter are underlined in red. The underlining has been eliminated in the transcription because it appears to have been added to the document later. In his response Col. W. F. Cloud said that he would cooperate with Ellithorpe and that Ellithorpe had "his full consent to act in any way he thinks proper." (Col. W. F. Cloud to Major Ellithorpe, November 5, 1862, Camp Bowen, Ellithorpe Family Papers).]

JOURNAL ENTRY

November 6, 1862

During the day we have taken possession of three Mills & comme[nce]d putting them in running condition[.]

The supply of wheat & corn is quite abundant. To the loyal we pay to the Rebels confiscate.

We bid fair to subsist the army very cheap & with but little expense to the Govt provided comissarys & Quartermasters render [?] just accounts—We sent this morning a strong force of Mounted Men & howitzers on a scout to the Creek Country to visit Taliqua [Tahlequah] Ft Gibson, & Grand Saline at the latter place we expect to manufacture salt in abundance & this is an article we stand in need of much[20]— The inhabitants here have been without salt for months, & are suffering extremely for the want of it[.]

From Lieutenant James H. Gillpatrick, November 6, 1862

1st Ind. Regt H. G.
Camp Bowen Ark Nov 6th 1862

Maj. A. C. Ellithorpe
Comdg 1st Ind. Regt

Sir

From Recent developments which have come to our knowledge we are fearful that a large amount of money placed in the hands of Lieut Col Wattles for the purpose of procuring change, and returning the same to the soldiers belonging to the several companies will be lost to the men unless prompt Steps be taken.

We therefore ask that you take such Steps as may seem to you most efficient to procure the return of the money to the Captains of the various companies to which it belongs. *[See chart]*

	his mark	Capt.
To-muck-mick-ko	X	"
Ah-hu-lu-tus-tu-muck-ko	X	"
Ock-to-ya-ge-ya-ha-la	X	"
Tom-me-tus-ti-nuck-ke	X	"
Go-ko-le-lo-ches	X	"
Tus-te-nup-chup-ko	X	"
Tulsefix-e-ko	X	"
John-neh	X	"

[*Note:* Captain Ah-hu-lu-tus-tu-muck-ko (or Ah-ha-la-tus-ta-nuk-ko) died of disease at Camp Moonlight, Ark., on March 23, 1863, and Captain Tus-te-nup-chup-ko died of disease at Fort Gibson on August 1, 1863. Captain Tulsefix-e-ko (or Tul-se-fix-se-ko) was killed on February 1, 1863. *Official Register of the Volunteer Force of the United States Army for the Years 1861, '62, '63, '64, '65*, pt. 7 (Washington, D.C.: Adjutant Generals Office, 1867), 364.]

Your obedient Servants
Witness
J. H. Gillpatrick[21]
1st Lt & Adjt

[*Source:* Kansas Historical Society, Ellithorpe Family Papers. *Note:* The word *his* is above each X, and *mark* is below each X.]

JOURNAL ENTRY

November 7, 1862

This morning another heavy scout was sent out to assertain if possible the precise location of Rains force[22]—They will be in by tomorrow—Should they be this side of the Boston Mountains we shall make a *drive* for them on a *double* quick—The Mills are tod[a]y reported in running order & the work of grinding has commenced & bids fair to prove a great success[.]

To William G. Coffin, November 7, 1862

Head Quarters 1st Regt
Indians Home Guards camp
Bowen near the line of the
Indian Territory November 7th 1862

Indian Supt
Col Wm G Coffin
and the Soldiers and Chiefs of
the Creek Nation at
Leroy Kansas

Gentlemen

Now being in command of the Creek Regiment it becomes my duty to again make an effort to restore the Regiment to its former proportions as well as to increase its usefulness towards the restoration of the Loyal ones to their own Country and homes[.]

To do this it must have the Individual strength of all Loyal Creeks and Seminoles. It must be remembered that those of the Nation who trust to the Government for protection are only a part of their number, the balance seeking to destroy not only the Government but the Loyal ones of their own Kin and now a mere diference of opinion that will divide the fraction remaining is unbecoming the patriotism of Loyal men and will prove disastrous to the perpetuity of the Creek Nation[.] Opothlesholan in his policy to distract the Indian Soldier from his obedience to the commands of the Government is unquestionably rendering to the Enemy most signal aid and comfort and a course which if persisted in will be visited with the severest censure. You will now perceive that we are on the border of the Indian Country and a very large portion of the Indians are now scouting through their own Territory[.] What I now desire is that *every man* who was enlisted as a soldier shall at once return to his command by the way of Fort Scott unless otherwise ordered by competent authority—For this end I will try to secure for each soldier his back pay making all due allowance for the bad counsel that have surrounded him. Herewith will be presented to the Chiefs and Men a communication for the captains and officers of the Regt[.] Special Agent Carruth is authorised to present these papers and accompany the soldiers under their officers (if any on duty) to these Head Quarters[.]

Very Respectfully
Your Obt Servant
A. C. Ellithorpe
Maj Comd Regt

[*Source:* National Archives, Record Group 75, Office of Indian Affairs, Letters Received by the Office of Indian Affairs, 1824–81, M234, roll 834, frames 1407–8.]

JOURNAL ENTRIES, NOVEMBER 8, 1862–NOVEMBER 10, 1862

November 8, 1862

Nothing of much importance has taken place today. Many of the inhabitants are coming to our lines claiming to be loyal & asking protection, large numbers of them are being sent North—What the end of this exodus from Dixie will be is yet to be seen—one thing is certain wherever our army goes the country becomes depopulated[.] Those who dont flee south, beg to be taken north—We today had a comissary train of about two hundred wagons arrive from Ft Scott & alsoe the arival of the Mail which to us is an advent of great importance—Some go away with a letter smiling with delight. Others with downcast looks, while some swear bitterly that the d—d mail is not worth the powder to blow it up—

Today I have discovered a most dastardly course of conduct which has been perpetrated by the Lieut Col S. H. Wattles of my regiment, during my absence[.]

He has managed to get into his hands about 4000 $ of money belonging to the soldiers & Interpreters of the Regiment—procured a leave of absence & taken the money with him—I have procured an order for his arrest, & Genl Blunt has promptly dispatched a messenger after him. I expect much difficulty with him when he returns—but knowing that I have right on my side I feel invincible & will not rest untill I bring him to justice. Genl Blunt seems anxious to aid me in fereting out his frauds.

The Genl is proving himself one of the ablest military men in the field[.] He pitches into the enemy wherever he finds them[.]

November 9, 1862

Today our scout returned from an exciting trip over the Boston mountains,[23] upon this side of the mountain we came upon a camp of Rebs. They were fairly surprised, & precipitously fled.[24] There were 400 of them & only 300 of us. We unlimbered the howitzers & let them bark at them[.] The shell fell amongst them killing two & wounding several[.]

They ran as if the de—l were after them[.]

November 10, 1862

We remained in camp all day, nothing new or exciting all are anxious to go forward & find the enemy[.]

Statement by Indians, November 10, 1862

List of persons to whom payment was made under assumed names.

(1) Jo-la-fix-se-ko Real name, Ah-ha-la-fix-a-ko

This Indian was induced to assume the name, and draw the pay due to one of those Indians now about from the Regt at Leroy amounting to $55.00

(2) (Po-ka-ko-che) Real name Fas-ha-jo

In this instance Fas-ha-jo, was induced to assume the name of (Po-ka-ko-che) *an Indian Deserter* before the time of payment. He is not certain what amount was paid to him- but he retained only $5.00. the balance being taken by the (manager)

(3) ("Too-sea") Real name "Go-bey."

Go-bey cannot tell whether money was drawn or not, since he did not receive any himself. He was instructed to answer to the name of ("Too-sea") when it was called by the Paymaster.

In Presence of
A. C. Ellithorpe, Maj Comdg
J. H. Gillpatrick. 1st Lt. & Adjt.

The above statement was made through the Interpreter Nov. 10th 1862. By the Indians implicated.

[*Source:* Kansas Historical Society, Ellithorpe Family Papers.]

JOURNAL ENTRIES, NOVEMBER 11, 1862–NOVEMBER 12, 1862

November 11, 1862

Today a large train of two hundred wagons arrived from Ft Scott loaded with provisions[.] weather still fine & nights cool—

November 12, 1862

Today we returned the train with some 100 families of refugees from the state going to the land of peace & freedom.

Chicago Evening Journal Article

THE ARMY ON THE WESTERN FRONTIER.

The Operations of Gen. Blunt's Forces in Northwestern Arkansas.

THE ENEMY ATTACKED AND ROUTED TWICE.

Destitution and Desolation Caused by the War.

Correspondence of The Chicago Evening Journal.
HEADQUARTERS OF THE 1ST DIVISION OF THE ARMY OF THE FRONTIER, CAMP EWING.[25]
Benton county, Ark., Nov. 12th, 1862.

We are now occupying one of the most wealthy counties in the State of Arkansas. Our army consists of the Kansas division, three brigades, commanded as follows: 1st Brigade by Gen. Salomon; 2d Brigade by Col. Weere; 3d Brigade by Col. Cloud—all under Brigadier General James G. Blunt. This division is now acting in conjunction with the division under Gen. Schofield, who at the present writing is some 25 miles north of here, at the noted Elk Horn Tavern, or perhaps better known as the Pea Ridge battle-ground. Schofield's and Blunt's forces may be set down at about 20,000 men, with an abundance of artillery, and generally well appointed arms.[26]

You have probably heard of the victory we gained over Gen. Cooper a few days ago at Maysville, near the line of the Cherokee nation.[27] Cooper's force consisted of about 5,000 men, all very well armed, and five pieces light artillery. Gen. Blunt started from north of Bentonville with a force of 2,000 men and several pieces of artillery. The advance reached the enemy's pickets about daylight the next morning. It was discovered that the enemy was fully aware of our approach, and evidently making arrangements for a retreat.

The advance force, consisting of only 500 men and two mountain howitzers, with General Blunt at the head, made the attack, and pitched in, in the most approved Western style. The enemy, supposing that our whole force was close at hand, commenced falling back, returning our fire from their five guns, with tolerable energy and skill. Blunt decided to charge their guns, and gave the word. Away went the gallant five hundred boys, with the gallant little General at their head. The enemy broke and ran. The guns were ours, and we had nothing more to do but to spur forward and keep in sight of one of the most scientific skedaddles of modern record. Our loss was five killed and twelve wounded; that of the enemy, as far as ascertained, 60 killed, 140 wounded, and 50 prisoners, with all their camp equipage, cannon and many small arms.[28]

We have dropped back fifteen miles, a little south of Bentonville, for a long pursuit would be useless, when the enemy gave unmistakable evidence of their superiority in a race.

Perhaps you would like to know what we are doing now. Well, then I will tell you, and I am sure you will approve of our Industry. We are in the vicinity of four flouring mills, with large quantities of wheat and corn in the vicinity. We have taken possession of the mills and gone into the *milling business.* We are now turning out about twenty thousand pounds of flour and meal daily, with which, together with the supplies we are getting from Fort Scott, we shall soon be able to settle down to a winter's campaign. We have just sent out a force to put the salt works in the Cherokee Nation at work. They will be able to make salt for the whole command. Hogs run wild; chickens abound; beef is plenty, and sorghum is cheap; and, I might add that sesesh are getting very scarce. Bushwhackers are about the only enlivening element we have. A volley from the thick jungles of brush now and then only serves to keep the boys' eyes open, and, though it is a little vexatious, it keeps us on the alert.

It is now that one realizes the horrors of war. The old homesteads are forsaken; the loom and wheel are idle; family relics are scattered in confusion over the once happy cabins—the inmates have fled, they know not where themselves, but evidently deeper into the gulf of treason and destruction.

The fearful ravages of the rebel conscript law are everywhere most apparent. Fathers, husbands and brothers, who would have remained quietly at home, have been forced into the rebel ranks—their families left to battle with want and the inevitable abuses that follow in the wake of an army. It is hard to witness the fears of those who are not responsible for this great calamity. They plead for their last cow, the last favorite family horse, and even for the last bushel of corn; but sometimes in vain—for while the commanders and officers generally feel deeply for the miseries of these wretched people, there is a swarm of unrelenting and unscrupulous thieves that have no mercy. It is, however, to the credit of Gen. Blunt, that he is exercising the most vigilant care that none shall suffer for bread, and that all plunderers are severely punished. Such families as desire to go North are furnished with comfortable transportation and rations.

This State (Arkansas) has got to go through the ordeal of depopulation. Men cannot live here without taking sides, and that means joining one army or the other, going South or North. It is the border over which the armies of both sides will traverse in every direction, consuming every thing available that will subsist an army, and how can the helpless families live when the substance of the country is consumed. The men have gone South; the families will generally go North. The severest pestilence or famine could not produce so great an exodus as is now going on. Our commissary train starts in the morning on its return to Fort Scott, and over one hundred families go with it. This occurs tri-weekly. Compute it, and see when the old State of Arkansas will be a wilderness again. If this desolation could only be visited upon the heads of those who plotted this unholy war, then the smoke of their destruction would be a sweet incense. But no; the unprincipled political originators of this calamity will ride in the official car of luxury until the treason is compounded; then we may fear that they will again occupy positions of favor, through the intercession of peace-makers and king-cotton apologists.

To-day two of our large scouting parties have returned—one from south of this point some 35 miles. The scout consisted of four hundred men, mounted, and two howitzers. As they approached the Boston Mountains, they discovered an encampment of some four hundred of the rebel State provost guard. The two howitzers were brought to bear within about seven hundred yards and the dogs let loose. Our men charged gallantly, and the chivalry again gave us an exhibition of their powers of locomotion. They abandoned their train and camp equipage and fled to the mountains in consternation. Having no use for the plunder we piled it together and made bonfires. After pursuing them over the mountains, over horribly, stony, and rugged roads, we gave up the chase. The condition of the country over which the scouts passed is the same as here. Almost every man is a conscript in the rebel army, and the families eager to flee any where for safety. Several with the butternut garb came to our lines, having just deserted from their conscription. They report that a large amount of clothing has just been received, as well as arms, from Europe. This will enable Rains to partially outfit his men.

Our scouts from the Indian country report the rebels under Cooper south of Fort Davis,[29] and still moving farther into Dixie. The whole of Cooper's force are disheartened, and say that there is no use to fight longer. Deserters from his army report great disaffection and a general belief that the South must yield, or the North will destroy them.

We destroyed a large tannery, with great quantities of unfinished leather. The whole Southern country is destitute of leather, salt and clothing. Every old loom, in every hovel throughout the whole country, only stops when our forces knock at the door. From this source the poor devils get all they have to wear.

Mrs. Gen. Rains left Sarcoxie, Missouri, to join her spouse five days ago, under escort of some 300 Missouri bushwhackers. She is truly an ugly specimen of secesh crinoline.

I shall give you in a few days the gratifying news of the capture of two important points on the Arkansas river. We are again in possession of Fort Gibson and the whole Cherokee country.

Rains, with a large force, is on our east flank, making his way carefully north, and will probably make a dash at Springfield, Mo., before long.[30] There will be troops enough to attend to him, I think in that quarter.

Here we are, away down in the enemy's country, even farther into Dixie than Rains himself, and intend to go still farther, thinking that we can fight the enemy in our rear fully as well as we can in front, and yet the "Grand Army of the Potomac" is "quiet." We are going to take the chances of whipping somebody or getting whipped, if they will only let us alone from headquarters, Gen. Blunt is one of the fighting Generals and don't go back, until after he is badly whipped.

The weather is at present fine. The country is well watered. The soldiers are generally healthy, and in fine spirits. Unless your grand armies make an advance before long, we shall cross the Mississippi a little lower down and attack the enemy in the rear, compelling them to fight, or we drive them across the Ohio river. If this should take place it will be necessary that our Generals in that quarter see that the women and children are moved back from the frontier.

CREEK.

[Published on November 25, 1862.]

JOURNAL ENTRIES, NOVEMBER 13, 1862–NOVEMBER 19, 1862

November 13, 1862

Today we broke camp & bid farewell to Camp Bowen we have consumed all the forage within 10 miles, & have moved south west—by west—on our way to Tahqua [*sic*] in the Cheroke nation we camp this evening 12 miles on flint Creek. good water, plenty of forage &c no news from the enemy. All in good spirits—day fine & night beautiful[.]

We march in the morning at day break[.]

Camp Babcock,[31] Near the Cherokee Line Arkansas, November 14, 1862

We marched this morning at sun rise & made a distance of about 12 miles, & our camp is now on flint Creek[32]—it is a fine little bottom & well supplied with corn standing in the field of good quality. My camp is in a turnip patch & we find this esculent a great rarity. The day has been beautiful—This afternoon a scout has returned from Taliqua & report that the enemy are concentrating in force at Kane Hill.

At Head quarters, the belief is prevalent that a large force of over twenty thousand are concentrating for the express purpose of fighting Blunts command[33]—if this is the case it is a concentration of *Coopers* & *Hindmans* forces, reinforced from *Rains*, & *Pike*. If this turns out then we shall have a hard fight. Our force here at this time will not reach over 8,000 men, though we have four Batteries, besides several Howitzers. If the Battle is where we can use our artilery, I have no doubt we can whip them, without it we shall have to retreat, & if our communication upon the North is cut off, our only outlet is west & into a country that is destitute of forage for man or beast[.]

Before tomorrow night we shall know the position of the enemy, & shall either fight or retreat immediately. We shall see what we *shall see*—

November 15, 1862

At 10 oclock A.M. an alarm came in to camp that the pickets of the 1st Brigade under Salomon were fired into by the pickets of the Enemy[.] we now stand 12 OClock with our men ready to mount & the Batteries in readiness to move[.] we are in hopes that the enemy are in force to make an attack the ground we ocupy is not the best but it will do very well.

November 16, 1862

Today is gloomy & Sunday it has rained all night & rather warm for the season of the year. No new tidings of importance from the enemy, other than that they have a force at Rays Mills,[34] about 15 miles from, our scouts & spies are out & if possible will get information as to numbers & character of their force[.]

Report gives them 8,000 cavalry & 4,000 infantry at the Mill & at Kane hill seven miles from the Mill. Genl Blunt is determined to fight. it makes no difference what their force is. One thing is certain they never will fight us when they know that we have an equal force—hence the only way to fight then is to give them the odds & take the chances of Whipping a superior force. The day has been a gloomy one—Genl Blunt came to my quarters & had a sociable converse—Night has again come on & a misty rain still is hanging over us making the camp very disagreeable[.] I have tod[a]y found out that one of the Lieutenants has been defrauding the Government out of something lik one hundred dollars, by drawing money upon false names.

Lieut Dobler is the guilty one & I shall bring him to speedy punishment[.][35] I this moment send for his arrest & place a guard over him during the night—

This is a duty that I dred to perform for the reason that it caries disgrace with it to the guilty part to a fearful extent.

November 17, 1862

This has been a gloomy day again, not over one hours sun shine—We have learned that the enemy at Rays Mills & at Kane Hill have retreated towards Fort Smith. We sent a scouting party of two hundred men to assertain exactly where they are mooving & what they intend doing—Today I sent in a statement concerning the misconduct of Col Wattles which will go forward to Washington, allso concerning Lieut Dobler—I think they will be dismissed from the service with disgrace—The rain is falling fast tonight & our camp is on low mudy ground, if it continues we must move to better quarters[.]

We today herd of the removal of Genl McClellan[36]—It gives general satisfaction to all parties in the Army here, & inspires a new feeling of hope that the war will now be brought to a speedy close[.]

Several hundred Cherokee & Creek reffugees came to our lines today. A few stragling Sesesh were taken, probably bushwhackers.

Forage begins to get scarce & poor—My negro has just brought me in a nice warm peach pie. *he is a brick—Bully for him!*

November 18, 1862

Still it rains slow but steady. The mud in camp is increasing. The weather is mild which makes the rain more bareable. Otherwise the sufering of the contrabands & refugees would be terible, they have no tents nor covering of any kind. many of them almost naked—as soon as the comissary train comes in we shall send all who are not fit for duty North. The night has brought no news. our scouts are out yet. The day will probably give us some news—

I called upon the Genl this morning—took breakfast with *Genl* Babcock[.] Ham, mackeral boiled potatoes, hard bread & coffee with *bad whiskey* for *desert[.]*

Two Southern Ladies called at the tent,—regular snuff-lickers, smokers & tobacco chewers, a fair specimen of Arkansas *She Rebels*—Their principal occupation is licking snuff, chewing, smoking, Eating hog & hominy & raising greasy squalling, sallow babies of a very inferior quality[.]

Camp Babcock, November 19, 1862

The night has been dark & rainy. The morning opens with increased rain. The ground is saturated, & the mud is getting very deep. The weather is growing colder. The whole country looks very gloomy—The prospect for active operations during such a state of weather is very unpropitious. The camp is gloomy & I fear that sickness will set in[.]

We are so remote from our own country that it is no ordinary task to make the trip, & our comissary teams will have a hard time to get through—at 12 Oclock the sun came out & the sky cleared up. The wind breeses up & turns cold. It now bids fair for good weather once more—Today I wrote to the Journal, to my wife & to L H Hapgood[37]—gave them rather amusing description of the country, people & things in general[.]

Took supper with Genl Blunt at his quarters, he goes one mile from camp to attend a party—Not feeling well I declined going[.]

The day brings no news of any importance, we are all anxious to hear the war news from the East hoping that our arms are meeting with success[.]

We think it strange that our Gun Boats are not yet in the Arkansas River—an Army cannot be maintained here long unless we get supplies by water, instead of by land. Our Gun Boats once in possession of that River it gives us a new base to work from, & places us in position to advance farther South—

This is one of the most important steps for our Govt to accomplish[.]

About one week ago a Lieut from cap Rab's battery was missing from our Camp on the Spavinaw.[38] today a party from My Regt & the Battery found his body about one mile from the old camp five of Livingstons men came upon him while he was in a house & shot him[.][39]

They then threw him down a steep bank first robing him of his boots pants cap & coat leaving him unburied. We have the names of the men who done the cowardly deed & when we get them they will pull hemp sure—I think of taking a weeks trip after this man Livingston & his gang of Bushwhackers, I am quite sure with proper plans I can capture or destroy the gang[.]

Chicago Evening Journal Article

FROM THE ARMY ON THE WESTERN FRONTIER.

THE DESOLATION OF WAR—THE DESERTED WOMEN AND CHILDREN OF ARKANSAS—FEMALE SNUFF-SUCKERS—FLEEING FROM FAMINE—ARMY MOVEMENTS AND PROSPECTS.

Correspondence of The Chicago Evening Journal.

HEADQUARTERS 1ST DIVISION OF THE ARMY OF THE FRONTIER, CAMP BABCOCK, ARK., November 19, 1862.

This is said to be the place where the "Arkansas Traveler" lived, and from the topography of the country, and the *physique* of the people, I have no doubt it is.[40] But few of the males live at home. Nearly all the houses contain widows and extensive families of poor orphan children. It is surprising how many widows there are in this country. Since the good old days of the "Traveler" this county has undergone a wonderful change. "Where is your husband?" "I have not got any." "Whose children are these?" "Mine, I *reckon*, but my husband is dead," or "went away several months ago." This is the invariable answer; and that such a class of people should live and have a historical existence in this great, progressive, enlightened Republic, is truly astonishing.

This is not a prairie country, but one everlasting jungle of dwarf brush, unfit for anything but fire wood. The farms are generally small and poorly tilled. Corn is the principal crop, except children, and such children!—sallow, puny things! You have heard of snuff-suckers and clay-eaters. Well, here you find them in all their ancient glory. The ladies mostly are addicted to this filthy habit. The process is as follows: The snuff is generally contained in a square four-ounce glass bottle. A small stick two or three inches long, with one end *chewed* to the condition of a small broom, is thrust into the bottle of snuff and then rubbed upon the gums of the teeth. The stick, or little broom, is then adjusted, prot[r]uding from one corner of the mouth, and the happy lady sucks away at the precious thing with all the vigor of a three-months' baby at its "sugared rag." Their teeth are black, eyes sunken, and all look as though they were enjoying a ripe condition of the yellow jaundice. The women do nothing, apparently, but lick their snuff, chew and smoke, eat hog and hominy, and raise an inferior quality of stupid, sallow babies. This is the inside, fire-side, home view of Rebeldom in Southwestern [northwestern] Arkansas.

I have just returned from a scout through the Cherokee country.[41] You will understand our location when I tell you that we are about one mile from the Cherokee line, sixty miles north of the Arkansas River, near "Bang's Mills." I find the country, the whole distance from here to Taligua, Park Hill, and on to Fort Gibson, one complete desolation, and still further on across the bridges, rivers, and through the whole Creek count[r]y, north of the Arkansas river, nothing remains but one barren waste. The country is deserted and given up to the destroyer—War.

Over seven hundred persons followed our scouts into camp, many of them the families of absconded rebels. They came from necessity. Starvation stares them in the face. The few bushels of corn that they have hid away in the cellars or garrets, for family bread, are seized and consumed by the scouting parties of one army or the other. This was their last hope, and when it is gone, they too must go where they can get bread. In the vicinity of Taliqua, the most fertile part of the country, there cannot be found a single feed of corn. The hogs and cattle are nearly all gone, and one might as well look in the traveled roads as in the fields for forage. Naked and half-starved children, women, white, Indian or black, pour into our lines for bread. Bread is now the cry. The evil genius of war has come at last—*famine*. There is no mistaking it—it is here, and these ignorant, deluded creatures are fleeing from it as from some terrible pestilence. The same work of destruction is going on throughout the whole State of Arkansas, and when the two armies consume the bread, which will soon be done, her people too must flee or starve. They have become satisfied that to go farther South is but another step to more certain destruction [paper creased obscuring words] the two armies will consume all the corn in the country.

The people of the Free States have not yet tasted the horrors of war. Let us hope that they never will.

The rebel forces commenced concentrating at Bay's Mill and Kane Hill.[42] Their object was undoubtedly to collect the breadstuffs and run the mill for winter supplies. They had no idea that we were so close to them, and as soon as they learned that our camps were within fifteen miles of them, they made a hasty retreat in the direction of Fort Smith. Although their numbers were probably far superior to ours, they would not give us battle. They fear Blunt and his flying field batteries. Their force at Kane Hill consisted of six thousand cavalry and eight thousand infantry, and yet they fell back. It is the impression now that they will either fight us in the Boston Mountains, or make a final stand at Fort Smith. That they intend to give us battle soon, is evident, and if we are ever defeated here, it will be by underrating the force of the enemy.

My next letter will be from a point nearer Fort Smith, and will probably contain more stirring news.

The weather is rainy, the roads bad, but the men in good spirits.

The news of General McClellan's removal has just reached us, and it is difficult to tell what the general impression is. We hope that some bold and decisive blows

may soon be struck by the great army of the Potomac.
CREEK.

[Published December 1, 1862.]

P.S.—This moment a scout has come in and reports one thousand of the enemy, mounted, southeast of us 12 miles—said to be from the command of Standwaiter [Stand Watie]. We shall be after them in half an hour.
C.

JOURNAL ENTRIES, NOVEMBER 20, 1862–NOVEMBER 21, 1862

November 20, 1862

The morning opens beautiful, clear & cool—but very pleasant—Still we remain in camp Babcock awaiting the arrival of our comissary train, A camp rumor is afloat that 3 of the Wisconsin 9th have been killed,[43] about 8 miles from here while foraging. The Bushwhackers are still hanging around[.]

I have this evening ordered a moove of the Rgt to better the camp ground. I have selected a location one mile in advance of all the rest of the army so that it gives me the advance in case of a fight[.]

We shall probably remain here three or four days yet.

The day has been fine throughout. Mud has dried up very fast[.] This evening again I had an invitation to a ball or party at the house of a noted Rebel—I decline going for various reasons to numerous to mention[.]

Genl Blunt & many other officers have gone, & will no doubt have a pleasant time[.]

I have today tried to get the Genl to let me advance to Rays Mill He says he will do it shortly.

I am of the opinion that unless we get there soon we shall find the mill put in such a shape that we cannot use it—

Camp Ellithorpe, November 21, 1862

This morning at sunrise we broke camp & mooved about one mile to the other side of the creek. My camp ground is as fine as could be desired. I am heartily glad to leave the low, stinking filthy place where we have been for several days[.]

I got no news from home yet, no intelligence from any quarter except around this Bushwhacking country.

My men are nearly all out on scouts[.] The morrow will probably bring a part of them in—I get no news from the enemy, except Camp reports. I have not seen the Genl today—from him I generally get the news of importance—My Lieutenants some of them think that I am very hard upon them. Two desire to resign. I will aid them in doing so[.]

Today we captured two men supposed to be bushwhackers—I have spent the most of the evening in reading the "*Arkansas Doctor*[.]"[44] It is rather an amusing piece of nonsense for the million, filled with stale sayings, old jokes, & foolish tales—It serves to kill time and amuses for the hour.

To Colonel Norton P. Chipman, November 21, 1862

Head Quarters 1st Ind Regt
Camp Babcock Arkansas
Nov 21st 1862.

Col N. P. Chipman
Chief of Staff, to
Maj Genl Curtis

Sir

I promised when I last saw you to write when I arived at the Head Quarters of this Army. I have delayed from day to day in hopes of having something to interest you. Well here I am in command of the Creek Regt Col Wattles having gone home on a leave of absence. Col Furnas as you know is not here hence I am the only remaining field officer left. Genl Blunt kindly put me upon his staff—but I saw that to keep the regiment alive I must take hold of it. I found it much demoralized & reduced in its morning reports to some 400. men[.]

I further found that we were approaching the Indian country & hence a greater necessity existed to keep together the Indian Regts—I at once sent messengers to

Leroy to call back the two or three companies there. I am informed that they have decided to come back & join the command & feel satisfied to enter their country from this quarter—Here we can obtain forage & have done so in tolerable abundance all the way down—while to have gone almost any other way we could not have subsisted our stock[.]

I have revived the old spirit in the Rgt & now feel confident that in battle I can give a good account of the I—Js [?][.]

I learn that Genl Blunt has approved the resignation of Furnas. Col Wattles will not probably long remain in the command for reasons which will pass through your hands I presume. Should this be the case, I desire to take the *Colonelcy.* I think I am entitled to it although Kansas influences may beat me & some outside man may get the position[.]

I have done nearly the whole work of raising & commanding this Rgt & still I have occupied a very subordinate position[.]

If you can honorably, & without prejudicing your own interests aid me in any maner, I shall esteem it a favor, & if oportunity offers will cheerfully reciprocate[.]

I presume you are well & frequently posted as to all our moovements. I will simply say that I think there is no prospect of a fight until we reach Fort Smith. I learn that the enemy are concentrating there in conciderable force. I could raise two or three fine companies of Arkansas boys *true to the country* as sharp shooters if I could get Genl Curtis to recommend the Sec of War to purchase the guns. They can be had for $35 each by the quantity—See what you can do in that quarter.

Bushwhackers are tolerable thick and pick off our men whenever they stray from camp.

Please drop me a line & post me as to prospects generaly[.]

I have the honor to be
Sir
Your Obt Servt
A. C. Ellithorpe
Maj Com 1st Ind Rgt

[*Source:* National Archives and Records Administration, Compiled Service Records of Union Volunteers from the State of Kansas, First Indian Home Guards, Record Group 94, A. C. Ellithorpe file. *Note:* Following the written summary of Ellithorpe's letter: "Answer[:] The General is glad to have a good account of the Indian Regiment[.] Hopes all of them will deserve and receive [?] full pay and many honors. S R Curtis Maj Gen."]

JOURNAL ENTRIES, NOVEMBER 22, 1862–NOVEMBER 23, 1862

Camp Ellithorpe, November 22, 1862

The day has been beautiful—one of those old fashioned Indian summer days.

I have today busyed myself in giving orders, infusing a spirit of discipline, & energy & urging the men & officers to activity & energy—The Regiment was in a confused condition when I came into it, no order, no disciplin, it was little better than a mob. Every man acted from his own impulses, & there appeared to be no head.

Order is fast being restored & we again have the appearance of an organized military force—My time is almost wholly ocupied attending to the home duties of the regiment giving me only occasional oportunities to lead scouting parties[.]

Two thirds of my regiment are now out on scouting—

I learn today that a man from the Kansas 10th Rgt is at work hard, to get to be colonel of the Rgt Kansas politics may accomplish it—but if it does, I resign *instanter.* Jim Lane is opposing me, all, in his power.

Camp Ellithorpe Arkansas, November 23, 1862

Sunday has again come & as fine an autumn day as ever shown upon a Western soil—I visited Genl Blunt in the morning & he returned the visit in the afternoon. The Genl usualy friendly, but there is an outside presence being brought to bear upon him, to induce him to endorse the recommendation of one Cap Quig of the Kansas 10th for Col of this Regt—Kansas politics may induce, or rather compel him to yield & make the endorsement[.][45]

If so—I of course will resign as I would not suffer any Cap. to pass over me by promotion—

We hear nothing from the train we have been expecting, some fears are entertained lest it may be cut off—if so we are in a bad fix.

We hear nothing from schofield & his command. They are north of us a long way.

To Brigadier General James G. Blunt, from Indian Officers, November 23, 1862

There is, we understand, a petition in circulation asking that you recommend some person with whom we are unacquainted, for Colonel of this Regiment. We are fully aware that said petition has been put forth by a few of the dissatisfied officers, some of them are under arrest upon charges of stealing, or swindling the soldiers & the Government. Our present officer in command, Maj. A. C. Ellithorpe, is fast bringing to light these frauds & clearing the Regiment of these swindling tricksters.

We hope should the resignation of Col. Furnas be accepted, that you will recommend & urge the promotion of the officer who has been with us from the first, and proved himself competent for the position, and worthy of our fullest confidence.

[*Source:* Annie Heloise Abel, *The American Indian and the End of the Confederacy, 1863–1866* (1925; repr., Lincoln: University of Nebraska Press, 1993), 123 n. 258. *Note:* After quoting from Blunt's letter, Abel wrote: "In February 1863, Blunt notified department headquarters of Wattles' resignation as lieutenant-colonel and urged that if Wattles would not accept the post of colonel, it be conferred upon Ellithorpe. It was at this stage that Coffin and his subordinates, protested against the assumptions of the military men. In transmitting a report of Agent Martin's, dated December 20, 1862, Coffin complained to Dole, 'If the programme as fixed up by the military officers, and which I learn Dr. Gillpatrick is the bearer to your city and the Solicitor General to procure its adoption, is carried out, the Indian Department, superintendents and agents, may all be dispensed with.'"]

JOURNAL ENTRY

Camp Ellithorpe, November 24, 1862

This has again been a day of unusual splendor, one of those fine balmy, matured autumn days[.]

A flag of truce came to our lines today from the command of Hindman its object was to effect an exchange of prisoners.[46] what the result has been I as yet am not aware.

Our command is on quarter rations, & our comissary train not yet heard from. Four prisoners escaped from Genl Head quarters last night one of them was a Rebel Colonel—This evening I write to Colonel Chipman & J. H. Lane, giving them an inside view of the *sculdugery* that is going on, in the efforts that are being made to supercede, or rather have a Kansas politician promoted as Col of the Regt[.]

Colonel Weir is still at the botom of the affair, assisted by Doctor Gilpatrick,[47] who is a nephew & brother in law of Genl Blunts[.]

The Doctor is in my opinion a very corrupt man, & will oppose any person who will not strike hands with him in all his schemes of peculation. It has stired up a large hornets nest, arresting the Lieutenants of my Regt & causing the Lieut Col to be arrested. But I am concious of being right, & hence I feel able to oppose & fight a legion of men who sustain fraud in any shape[.]

Chicago Evening Journal Article

FROM THE ARMY ON THE WESTERN FRONTIER.

Correspondence of The Chicago Evening Journal.

HEADQUARTERS FIRST DIVISION ARMY OF THE FRONTIER, ARKANSAS, FLINT CREEK, NOVEMBER 24, 1862

We are slowly approaching Fort Smith and will very soon make the rebels run or fight. There is no doubt but they are concentrating a large force at that point. From positive information we may set them down at 25,000. Many of them are poorly armed and very much disaffected. This class comprises mostly the conscripts from Arkansas. They have about twelve pieces of 10-pounder guns. The rebels all admit that if we get Fort Smith the cause of the Confederacy is lost in the Southwest. We shall have it inside of ten days; this you may set down as a fixed fact.

Confederate money here is the only thing that can be used except specie. "Greenbacks" wont go; the people think them worth less than the paper they are printed on. It is truly astonishing to see what confidence they have in their rebel shinplasters. This morning some of our soldiers went to the house of a wealthy citizen (rebel), to purchase apples. The lady replied that she would not take our money in payment, nor would she sell even to "Feds." This blocked the game, and the large pile of fine apples in the cellar remained untouched. But an idea struck one of the boys, and he resolved to have some apples by strategy. The General had given orders that nothing in the houses should be molested; hence strategy must be resorted to. One of the soldiers was stripped of his uniform and clothed in the secesh garb of "butternut." A small pile of confederate shinplasters in his pocket properly prepared him for the enterprise. Two soldiers, with fixed bayonets, marched him to the kind lady's house as a prisoner. The prisoner then told his tale of suffering, not only of himself, but of his many companions, also prisoners. The good lady sympathized deeply with him, and sold him a bushel of apples for a fifty-cent confederate plaster. The prisoner shouldered the apples, and the guard marched him to camp. The strategy worked, and the boys are now doing a thriving business with fifty-cent shinplasters and manufactured prisoners, to the complete peaceable conquest of the rebel apple pile. How long before the old lady will smell a large rat is yet to be seen.

Today we had three men shot by the bushwhackers of Livingston's band, who hover upon the outskirts of the army. Yesterday we found the mangled body of a Lieutenant in Captain Rabb's battery, who was murdered some days ago, while at the house of one of the citizens buying butter. Vengeance will be dealt out to them with interest.

I will keep you posted in all matters that are admissible to go to the public. In the meantime you may expect stirring news very soon from this quarter.

CHEROKEE.

[Published December 4, 1862.]

JOURNAL ENTRY

November 25, 1862

The morning is cool[;] the night has been frosty but clear.

The day looks like a storm[;] the air feels like snow.

At noon I visited Genl Head quarters, herd no news of importance. This afternoon all the Captains came to my quarters & asked permission to sign a petition, to Genl Blunt requesting that he recommend my appointment as Col of the Regt[.] The feeling is unanimous with all the Indians. four of the White Lieuts have signed a petition to have Captain Quig appointed[.]

We have herd from the train & I expect Col Wattles with it. There will be music when he gets here. he will either own up to his rascality or play bluff & undertake to browbeat, & sustain himself—If he pursues the latter course he will find a hard road to travel & will be crushed deeper than ever. A mild policy is the only course that will let him out without the severest punishment. I cannot conceive how he can ever hope to clear himself from the offences he is guilty of—I called upon Genl Salomon this afternoon. he is in good spirits, but evidently very much disgusted with the maner in which the expedition is conducted. There is no feeling of friendship existing between himself & Genl Blunt. General B has the utmost disgust for him & freely expresses that Salomon is a *God Damned Coward*[.] One thing is sure if Salomon is a coward, he has the qualities of a very courtious Gentleman & possesses a fine military education, & has one of the best disciplined Regts in the service.

To Colonel Norton P. Chipman

November 25, 1862
Head Quarters 1st Ind Regt
In camp on the Cherokee Line
Nov 25th 1862.

Col. N.P. Chipman
Chief of Staff
Dept of Missouri

Sir

A few days ago I wrote you perhaps a tedious letter & possibly trespassed upon your time, with affairs foreign to your duties—I venture again to drop you a word upon the same subject matter.

I find that my impressions have proved true & that the Kansas politicians are still at work—The facts are briefly these[.]

When I arrived Lieut Col Wattles of this Regiment obtained a leave of absence. This involved the necessity of my taking command, I done so—

In the course of a few days, while working to find the bottom of affairs in the Regt I stumbled upon a series of high handed frauds, both upon the men & the Govt—I will here observe that I found the command in almost a state of disolution—I found that the Interpreters of the Regt had received *no* pay—I immediately went to work to assertain the cause—Investigation resulted, in finding that the Quartermaster had issued the proper vouchers to pay them & that they were delivered to the commdy officer to hand over to the proper persons. The vouchers were issued according to the list, & at the request of the Commdy officer Lieut Col Wattles, he took them to Genl Blunt, & they were "ordered paid."

Col Wattles then drew the money on them while at Fort Scott, on I think the 15th of October. The army then moved south. Col Wattles told the Interpreters that he could not get their pay then but would have it fixed before long—Thus matters rested untill I arrived, & thus he went away, having in his possession $649.69/100 belonging to the interpreters of the Regt. alsoe over $1500—of money belonging to the soldiers of the Regt which he induced the Captains to place in his hands to get changed into small change in order to make the proper change to each man.

I at once made the facts known to the Genl & he promptly ordered his arrest & return to the command. I alsoe found that some of the Lieutenants (white men) had induced some poor ignorant Indians, who were not soldiers, to answer to the names of dead men, & even inserted some names upon the muster rolls, & thus drew full pay upon these names, giving the Indians *five dollars* apiece & pocketing the balance of the three months pay themselves. These men I at once placed under arrest, & have reported the facts.

All this you may suppose has stired up quite an excitement, & the thing is getting warme[r].

In the mean time, the friends of these men in the regiments from which they were detailed, have put in circulation a petition, to have one Cap Quig from the Kansas 10th made Col of this Regt. I understand it was put in motion through the influence of Col "Weere" The man who commanded the last summers "Indian Expedition["]. You know his history & know how he *likes me*. Now I have no idea that the Department will consent to such an act, to the detriment & prejudice of other officers in the Regt. Yet Kansas politicks has done a great many strange things & it may run even this through the mill. I am now the only field officer here Col Furnas has resigned, & Col Wattles ocupies the position that will hardly insure his remaining in the command long. Now Col I write you as a citizen—not officialy—that you may be personaly posted—I have made all of my statements through the proper chanels, but these things sometimes fail *to be in season*. An application will go forward for me as is customary in such cases, hence I leave you to pursue such a course as you think will best sustain me in trying to do what is right & promoting my interest in an honorable way.

There is no news more than when I wrote you before. Nothing but Bushwhackers are discoverable. we hear that a large force is concentrating at Van Buren & Ft Smith, this is probably true.

Please drop me a short line & as ever
I have the Honor to be
Your Obt Servt A. C. Ellithorpe

[*Source:* National Archives and Records Administration, Compiled Service Records of Union Volunteers from the State of Kansas, First Indian Home Guards, Record Group 94, A. C. Ellithorpe file.]

JOURNAL ENTRY

November 26, 1862

Late last night my scouts returned from a trip beyond Maysville. They brought in 400 head of cattle belonging to the command of Col Stand Waitie. on their return they were fired into by bushwhackers killing one & mortaly wounding two of our men. They succeeded in getting one of the scamps, & left him quietly suspended by by [*sic*] the neck to a limb of a tree[.]

The fellow after firing upon our men, wheeled & ran making good his retreat some three miles to a log cabin in the woods[.] when our scouts came up he was divested of his arms & played the *inocent*, & *Union* to perfection. But a search revealed his discarded arms & his swetty horse, with his back wet & hot from the saddle—In 10 minutes he swung a lifeless corse from a tree, & left hanging there a warning to piratical brush murderers—My scout desolated the houses in the vicinity as a warning to such acts in the future[.]

They may bushwhack but I will follow them with the torch & the halter untill they sease this mode [of] warfare—

Our comissary train came in this evening in good order, about two hundred wagons—

We learn that quite a number of the enemy are in the brush along the Spavinaw river. This P.M. we sent a large party down to Dutch Town to run the Mills there.[48] These mills are capable of running 12000 lbs every 24 hours[.] This would support our whole command, if properly run.

There can be about 5000 bus[hels] of wheat found surrounding.

CHAPTER 4

THE PRAIRIE GROVE CAMPAIGN, NOVEMBER-DECEMBER 1862

Death has reaped a terrible harvest to-day.
—ALBERT C. ELLITHORPE, *Chicago Evening Journal*, December 23, 1862

This chapter covers only thirteen days, but they were action-packed and marked by Albert C. Ellithorpe's participation in the Cane Hill engagement and the battle of Prairie Grove. Ellithorpe wrote in his journal on each of the thirteen days, with two *Chicago Evening Journal* articles providing more detail but less of a personal emphasis. In these accounts Ellithorpe often referred to the region of "Kane Hill." Cane Hill is a large plateau that sprawls across an area southwest of Fayetteville, Arkansas. During the war the plateau was an agricultural region, and the "principal settlements, Boonsboro and Newburg (known today as Canehill and Clyde), occupied the winding valley carved by Jordan Creek."[1]

Confederate major general Thomas C. Hindman took command of the Trans-Mississippi District after the Pea Ridge defeat in March 1862. An aggressive and energetic commander, Hindman created a new army after the departure of Maj. Gen. Earl Van Dorn's force by overpowering civilian leaders and bringing greater order to the war effort. Now this fiery administrative genius hoped to deal a fatal blow to Brig. Gen. John M. Schofield's divided Army of the Frontier. Brig. Gen. James G. Blunt's Kansas Division, which Ellithorpe was part of, was stationed in northwestern Arkansas (map 2), with the army's other two divisions over one hundred miles away, near Springfield, Missouri.[2]

The action started when Brig. Gen. John S. Marmaduke and his Confederate cavalrymen entered the Cane Hill region to forage. Discovering Marmaduke's initiative, Blunt ordered his troops to counter this action. Marching from Camp Babcock in northwestern Arkansas early on the morning of November 27, the men moved south, passed through Cincinnati, and then headed southeast to Rhea's

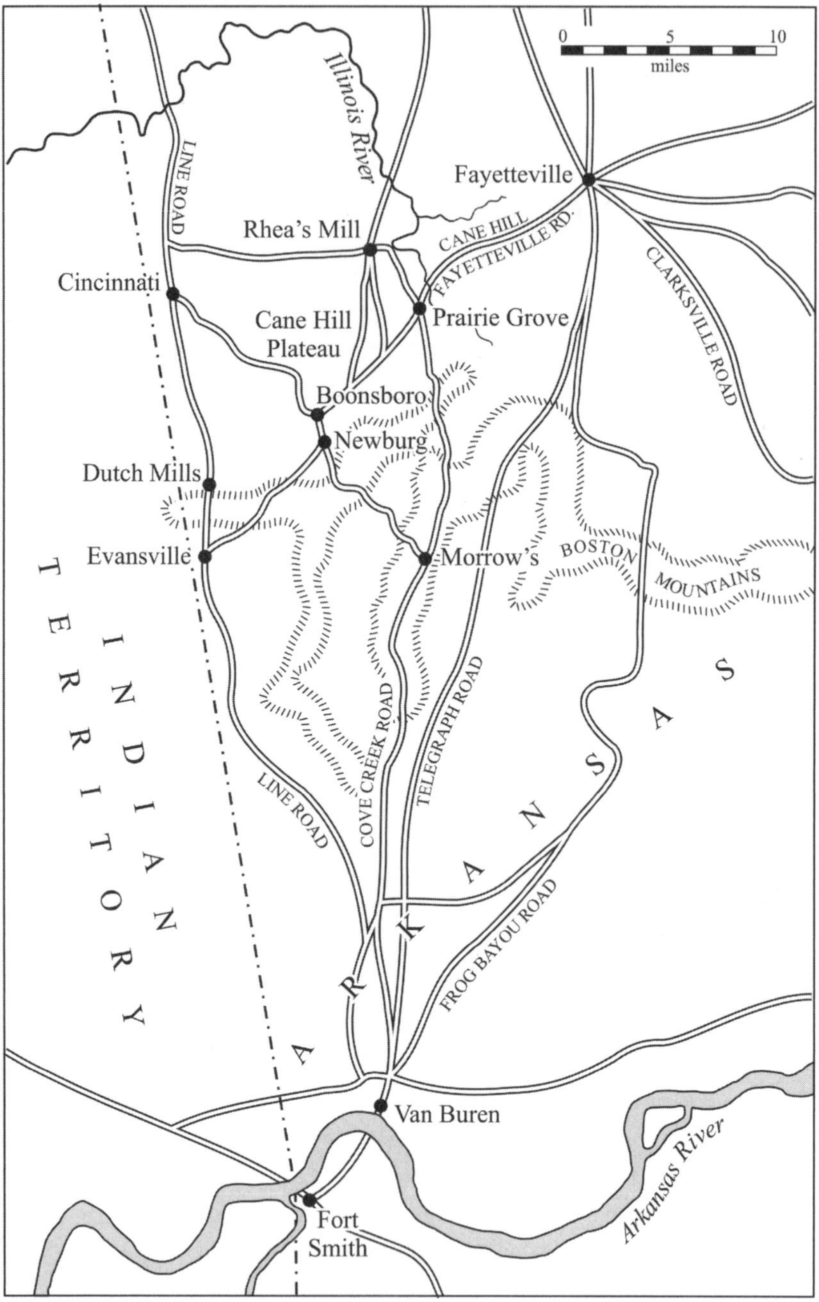

MAP 2. Northwestern Arkansas. Map by Mary Lee Eggart.

Mill. The next day Blunt's men marched south toward Boonsboro, where they forced the Confederates into a twelve-mile retreat through rugged terrain. Ellithorpe described ably this engagement at Cane Hill in his journal and in a *Chicago Evening Journal* article. Following this exciting action, his brigade commander, Col. William F. Cloud, ordered Ellithorpe to take one hundred men on a scout to Evansville on December 2. Located southwest of Boonsboro, near the border with the Indian Territory, at Evansville they were "to drive the enemy down the line road and then co-operate with the Com'd under Capt. Camerson 2nd K. V. [Kansas Volunteers] and return with him to this place." Ellithorpe reported that this small venture was successful.[3]

During the interlude between Cane Hill and Prairie Grove, Ellithorpe preferred charges and specifications against Lt. Col. Stephen Wattles due to his misappropriation of pay. As a result, Wattles was arrested, but he was soon reinstated as commander of the First Indian Home Guards by Blunt on December 5, two days before the Battle of Prairie Grove battle. Also, Ellithorpe was ordered to repair a gristmill, possibly the 1830s-era Pyeatte-Moore Mill in Boonsboro. Using his mechanical skills, Ellithorpe successfully repaired the gristmill; parts of this mill survive to the present day.[4]

Military action heated up again when Hindman's army of twelve thousand men moved north in an effort to destroy Blunt's troops, who were now even farther away from the rest of the army. Realizing that Confederates were on the march again, Blunt called for help from Brig. Gen. Francis J. Herron, who was camped with two divisions near Springfield. In one of the most impressive feats of the war, Herron's men marched over one hundred miles in "a period of three and a half days . . . and went directly into battle at Prairie Grove." Blunt and his men retreated from the Cane Hill region, and then, on December 7, marched cross-country to Prairie Grove, where Hindman's men, situated atop a ridge, were locked in combat with Herron's weary soldiers.[5]

When the First Indian Home Guards reached the battlefield, the men dismounted and positioned themselves to the right of the Twentieth Iowa Infantry, one of Herron's units. Blunt's and Herron's divisions were now united. Giving "a chilling war yell" that a Confederate defender called "one of the 'most horrible . . . I ever heard,'" the First Indian Home Guards, with the Twentieth Iowa on its left, advanced across a wheat field. Confederate soldiers saw African Creeks in the regiment wearing "federal uniform" and "wearing officers' swords," labeling it "disgusting." The men "rapidly penetrated to the line of battle of the enemy, which gave way on our approach." The green Twentieth Iowa then fired accidentally into part of the Home Guards's left flank. To warn the Twentieth, "some of the Indians came running back through the wood to the right, gesticulating violently and pointing toward the direction whence they came. At this moment an officer shouted to me that we were firing on friends." Wattles acknowledged that the friendly fire caused "a five-minute panic," but then his men rallied. The Twentieth Iowa retreated with the First Indian Home Guards, and both spent the remainder of the battle supporting Hopkins's Kansas Battery. By the end of the action Ellithorpe had fired thirty-two shots with his Henry rifle.[6]

The First Indian Home Guards reported casualties of two killed and four wounded, but this total was an underestimation. Wattles wrote that the Indian soldiers "report no wounds but such as the necessities of the case demand." By contrast, the Twentieth Iowa reported losses of nine killed and forty wounded. Ellithorpe may have imitated his Indian soldiers by refusing to report an injury. He made no mention of a wound in his diary or other surviving wartime writings, but in an 1876 biographical piece the writer stated that Ellithorpe "was wounded" at Prairie Grove, and by 1897 the injury was described as a severe wound. In his 1901 pension application, Ellithorpe wrote that he had "two gun shot scars, one in hand one in thigh," with the implication that these were wartime injuries. Wattles praised three Indian officers as well as "Major Ellithorpe and all the other white officers [who] were particularly active and efficient during the whole day." Brigade commander Cloud commended both Ellithorpe and Wattles for their conduct, along with officers and men from some other units. Ellithorpe had again performed well in a combat situation, but his most significant challenge remained within his regiment.[7]

JOURNAL ENTRIES, NOVEMBER 27, 1862–DECEMBER 1, 1862

November 27, 1862

Today the comissary train arrived all safe with a large amt of provision,—but there will be no distribution of stores for an order has just come to put my comand in readiness to march without train, & with 3 days rations of hard bread & salt, with the ambulances[.]

This looks like a fight on hand[.] The enemy are at Boonsborough & Kane Hill in large force. Our intention is to make a suden decsent upon them & if possible surprise the whole force[.] We march at day break—Hence I close my journal for the present & await if ever an oportunity to record the events that may transpire during the time.

November 28, 1862

The day was ocupied untill 10 Oclock P.M. in making a forced march towards Boonsborough or Kane Hill. no incidents only we hear that the enemy are in force at Boonsborough 7,000 strong, & say they are determined to give us battle[.]

We camp within 10 miles of them.

November 29, 1862

This has been a day o[f] stirring events.[8] The future history of this war will give it a place upon its pages—I will very briefly relate the principal features of the day.

We broke camp ~~last evening~~ this morning at 5 Oclock, & quietly took up our line of march, everything arrainged to make a vigorous attack upon the Enemy. The order of march was 1st 3d Brigade 2d Brigade & first Brigade with ~~three~~ 4 Batteries of 6 guns each & 6 mountain howitzers.[9]

My Regt was in the 3d Brig and occupied a central position in line of march. We passed Rays Mills about sun rise & struck the pickets of the enemy at 9 Oclock.

This 10 miles march was over two mountains, with extremely rocky & rug[g]ed roads. The first Picket of the enemy was captured with one killed. This alarmed the enemys Grand guard & he immediately put himself in readiness for battle, planting two Batteries of 4–12 lb guns comanding the ravine entering the town[.][10]

We discovered the trap & left the main road in the ravine & assended the mountain & planted our batteries in a position com[manding] theirs alsoe com[manding] the Town—this was done unobserved by the Enemy[.]

Our guns opened upon him by surprise doing great damage & compelling them to retire[.]

From this moment the retreat commenced & we fought them for a distance of *ten miles*[.]

The retreat ended in a run & complete rout. The forces of the enemy was about 7,000, ours not over 5,000.[11]

Our loss will foot up 30 killed & 75 wounded. That of the enemy thrible [treble] our numbers[12]—

My Regt fought well & all the officers performing their duties bravely. How I performed mine the records of the genl Report will tell perhaps—I have no reason to complain of the compliments paid me by the Genl[.]

November 30, 1862

Today we have busied ourselves in burying the dead, taking care of the wounded & providing ourselves with something to eat. We brought nothing with us but *hard bread* & *Salt.* no tents and but one blanket[.]

The nights are cold, & we lay on the ground in the open air.

December 1, 1862

Today our company & staff wagons came up, our camp is pitched & we again commence to live like human beings. I will describe this Town of Boonsborough or Kane Hill—At some more conveniet oportunity & when I have the time to devote to it—now I am tiard [tired] & can hardly sit up to scratch these few words—

To Colonel William F. Cloud, December 1, 1862

CANE HILL, ARK., December 1, 1862.

Col. WILLIAM F. CLOUD,
COMMANDING THIRD BRIGADE.

SIR:

I have the honor to report that my regiment was engaged, during the battle of the 28th instant [ultimo], in a skirmishing fight over the hills and through the ravines and woods, a distance of about 4 miles. I found the men willing and eager to engage the enemy. All the company officers were prompt and at their posts. Lieutenants [A. F.] Bicking,[13] [F.] Crafts,[14] [F. J.] Fox,[15] [S. C.] Hall,[16] and [E. C.] Manning,[17] proved themselves competent for the emergency. Adjutant [J. H.] Gillpatrick rendered efficient service throughout the day. I learn that 1 of our men only is killed and 2 slightly wounded.

I am, with respect, your obedient servant,
A. C. ELLITHORPE,
MAJOR, COMMANDING.

[*Source:* United States War Department, *War of the Rebellion: A Compilation of the Official Records of the Union and Confederate Armies,* 128 vols. (1880–1901; repr., Harrisburg, Pa.: National Historical Society, 1971), ser. 1, 22, pt. 1, 48.]

Chicago Evening Journal Article

THE ARMY OF THE WESTERN FRONTIER.
Account of the Battle of Kane Hill, Ark.
Correspondence of The Chicago Evening Journal.
KANE HILL (or BOONEVILLE), Arkansas.
Headquarters Army of the Frontier, 1st Div., December 1, 1862.

Again we have put the enemy to flight. I will briefly give you the particulars of the "Battle of Kane Hill," or Boonsborough.

Gen. Blunt's division of the army, consisting of three brigades, four batteries, and six mountain howitzers, under the command of Gen. Salomon, 1st brigade, Col. Ware, 2d brigade, and Col. Cloud, 3d brigade, were in camp near Lindsey's Prairie on the evening of the 27th. Orders were issued for detachments from each regiment to move at daylight on the morning of the 28th, with three days' rations of hard bread and salt in their haversacks. Most of the artillery was ordered to move, and all the ambulances accompanied the column.

Promptly at daylight the column was put in motion, Gen. Blunt commanding in person. The country over which we passed (southeast) was extremely rugged, rendering the passage of our artillery and ambulances slow and tedious. Nine o'clock in the evening, however, found us within ten miles of our enemy, who were camped in a force from seven to eight thousand strong at Boonsborough. From our scouts we learned that they were determined to fight at this point. The rebel forces were under the command of Major General Marmaduke,[18] Brig. Gen. Shelby,[19] and other lesser Confederate lights, such as McDonald,[20] Quantrell,[21] Livingston, &c. It was a concentration of all the "bushwhacking" gangs, united to Marmaduke's forces. It was evident that they were driven by necessity to hold, if possible, the section of country compaising [*sic*] Boonsborough, Kane Hill, Roy's [*sic*] Mills, and Dutch Mills, all within a radius of fifteen miles, and comprising the greatest wheat growing and flouring section in Arkansas.

At 4 o'clock on the morning of the 29th the column was put in motion, the 3d brigade in the advance, under Col. Cloud, in the following order: the Kansas 2d cavalry, Col. Bassett,[22] Capt. Rabb's Indiana Battery, the Kansas 11th Infantry, Col. Ewing, the rebel battery,[23] taken at Fort Wayne, the 1st Indian regiment commanded by Major Ellithorpe; next Colonel Weere's brigade, and the rear brought up by Gen. Salomon with his brigade. The column moved as rapidly as possible over the mountain roads; indeed one of the mountains was so precipitous that the men had to lay hold of the guns and assist the jaded animals to make the ascent. These difficulties did not deter the men or officers; silently as possible we pressed forward, hoping to get in sight of the enemy's camp without alarming them. The advance scout ascertained the position of the enemy's pickets, and "took them in," killing one and capturing the rest. This alarmed their grand guard, although but a few shots were fired. Immediately the whole camp was alarmed and quickly formed in position, planting two batteries of four guns each, intending to rake us as we filed through the narrow ravine that led to the town. Gen. Blunt was not to be caught in this kind of a trap. The column was at once moved from the main road up the steep hillside and through the thick brush, completely out of sight of the enemy. A position was gained upon the top of a hill overlooking the town and the enemy. Three mountain howitzers, put in position, at once commenced the battle; some twenty shells were dropped amongst them before they could reply. While they were engaged in changing position, Capt. Rabb, with his battery, gained a favorable site and opened with four 12-pound guns, with terrible effect, dismounting one of their guns and disabling another. By this time the enemy had located two of their guns, and paid their compliments to Capt. Rabb, by way of killing and wounding five of his men and killing six horses.[24]

Now the battle became general, and the artillery duel continued some fifty minutes, when the enemy withdrew their batteries and commenced to fall back to a new position. The regiments comprising the 1st brigade rapidly advanced, covered by the artillery. Deafening shouts went up from our lines as they pressed forward. The rebels could stand it no longer, and now the skedaddle commenced. From one hill to another, through deep ravines, up and down mountains, and through the woods, they fled, occasionally making a stand in some masked place, until charged and shelled out. Thus the battle continued, the retreat and pursuit, from 10 in the morning until dark.

Almost every rod of ground was fought over for a distance of ten miles. Both armies were exhausted. Cavalry regiments dismounted and fought through the brush; artillery horses dropped in the harness, and men would seize the ropes and drag the guns forward. The closing scene was between sunset and dark. The enemy made a stand in a deep ravine. Our howitzers had not yet come up; our men, impatient, made a charge—cavalry men on foot, with sabres and pistols, infantry with bayonets, and Indians with rifles, in the very thickest of the woods. The cheering of the white men, the shrill war whoops of the Indians, the clashing of sabres, and the incessant roar of small arms, converted this remote mountain gorge into a perfect Pandemonium. The enemy gave way, and darkness prevented further pursuit. Thus ended the battle of Kane Hill. At this writing I have no idea of the loss of either side, and it would be but guesswork to estimate it. Yet it is evidently much smaller than if the battle had been in an open country. The trees would stop the shot and shell frequently before they reached half-way to the enemy. The firing of the enemy was very wild, as is evident from the marks upon the trees, the balls lodging from four to ten feet over our heads.

The whole force of the enemy have retreated to Van Buren, and will probably cross the river near there.[25] This they will be compelled to do, as there is no forage in that vicinity. We have taken their last hope of subsistence in getting possession of the five flouring mills and the wheat surrounding. This is a greater loss to the rebels than a dozen batteries.

As soon as I "post," I will give you the leading items transpired and transpiring.

BOONEVILLE.

[Published on December 11, 1862.]

JOURNAL ENTRIES, DECEMBER 2, 1862–DECEMBER 3, 1862

Camp Kane Hill, December 2, 1862

Today I have been on a scout to Evansville in command of a force for the purpose of driving down the Cherokee line road the enemy posted along that road. it was a very difficult task to perform & a dangerous one, for it was over the strip of country between the two armies & alternately ocupied by both forces. I have performed the task & captured 9 of the *rebs* amongst the number is one Captain [&] one Lieut—

I have not lost a man, but stood a great chance to loose my whole comand[.]

Many things have occured during the day worthy of note—but I have no time to write them now, but will leave it for leisure days[.]

Camp Kane Hill, December 3, 1862

An order came appointing me to superintend the Kane Hill grist mill.[26] I have taken it in hand & shall soon know what I am able to do with it. I have spent the whole day in superintending the repairs preparatory to starting it.

The mill may be run either by water or steam.

To Brigadier General James G. Blunt, December 3, 1862

Head Quarters 1st Indian
Regt Home Guards
Kane Hill Arkansas
December 3d 1862

Brig Genl James G Blunt
Com 1st Div Army Frontier

Sir

My former statement to you dated November 16th 1862 relative to the conduct of Lieutenant Colonel Stephen H Wattles of this Regt, in regard to his having drawn the several sums of money appropriated to pay the Interpreters of this Regt, & his failure to apply this money to that purpose, I had deemed quite sufficient for your official action. I have since learned that I am compelled to prefer charges in form.

Herewith please find the charges & specifications. I desire that this brief explanation shall accompany all the papers in the case[.]

I have the Honor to be Sir
Your Most Obedient Servant
C Ellithorpe
Maj Com 1st Indian Regt H. G.

Head Quarters 1st Indian
Regiment of Home Guards
Kane Hill Arkansas
Dec 3d 1862

I prefer the following charges & specifications against Lieutenant Colonel Stephen H Wattles of the 1st Indian Regiment of Home Guards[.]

Charge 1st

Embezlement of money belonging to the employees & Interpreters of the 1st Indian Regiment of Home Guards[.]

Specification 1st That the above named Col Stephen H Wattles did receive from O. S. Coffin Acting Quartermaster for the above named Regiment certain vouchers bearing date August 31st or thereabouts (1862) drawn & made payable to the following named persons, & for the following named Sums, for services alledged to have been rendered as Interpreters for the above named Regiment *To Wit*—"*Toney*" $166.66/100 "*Richard Bruner*" $83.33/100 "*Ned*" $83.33/100 "*Dick*" $83.33/100 "*Jim*" $83.33/100 "*Charlie*" $83.33/100 "*Frank*" $83.33/100

Specification 2d That the said above named Col Wattles did present the said several above specified vouchers to Brigadier Genl James. G. Blunt & procure thereupon his, the said Blunts, order to pay the same, & that upon the orders of the said Genl Blunt, to pay the said several vouchers, he the said Col Wattles did present the said vouchers to Captain J. G. Haskel Division Quartermaster & procure the payment thereof, upon the 15th day of September 1862[.]

Specification 3d That the said above named Lieut Col Wattles has not up to the present time accounted to the said several Interpreters in whose favor the said vouchers were issued, nor has he informed them that he had received their pay upon said above named vouchers and the said Wattles has frequently, since drawing the money upon said vouchers, told the several Interpreters that he had not drawn their pay, but that he the said Wattles had writen to the President of the United States about it, & so soon as he got the money he the said Col Wattles would pay the same over[.]

Specification 4th That but one of the said Interpreters got the voucher issued to him[.]

Specification 5th That the above named Lieut Col Stephen H Wattles, did obtain a leave of absence on or about the 2d day of November 1862 for a length of time sufficient to go to Michigan & return therefrom, and he the said Lieut Col Wattles did immediately procede on his journey, without paying the said interpreters, the money due them, and further, that upon his being requested to pay them, the Interpreters, he the said Lieut Col Wattles replied "that he had not drawn their mony[."]

Charge 2d

Drawing money from the Government upon a fictitious name, or fraudulently[.]

Specification 1st That the said Lieutenant Col Stephen H Wattles did cause to be isued two of the above named vouchers as follows, one to the name of "*Richard Bruner*" & one to the name of "Dick" whereas both of the above names belong to one & the same person, both vouchers above named were each for the sum of $83.33/100 as specified in the first specification of charge 1st [.]

Specification 2d Further that the said Lieutenant Col S H Wattles, did report the name of "*Ned*" as an interpreter, to the Quartermaster & did procure the isue of a voucher thereon for the sum of $83.33/100 & that he the said Wattles did procure the order of payment thereon from Genl Blunt & did draw the pay thereon from Capt J. G. Haskell Division Quarter Master. Whereas the said "*Ned*" was not an interpreter, nor was he used as such, or recognized as such in the regiment—but on the contrary the said "*Ned*" was employed & used as the body servant of the said Lieut Col S H Wattles, & further that the said Wattles did draw pay for the said Ned as one of his servants, from the United States pay Master[.]

A. C. Ellithorpe
Maj 1st Indian Regiment Home Guards

[*Source:* National Archives and Records Administration, Compiled Service Records of Union Volunteers from the State of Kansas, First Indian Home Guards, Record Group 94, Stephen H. Wattles file.]

JOURNAL ENTRIES, DECEMBER 4, 1862–DECEMBER 7, 1862

December 4, 1862

This morning I had the mill ready for operation & got up steam[.] I find upon tryal that I can turn out about 12,000 lbs of flour every 24 hours. I have got it in fine operation & making bread for the command very rapidly[.] how long we shall run it is uncertain, for the enemy are within 12 miles of us in force 20,000 strong, & may march upon us at any hour. I shall run the mill untill the bulets begin to whistle[.]

Kane Hill, Arkansas December 5, 1862

At 9 o'clock this morning news came in that our pickets on the mountain road were attacked & that the force of Hindman & Marmaduke were advancing in full force. In an hour our trains were hitched up & all our forces under march to the several assigned positions. we remained in position untill 2 Oclock, & then assertained that there was nothing but a picket skirmish. we were ordered to retire to camp.

Lieut Col Wattles came in last night under arrest. this morning he was released by order of Genl Blunt & placed in command of the Rgt again. I am not made aware if this is permanent or not[.] If so, I am of course compelled to resign, as I will never serve in a regiment with him. Tomorrow I shall learn the intention of the Genl—

December 6, 1862

Nothing new but the same movements as yesterday[.]

Sunday (*Battle of Prairie Grove*), Kane Hill Arkansas December 7, 1862

Last night our camp was kept in condition to march at half an hours notice. Rumors still come in that the enemy are making demonstrations upon our pickets. they have advanced driving our pickets to the north side of the mountain & are now appearing upon this side in increased numbers. Again our command is put in battle position[.]

At 9 Oclock this A.M. we found that Hindman with his whole force is passing our left flank & rapidly approaching our rear. Our ~~wag~~ train was put in motion at 8 Oclock & ordered to procede to Rays Mills, north 10 miles[.]

Our whole force was immediately ordered to march rapidly to keep Hindman from cutting off our train[.]

Our two armies were only about five miles apart & running parallel[.]

At two oclock we came in sight of the Mills & herd the booming of canon away on our right upon the Van Buren & Fayetteville Road[.]

This proved that Genl Herron had met the forces of Hindman & they were fighting.[27] Our forces pressed forward, towards the left flank of the enemy & about ½ past two our batteries were at work & 5000 of our Division engaged with the left of the enemy[.]

The Battle had now become General along the whole line[.] We had formed the junction with Genl Herron & nothing now remained to be done but to fight[.]

The strength of the enemy was 25,000. ours all told combined with Herrons division only 15,000[28]—The battle raged with fearful slaughter untile ~~sund~~ dark when the enemy retired sulenly leaving to field to us—The victory was ours & Hindman with his grand army was whiped—our troops tiard & hungry. Camped on the field without fire, food or blankets[.]

Thus ended one of the most sanguinary battles ever fought in the West—It is called "*the battle of prairie grove*[.]"

My regiment was engaged throughout the entire battle & the most of the time fought well[.]

Chicago Evening Journal Article

THE GREAT BATTLE AT PRAIRIE GROVE, ARK.
Letter from Our Own Correspondent.
HEADQUARTERS ARMY OF THE FRONTIER
RAY'S MILLS, Ark., December 7, 1862.

Death has reaped a terrible harvest to-day. The "Battle of Prairie Grove" will be long remembered by the people of the West, and it will fill a conspicuous place in the future history of this cruel and unholy war.

You have probably got most of the particulars of the battle by telegraph, but a brief history of it may prove interesting to many of your readers.

Since the battle of "Kane Hill" the forces of Gen. Blunt have been occupying a radius of country of some sixteen miles, comprising Dutch Town Mills, Boonsboro, or Kane Hill and Ray's Mills, the great wheat and corn district of Arkansas. Gen. Salomon's brigade occupied Ray's Mills; the other two brigades Dutch Town and Boonsboro.

On the morning of the 5th Gen. Blunt learned that the enemy were making preparations to cross Boston Mountains and attack us at Boonsboro. During the day the enemy advanced his pickets, driving ours over the mountains. Both armies then commenced strengthening their pickets. During the night severe skirmishing was going on in the mountains, our pickets slowly retiring towards Boonsboro, and the enemy approaching within two miles of our main lines. During Saturday, the 6th, the enemy continued to hold his position at the foot and upon the north side of Boston Mountains, upon the same ground where we had fought and whipped them on the 29th ult.

We had learned positively that Hindman had reinforced Marmaduke with about twenty thousand men and fourteen pieces of artillery. This was evidence conclusive that the enemy were planning to overwhelm our small force, knowing that they would have nothing but the division of Blunt to oppose them. But Gen. Blunt, upon the first intimation of Hindman's reinforcement, ordered the command of General Schofield forward [*sic*] upon forced marches. At ten o'clock on the morning of the 7th (Sunday) we discovered that Hindman had essayed to trap us. His demonstration upon our front was only to cover his flank movement upon our left with his entire army of 25,000 or 30,000 men, and before we had discovered his intention, his whole force was far on its way towards Ray's Mills, where he intended to fall in our rear and "gobble us up." Let us see how he succeeded.

Immediately our two brigades were "about faced" and ordered to Ray's Mills in a double-quick, a distance of ten miles, our trains taking a road parallel and a little west of us. Now commenced the strife. Hindman had fully four miles the start with the front of his column, his men enthusiastic with the prospect of gaining our rear and cutting off our trains of over two hundred wagons, and a fresh supply of commissary stores. This army was upon what is called the "Wire road," leading from Fayettesville to Van Buren; while Gen. Herron, of Schofield's division, was on the same road, making a forced march to reinforce Blunt at Kane Hill, or Boonsboro. About three miles, a little south of east from Ray's Mills, Gen. Herron and Hindman ran together similar to two locomotives, both rather thunder-struck at this unexpected meeting. Now the fun commenced. The men were speedily formed, the guns unlimbered, and the "war dogs" let loose. Blunt's division heard the first roar of the cannon, and were west upon the flank about 3 miles. The booming of every gun seemed to add strength and speed to man and beast. Leaving the main road, we took a straight shoot over fences, ditches, through fields of chapparell and thorn brush, until we came to the enemy's lines upon their left flank. Here they were just making a movement to flank Herron with a force of over 7,000 infantry. Herron's forces fought like tigers, but the enemy were overwhelming them with numbers. Our (Blunt's) guns were unlimbered and two full batteries belched forth shell and shot into the enemy's left. This was sweet music to the ears of Gen. Herron and his brave boys. The roar of our first guns had hardly died away, when a thrilling cheer went up from Herron's whole division that drowned for a moment the din of battle. Cheer upon cheer was sent up from their lines, as our booming cannon told them that Blunt had come to the rescue! Our lines were speedily formed, and in less than half an hour the whole line, from Herron's left to Blunt's right, was engaged. It was now about two o'clock, and one of the most lovely days that ever beamed on a Western climate.

The enemy fought with desperation. They were covered through the entire length of their lines with a small growth of timber and upon the heighth of land; while our entire forces were upon the open, level ground fronting the timber. This gave them a very great advantage. Again and again our infantry would charge into the woods from the open fields and drive them back, and in turn they would charge our men and drive them again to the edge of the opening. Thus the battle wavered until darkness began to set in, when our troops were ordered to withdraw from the woods to the open fields, in good order. The batteries were all set for this movement. The enemy supposed us retreating, as our cannon were still, and they came charging to the very open fields, with hideous cheers. The whole skirt of the woods was filled with them. Our fifty cannon poured a volley of grape and canister into their lines that struck them dumb. Our guns were not sixty yards from them. They rallied and attempted to charge the batteries, many of them almost reaching the mouths of the cannon; but another volley of canister sent them howling to the wilderness, and closed their fire. A few rounds more of shell into the bush and the battle was ended. Darkness was upon us. A few hearty cheers went up for the Stars and Stripes, and all was hushed but the groans of the wounded and dying. The field was ours. A noble victory had been won, and Hindman had been outgeneraled.

I cannot give you the thousand incidents of personal bravery that occurred through the day. It is sufficient to say that all our troops did nobly. None but those fighting under our glorious flag could have fought so bravely.

Flags of truce were sent from both lines to pick up the wounded.[29] The whole night was occupied in this work. The wounded were scattered through the brush and woods, and the darkness made the work slow and tedious.

Our loss will reach over one thousand men; that of the enemy will easily double ours.[30] Hindman has fled with his great army over the mountains again, and will not, probably, make a stand until he reaches the Arkansas river.

Gen. Blunt and Gen. Hindman had an interview the next morning after the battle, at the solicitation of the latter. The subject matter of the interview was unimportant, farther than an arrangement for the exchange of prisoners, and the acknowledgment of Hindman that he was whipped severely. The prisoners taken say that our artillery slaughtered them terribly. Nearly all express a wish to see the war ended, and the wounded seem to rejoice that their wounds will let them out of the rebel service.

CHEROKEE.

[Published on December 23, 1862.]

JOURNAL ENTRIES, DECEMBER 8, 1862–DECEMBER 10, 1862

Monday December 8, 1862

This day has been ocupied in burying the dead & caring for the wounded, At my leisure I will here give a short description of the battle field[31]—

December 9, 1862—*Battle Ground*

The whole of today has been consumed in caring for the dead & wounded. Burial parties from both armies have worked side by side all day. The hospitals are filled.[32] we have lost over 1000 men the enemy nearly three times that amount. I will give the particulars of several interviews with some of the officers of the enemy at leisure.

December 10, 1862—*Rays Mills*

Today we mooved our camp three miles from the battle ground to Rays mills.

CHAPTER 5

REGIMENTAL TURMOIL, DECEMBER 1862–JANUARY 1863

The sooner our army is rid of these scheming, unprincipaled vilains, the better for the country.
—ALBERT C. ELLITHORPE, December 11, 1862

After a winter campaign Civil War armies typically settled into camp, but the Army of the Frontier remained active. From December 11, 1862, to January 8, 1863, the disgraceful episode involving Lt. Col. Stephen Wattles concluded, officers jockeyed for command of the First Indian Home Guards, and lightning raids into the Indian Territory and to Van Buren, Arkansas, occurred. Albert Ellithorpe penned five *Chicago Evening Journal* articles and wrote in his journal each day, except for the period between December 23 and 31, when he actively campaigned.

Ten days after Prairie Grove, Wattles was returned to arrest for his theft of the interpreters' pay, and Ellithorpe again commanded the regiment. In the meantime Wattles repaid the money and informed Ellithorpe that he would resign his commission because of poor health. Persuaded by this promise, Ellithorpe dropped his charges against Wattles in a December 19 letter. Wattles soon became so ill from piles, diarrhea, and rheumatism that "he could not ride a horse, and was taken in an ambulance" to Neosho, Missouri, to recover. In March 1863 Surgeon Andrew J. Ritchie of the Second Indian Home Guards reported that Wattles had received a forty-day medical leave due to a heavy loss of blood caused by hemorrhoids. In spite of these afflictions and his promise to resign, Wattles remained as commander until the end of the war and even received the coveted promotion to colonel on February 19, 1863. Bad deeds never seemed to stick for long to Wattles. He never was charged with attempting to sell government property in previous months, and he was not court-martialed for stealing money from some of his soldiers. Wattles commanded the regiment at Honey Springs on July 17, 1863, the largest and most significant battle in the Indian Territory, but left the regiment four days later, either for medical reasons or to serve on court-martial duty in Springfield, Missouri. A master of self-promotion, Wattles attempted to get a leave in August while serving on court-martial duty by claiming to "have been actively engaged in the field for two years," a fairly nervy claim in light of his lengthy absences from the regiment. In 1865 Wattles was under arrest at Fort Gibson in the Indian Territory for unstated reasons. How such a man managed to hold onto his position ranks as a minor mystery.[1]

During the denouement of the Wattles affair, Ellithorpe complained of corruption within the army and declared in his diary on December 14, "It is better to pursue the plain course & leave the service rather than resort to the underhanded means necessary to procure a promotion." And yet in a January letter to Col. Norton P. Chipman, Maj. Gen. Samuel R. Curtis's chief of staff, Ellithorpe expressed a desire to command the regiment.

Guerrilla warfare continued, even though these fighters had lost the protection of tree foliage. Ellithorpe wrote of two military raids in his newspaper articles: one to Fort Davis in the Indian Territory and the other to Van Buren, Arkansas. Ellithorpe participated in the first, which left camp on December 23. Commanded by Col. William A. Phillips, the force traveled quickly into the Indian Territory, through Tahlequah, and then across the Arkansas River. Fort Davis, a log structure located across the river from Fort Gibson, was burned along with its supplies by Phillips's men. On December 27 a Federal force marched southward across the ruggedly beautiful Boston Mountains and the next day attacked Van Buren on the Arkansas River. Both raids were well conceived and cemented the Army of the Frontier's reputation as an aggressive force.[2]

In his articles from this period, however, Ellithorpe did not focus solely on military events. Histories seldom show "the decisive role of military forces in the struggle for emancipation," a claim that makes Ellithorpe's mention of the flight of four hundred African Americans and African Indian slaves from the Indian Territory with Phillips's force quite intriguing. The breakdown of slavery and the issuance of the Emancipation Proclamation on New Year's Day elated Ellithorpe. "The spirit of freedom is abroad," he exclaimed, "and it can never be suppressed." Ellithorpe honed in on the importance of the military in emancipation by writing in his January 29, 1863, *Chicago Evening Journal* article "that the slave is now free, in all that portion of this Western country where our arms have been victorious, is beyond a doubt; for they have forsaken the masters and flocked to our lines. Many of them pass on North; many find ready employment in our army. These will never again be returned to bondage." Another milestone was soon reached with the creation of the Indian Brigade under Colonel Phillips, a move encouraged by Secretary of the Interior Caleb B. Smith and Indian commissioner William P. Dole. Previously serving in separate brigades, the three Indian regiments were now united and remained so until the conflict's close.[3]

JOURNAL ENTRIES, DECEMBER 11, 1862–DECEMBER 14, 1862

December 11, 1862—Kane Hill Camp

Late last evening an order came to put the Regiment in readiness to march at 8 Oclock in the morning—destination to our Old camp at Kane Hill.

The distance is 10 Miles & we arived here at 2 oclock P.M. & went into camp precisely in the old place. My tent is pitched over the same 10 ft square of ground as before. I[t] seemes strange that since we left here on Sunday Morning, that we have been 10 miles & fought one of the most severe battles ever fought in the West[.]

Yet it is true—The hospitals of the enemy are established in this place, & over a dozen buildings are filled with their wounded[4]—Tomorrow if nothing hinders me I shall visit their hospitals & will give the result of my inspection—

Yesterday I preferred charges against Lieut Col Wattles. I am forced to this course in order to preserve the integrity & well being of the Regt as well as to set an example & prevent the recurence of like dishonorable & fraudulent acts. I regret excedingly that any officer ocupying so high & honorable a position, should so far forget his own interest, & his sworn duty to his country as to resort to fraudulent transactions for pecuniary gain, but so it is. a covetuous man will bring disgrace upon himself & upon any cause he may chance to be connected with—This is by no means an isolated case, for there are hundreds who follow the army for the sole purpose of money & profit. They have no patriotism, no love of country, no thoughts for the future good of the nation, but only self, *mony, mony.*

The sooner our army is rid of these scheming, unprincipaled vilains, the better for the country. I may fall in the attempt to correct this evil in the Rgt, yet I will do my duty let come what will[.]

December 12, 1862 Kane Hill

At 3 oclock this morning we sent a scout of one hundred men over the mountains by the way of Evansville. Our object is to learn the real position of the enemy, & if he is mooving across the Arkansas River—

Today I have visited the Rebel Hospitals, many buildings are filled with them. They are all well clothed with warm homemade manufacture, good shoes &c[.] This disproves the common idea that the Rebel army is in a condition of suffering & destitution[.]

Their food is not so ~~of~~ various as ours, but they have the army staples *bread & meat* in abundance—Salt is scarce with them & much suffering & inconvenience arises therefrom—

The wounded express themselves in many different ways, some are sick & tired of the war—some have no hopes of success—others think they are sure of success & are determined to stick to it untill they die, or gain the liberty of the *south*—I find all classes very ignorant with regard to what is going on in the Nation, & in European country. Most of them truly think that thus far they have gained great advantages over us in a military point of view—They claim most of the great battles & have the faith to think that they will surely conquer us—This may not be impossible. Many things may conspire to render our government very impotent[.]

Our Govt from the commencement has been constantly embarassed by the continued efforts of a class of men who have simpathised with the corrupt local institutions of the South upon the question of Slavery—& it is yet to be determined if we are not ~~yet~~ compelled through this same element of Northern Democratic influence to recognize the independence of the South or accede to disgraceful terms of compromise. European interference may hasten this conclusion. We may yet be compelled to war with foreign Powers, & if so the struggle will be protracted & terific—Our people hate England with a holy hatred & a war with that power would be entered into by the masses with an enthusiasm seldom if ever witnessed before[.]

Kane Hill Arkansas, December 13, 1862

This morning the Sky was overspread with clouds, heavy thunder boomed from the West & a very heavy rain set in—warm like a summers shower—

My Scout returned from south of Boston Mountains & report the enemy retreating across the Arkansas River—I am not convinced that this is the truth[.]

I am of the opinion that they are determined to give us battle as soon as we cross the mountains[.]

Kane Hill Arkansas, December 14, 1862

Again the day has been very rainy—mingled with hail. though very warm. The rain has fell in torents swelling the small streams in the mountains, so as almost to prevent our pickets from proceding at a reasonable distance from camp—The only news we can get from the enemy is that they have gone out of our reach—I presume however that they are camped somewhere the other side of the mountain[.]

Today Lieut Loring of Genl Blunts Staff came to our camp & brought the money which Col Wattles caried away belonging to the men & paid the same over to the Capts of the different Companies.[5]

This man Loring is the sworn friend of Col Wattles & is doing all he can to smothe over his frauds & is in my opinion using his influence with Genl Blunt to ease the charges down & if possible make him think that everything is right—

He will work to defeat the convening of a court martial & I am inclined to think that unless I use unusual diligence he will accomplish this end—

I am determined that the whole affair shall be honorably adjusted & that he (Wattles), if guilty shall be punished & even through every officer in the command favors him I will pursue the affair untill justice is done—I have no fears that it will defeat me in any promotion I am entitled to from the fact that I care but little whether I am promoted or not—I find that there is so much corruption, & that it requires so much wire working to get ones just dues, that it is better to pursue the plain course & leave the service rather than resort to the underhanded means necessary to procure promotion[.]

I am however determined to vindicate my own rights let what come may—Today I have written to the journal & yesterday to *Maria*[6]—Col Wattles is still in Command, & doing all he can to demoralize the regiment.

His day will soon be run if I judge rightly—Today is Sunday & I must spend it inside my tent, & hear the rain patter upon the outside[.]

Chicago Evening Journal Article

FROM THE ARMY OF THE FRONTIER.
Letter from Our Own Correspondent.
KANE HILL, Arkansas, December 14, 1862.

Six days have now expired since the "Battle of Prairie Grove." We have had ample time to review all the movements *militaire*, and sum up the total, as well as the general results.

That the "Battle of Prairie Grove" has been one of the most important yet fought in the Southwest is quite evident.[7] It has given us complete possession of that portion of the State of Arkansas that afforded the greatest amount of supplies to the enemy. This valley, or range of country, north of the Boston Mountains, some thirty miles wide, extending from the Cherokee line on the west to the centre of the State east, may be considered the great grain-growing region of the State. All that portion of the country south of the Boston Mountains and along the line of the Arkansas river, has been exhausted by the numerous rebel forces concentrated in that region. From Ft. Smith to Little Rock the country is entirely stripped of everything that will subsist man and beast. The importance of holding this valley was duly appreciated by Generals Hindman and Marmaduke, and to this end they concentrated every available force to drive us out of the valley and once more gain possession of the mills and granaries.

It was a concentration of all the various troops of the various commands for one grand purpose. This will be seen from the order or proclamation of Gen. Hindman to his army just preceding the battle.

I herewith inclose you a certified copy of Maj. Gen. T. C. Hindman's "Address to his Troops":[8]

> HEADQUARTERS 1ST CORPS TRANS-MISS. ARMY.
> IN THE FIELD, December 4, 1862.
>
> SOLDIERS!—From the commencement to the end of the battle bear constantly in mind what I now urge upon you.
>
> First. Never fire because your comrades do, nor because the enemy

does, nor for the sake of firing rapidly; always wait until you are *certainly* within range of your guns, then *single out your man*, take deliberate aim as low down as the knee, and fire. Second. When occasion offers, be certain to pick off the enemy's officers, especially the mounted ones, and kill his artillery horses. Third. Do not shout, except when you charge the enemy; as a general thing keep silent, that orders may be heard. Obey the orders of your officers, but pay no attention to idle rumors or the words of unauthorized persons. Fourth. Don't stop with your wounded comrade—the Surgeon and Infirmary Corps will take care of him: do you go forward and avenge him. Fifth. Don't break ranks to plunder; if we whip the enemy all he has will be ours; if not, the spoils will be of no use to us. Plunderers and stragglers will be put to death upon the spot. File closers are especially charged with this duty; the cavalry in the rear will likewise attend to it.

Remember that the enemy you engage have no feelings of mercy or kindness towards you. His ranks are composed of Pisi [Pin] Indians,[9] free negroes, Southern tories, Kansas Jayhawkers and hired Dutch cut-throats. These bloody ruffians have invaded your country; stolen and destroyed your property; murdered your neighbors; outraged your women; driven your children from their homes, and defiled the graves of your kindred. If each man of you will do what I have here urged upon you, we will utterly destroy them. We can do this—we must do it. Our country will be ruined if we fail. A just God will strengthen our arms and give us a glorious victory.

T. C. HINDMAN, Maj. Gen. Com.
Official:
R. C. Newton, Ass't Adj't Gen'l.

From this document you will see that the rebel General staked his all, in the hopes of gaining a large victory.

His failure has been complete, his grand army has been put to flight, and suffered a terrible destruction.

Their loss will reach 2,500 killed and wounded, 1,000 from desertion up to the present date, and they still come in every hour. Their wounded are nearly all inside our lines, and are being concentrated at this place by details of their own men and ambulances under flags of truce. A few of their dead up to yesterday remained unburied.

From our scouts we learn that Hindman with his whole force is making his way rapidly down the river.

Marmaduke is hovering in and about Van Buren. Shelby is under arrest in consequence of some mismanagement during the battle. The force of Marmaduke will probably follow Hindman very soon. Speculation is rife as to their object in moving in this direction.

It is quite apparent to me that it is for the purpose of making an attack upon Gen. Steele, and then uniting with the main army of the Mississippi.

Whether this movement is intended as a complete abandonment of this section of country, cannot be positively determined until we advance our lines farther in the direction of Fort Smith.

From prisoners and deserters we learn that the Arkansas conscripts were forced to the front during the battle, and compelled to fight—guarded and forced on by the butternut rebels of Missouri and their regiments of regulars from Texas. Thus the partially loyal men of Arkansas, who would have been glad to remain quietly at home, have been forcibly conscripted, led to the front ranks and slaughtered like so many sheep. General Hindman is guilty of these murders, and upon him should the bitterest curses of the widows and orphans of those slaughtered, murdered, conscripted men, be invoked. Heaven can never forgive such a heartless, cold blooded outrage upon innocent men, women and children. A perfect system of terror has prevailed wherever the rebel army has possessed the country. Any man refusing to volunteer was conscripted, and a strong Provost guard of Missouri renegades have guarded every road leading from the State—thus preventing any man from going out, hanging or shooting all who tried to escape. Can anything more terrible than this state of affairs be conceived, in a civilized country.

What punishment can be inflicted upon such fiends as Hindman, Marmaduke, Rains and others, that will justly compensate them for this devilish work. An eternity of Parson Brownlow's "old fashioned orthodox hell" would fall short of meting out to them their just deserts.[10]

Who have won laurels in the battle of "Prairie Grove?" There may be various opinions regarding this—but history must not forget Gen. Herron and the troops under his command, who nobly held the entire force of the enemy at bay until the arrival of Gen. Blunt's forces. Herron fought like a real spotted Bengal tiger. Then Blunt came up, and, with his usual rough and ready pitch-in-style, made the mountains ring with his artillery thunder. Col. W. F. Cloud, commanding the 3d brigade of Blunt's division, again proved himself one of the best officers in the field. Every body fought well and deid [*sic*] credit to the Government and the noble cause for which we fight.

The rain has been pouring down for the last twenty-four hours in torrents, more like the thunder showers of August. Yet we may expect cool weather very soon. The streams in the mountains are swelling so as to make them temporarily impassable.

Two flags of truce came in last night, one from Hindman and the other from Marmaduke. Hindman asks permission to examine the battle field and make a *map* of the same, and the approaches thereto. This, indeed, was a very singular request. It is unquestionably for the purpose of enabling him to make a plausible defense, in his official report for his unfortunate defeat. It is hardly necessary to add that General Blunt declined the request.[11]

PRICES CURRENT AT FORT SMITH.[12]

Long Boots [/] pair	$75.00	Confed.	Money.
Short tops	40.00	"	"
Wheat [/] bu	10.00	"	"
Corn	8.00	"	"
Colt's Revolvers [/] pair	175.00	"	"
Coffee [/] lb	5.00	"	"
Sugar [/] lb	2.00	"	"
Tea [/] lb	10.00	"	"
Tobacco [/] lb	5.00	"	"
All articles of clothing are extremely high.			
Calico [/] yard	$3.00	Confed.	Money.
Common factory [/] yard	2.00	"	"

This furnishes a dear lesson and may be termed "paying dear for the whistle."

Conscripts are compelled to furnish their own clothes, and it is the "veritable butternut," and by the way the most appropriate uniform that can be worn in this country—it is precisely the color of the dead forest leaves and the soil. For bushwhacking operations it converts the individual "reb" into a complete masked battery.

While upon one of our daily scouts the other day we encountered the enemy's pickets. One of their number, more daring than the rest, made a charge upon one of our cavalry, crying out, as he charged forward, "here goes, boys for a *Fed, a pair of boots and a navy.*" He missed fire, and the next instant he went reeling from his horse, with a *navy* bullet through his head. These little encounters are of daily occurrence and keep up a constant school of excitement, a little dangerous but very instructive and beneficial to the soldier.

CREEK.

[Published December 26, 1862.]

JOURNAL ENTRIES, DECEMBER 15, 1862–DECEMBER 19, 1862

Kane Hill, December 15, 1862

Today I went to Rays mills to the Head Quarters of Genl Blunt in company with Col Wattles & three of the Indian Captains[.]

They are anxious to get into their own country & do not wish to be used as Soldiers against none but Indians. Genl Blunt promises them that they shall go into winter quarters, as soon as the enemy retires from this side of the Arkansas River[.]

Col Wattles wishes me to withdraw the charges against him & proposes to pay up everything & then resign—I have no confidence in his sincerity & well know that if I release him, he will turn upon me with all the malignity & fury of a Devil, I shall not let him steal any march upon me if I can help ~~for~~ it. No man shall ever decieve me the second time with permision—

Cane Hill, December 16, 1862

The day has been very fine—The pleasant sunshine & the pure clean air has been a magic tonic upon the whole army—business & bustle cleaning up—brushing coats caps & blacking boots—airing blankets & putting camp in order has been the in vogue throughout the day[.]

I have again taken possession of the Cane Hill mills & put them at work—Some pi[e]ces of the engine have not yet been returned—preventing my starting the engine—so I have to run the water portion of it. The swolen streams are fast receding though the roads & fields are soft & quite impassable[.]

We today bought a barrel of cider & several bushels of apples—quite a rarity in Dixie[.]

No news from the enemy one of our men was wounded last evening within one mile of our camp by a bushwhacker[.] we are scouring the mountains & bluffs in every direction hunting them out of their holes—

Colonel W—still cries for quarter & secretly is plotting how to evade his rascality—& if possible to disprove my charges.

Cane Hill, December 17, 1862

The day has again been fine—Col W—was again arested upon order of Genl Blunt—I again assumed command of the Regt—I [am] now fully aware that a move is on foot by several parties implicated in the frauds, to help him through a court Martial. They alsoe desire to root out every officer in this command if possible, that they themselves may be promoted to the vacant positions[.]

They will find music a plenty before they get through. I shall put the Regt in as good shape as possible while I remain in it. Even if I fully sustain the positions I have taken, I shall not long remain in the Regt—I am disgusted with the corruptions of the Army—

Cane Hill, Arkansas, December 18, 1862

Again the day has been fine. Yesterday I went to meet a flag of truce from the enemy under escort of the rebel Col McGinis—he is very much of a gentlemen & a man of talent—he comes with some two hundred of our prisoners for exchange—

I met him upon the Boston Mountains some ten miles from Camp[.]

He appears to be in rather low spirits & seems to performe his duties with an effort that does not argue well for his hope in the Rebel cause[.]

Col W—last evening went to Genl Hd Qurs—probably for the purpose of setting the fires to vindicate his cause[.]

The Indians are becoming very uneasy & desire to go direct to their own country—I have today held a Council with them & quieted them as much as possible—They think me sincere sometimes & again think that I am perfectly right—Some of the white lieutenants are doing all they can to make the Indians dissatisfied[.]

Cane Hill Arkansas, December 19, 1862

Genl Blunt yesterday visited our Brigade. There came with him the

Rebel Col McGinis, wine passed & a good time generally was had over the diner table[.]

Lieut Col W—returned today I think he has become satisfied that it is no use for him to fight aginst the charges I have prefered—He has writen out his resignation, & has today in company with Lieut Loring of Blunts Staff paid over to all the interpreters the money due them—Thus I have accomplished what I desired—viz to get the pay of these men & the return of the $1,500 belonging to the Indians. He now asks me to withdraw the charges, upon the ground that everything is settled & that the Govt is not wronged—I have agreed to write a letter to Genl Blunt withdrawing the charges if he thinks it proper for the purpose of permitting him to resign—I have thought that perhaps this was done for the purpose of getting me into a scrape—but I am well fortified[.]

To Brigadier General James G. Blunt, December 19, 1862

Head Quarters 1st Ind Regt H. G.
Camp Cane Hill Arkansaw
December 19th 1862

Brig Genl James G. Blunt
Com Army Frontier

Sir—Since I prefered the charges against Lieut Col S. H. Wattles—He has paid over to the several Interpreters,—through Lieut Loring,—the full amount due them. I am excedingly gratified that this has been done. He has alsoe manifested the greatest desire to rectify every act that would have worked injuriously to them—Taking the explanations he gives, I am now satisfied that the ends of justice would not, perhaps, be furthered by further investigation. Should it be consistent & admissible, I will withdraw the charges.

A C Ellithorpe
Maj Commdy

[*Source:* National Archives and Records Administration, Compiled Service Records of Union Volunteers from the State of Kansas, First Indian Home Guards, Record Group 94, Stephen H. Wattles file.]

JOURNAL ENTRIES, DECEMBER 20, 1862–DECEMBER 22, 1862

Cane Hill, Arkansas, Dec 20th 1862

The day has been mild but cloudy. has much the appearance of a storm. A heavy scout has been sent out to ascertain if the enemy have made any advance upon us. Forage is getting scarce & will compell a movement from this place very soon.

Col W—today paid up the balance to the interpreters I alsoe demanded that he pay his servant—I have withdrawn the charges against him, conditionally & if he now behaves himself I shall let him alone—He has tendered his resignation & it will be accepted[.]

Many Citizens have today come to the camp to recover horses taken from them[.]

They are all Rebels but claim to be good union people when we are here—They deserve to loose all to punish them for their treason[.]

Cane Hill, December 21, 1862

Sunday—The day has been quite pleasant—I have spent the day in writing to Maria & quite a long letter to the Journal[.][13]

Nothing has transpired worthy of note. I went a mile to the grist mill for a walk—

Rebel horse hunters still throng the camp. I shall start them soon—

No [?] news from the train upon which I expect [illegible word.]

I go to bed—

December 22, 1862

An order comes this morning, directing me to take all the available men of my regiment & report at 11 A.M.—We are directed to go to the Indian Country—we take 6 days rations of hard bread & salt the expedition will be a very hard one[.]

Chicago Evening Journal Article

FROM THE ARMY OF THE FRONTIER.

Correspondence of The Chicago Evening Journal:

ARMY OF THE FRONTIER, ADVANCE PICKET, BOSTON MOUNTAINS, December 23.

"Boston Mountains" is as indefinite a place as the "Michigan Pineries." These mountains extend over quite a portion of the western part of Arkansas, north of the river. But I will make my present location more definite by saying that we are on the top of the last mountain or range, some eighteen miles south of Cane Hill, and some twenty-eight miles north of Van Buren.

I have just run up here to take a peep at [t]he rebel pickets. Since Gen. Hindman's retreat from Prairie Grove, these mountains have been rather neutral ground. He has set his pickets at the south base of this mountain, upon what is called the "Cove Creek road," well knowing that there are but two tangible places to cross with an army: the other, west, some eight miles upon the "Line road," so called from running near and parallel to the line of the Cherokee nation.

It would seem to those unaccustomed to a rough country almost impossible to march an army through such a rocky, mountainous, wooden country as this, where infantry, cavalry, wagons, and cannon are strictly confined, to the narrow roads, so densely skirted with timber and brush as to make it impossible for a horseman to pass the train at the sides. The column must march as it starts: no change can be made, unless, occasionally, where an open field or clearing is found. Flank movements are rather out of the question in most places; in fact movements of any kind are make with the greatest difficulty, except movements on a sliding scale down some steep precipice where the man and the mule are vigorously contesting the question of which shall ride: and it is frequently hard to determine which has the top side the most.

Upon the road we met a flag of truce from Hindman, with some two hundred of our prisoners, most of whom were taken early in the morning from the command of Gen. Herron, prior to the battle of the 7th inst. The flag was escorted by one rebel, Col. McGines, evidently a man of mark in the Southern Confederacy. The prisoners had been stripped of their cavalry overcoats, blankets, &c. in many instances, their good boots exchanged for toeless sandals of the rebels. This is an outrage that should be visited with prompt retaliation. The intelligent prisoners report the following condition of affairs at Van Buren and Fort Smith:

The food of the rebel army consists of corn meal (without sifting) and fresh beef without salt. This is the total of their *fodder.* The process of preparing the meal for food is as follows: A cloth or handkerchief is laid upon the ground, and the meal, with nothing but water, is kneaded upon it; the round ball, called a *dodger,* is then covered up in the ashes and coals until baked. Quilts and comforts are used instead of blankets. The character of their arms is much superior to what we have given them credit for; a good quality of double-barreled shot guns, Enfield rifles,[14] United States muskets, Colt's and Merrill's carbines,[15] Mississippi yagers and back-woods rifles.[16] They were supplied with some 25 pieces of well-appointed cannon, mostly brass, and a few steel Parrott guns.[17]

Over one-half of the troops are Arkansas and Texas conscripts. In bulk they shout for Jeff. Davis and the Southern Confederacy, but in small private knots they are constantly concocting schemes of desertion. The army which fought us on the 7th inst., at Prairie Grove, consisted of eighteen regiments of infantry and ten regiments of cavalry, with twenty-one guns.[18]

Van Buren is converted into a filthy military camp; business is suspended, and the people are simply *staying*, filled with the greatest consternation, and expecting our advent daily. Fort Smith, five miles across the river, is in a similar condition; goods are being removed, and a general unquiet exists. The rebel Generals are laboring hard to infuse order and unity into the ranks of the soldiers, and making strenuous efforts to brace up the confidence of the people; but they "refuse to be comforted." At this juncture the appearance of two or three of our "iron mud turtles" in the river would would [*sic*] make confusion confounded. Why don't they come?

We passed down the southern slope of the mountain—struck their first picket and paid our respects by sending a howitzer shell amongst them. They impolitely showed us their butternut coat-tails and left at a 2:40 gait. They claim, amongst the Southern people, that they whipped us terribly on the 7th inst. The papers there herald a great and glorious victory. If they could fight as well as they can lie, they would wipe us out in ten days.

Our army is healthy and in the best of spirits; well fed, well clothed, and, above all, well Generaled. You will perhaps remember that I prophesied to you, some three months ago, that the little man Blunt would make a mark. He don't wear a pair of No. 9 pegged stogy boots with his pants resting on the top of them, with that same old gray coat that went through the Kansas war of '56, for nothing. He is a great strategist, and the most wonderful feature of his strategy is, in first finding where the enemy are, immediately sending a bomb-shell at them, and then going himself to see where it struck. Western men will readily comprehend this. It may, however, require a stretch of the imagination for Potomac strategists to fully comprehend this kind of Western strategy. From twenty-five to thirty deserters come to our lines daily. If this should keep up until spring, Hindman will be compelled to *go out recruiting.* The enemy have been compelled to abandon the use of cavalry—they cannot obtain forage. Corn is so scarce that they will not even distribute it to the soldiers to parch. What stock they have is subsisted in the cane-brakes along the bottomlands of the river.

They have three steamers running between Van Buren and Little Rock,[19] transporting provisions, forage, &c. This is now the main dependence of their army.

The Indian countries north of the river are free from any considerable rebel force, but the Indian families cannot go home this winter, for the reason there is nothing for them to live upon. The early spring grass will call them home to their own firesides.

I will keep you posted as we pass along. Many incidents occur that I have no time to relate—facts, bombshells and bullets are articles we deal in mostly.

CREEK.

[Published January 8, 1863.]

JOURNAL ENTRY

January 1, 1863

Another year has passed away, & still the war continues & still I am in the field—I had hoped before this day that I would be at home quietly with my family. But the fortunes of war have kept me still in the army[.]

I this day returned from my expedition to the two Indian countries, Cherokee & Creeke. The trip has been a hard one, but very successful. We proceded by the way of Taliqua & Park hill, to Fort Gibson here we stayed over Christmas, the only inhabitants here are Indians & negroes, all in a state of destitution[.]

Fr[om] here we crossed the Arkansas river one mile below the mouth of Grand River & sudeny [suddenly] made a dash upon the Rebel Fort Davis & burned the whole concerne, with all the stores & Rebel Govt property—

I then tooke a party of 200 men & made a dash five miles up the river to the Old Creeke Agency driving the forces of McIntosh & burning all the Rebel Govt property I could find[20]—

Chicago Evening Journal Article

FROM THE ARMY OF THE FRONTIER.

Delayed Letters to The Journal.

HEADQUARTERS ARMY OF THE FRONTIER,
CAMP RHEA'S MILLS, ARKANSAS,

January 1, 1863.

In my last I wrote that I would soon give you important news from this army. The policy of Gen. Blunt is not to lay still over one week at a time, and to this he adheres most religiously.

The enemy, for the past two weeks, have occupied the country south of the Boston Mountains, and camped mostly near Van Buren and across the river at Fort Smith. Since Hindman's defeat at Prairie Grove, they have been preparing for our reception, upon ground of their own choosing. The removal of Hindman has undoubtedly operated to disaffect and derange the general plans of their campaign. On the 24th inst. Gen. Blunt, with a large force, gave orders to march without transportation—no one knew where. The movement was made with the utmost secrecy. Six days' rations were taken in haversacks. The line of march, however, soon indicated the destination. The forces of Hindman (now commanded by Johnson) were to be attacked in their encampment south of the mountains.

Early on the morning of the 26th we drove in the advance pickets of the enemy, five miles out of Van Buren. The picket was hard pressed by two regiments of our best cavalry, up to the very lines of the encampment; nor did the charge end here. Gallantly our troops pushed forward upon the main force, who, taken completely by surprise, fled in the greatest confusion and consternation. Van Buren was ours, with a large amount of supplies and stores for army purposes. Six steamboats were captured, loaded with corn and commissary stores. Having no immediate means of transportations, the steamers were burned; also, many wagons and a portion of the town.[21] Our batteries were put in position, and the enemy driven from Fort Smith in confusion. The enemy replied from the opposite side of the river for a short time, but our artillerists proved vastly superior, and they abandoned their position and fled out of reach. Our loss was trifling—only one man killed; the enemy's loss is not yet accurately known.[22]

When we consider the great loss of stores and destruction of rebel property, together with the moral effect of driving them from their stronghold, this may be counted as a very important victory, not inferior, perhaps, to any gained during the campaign. The whole country north of the Arkansas river may now be considered free of rebel forces. Nothing is left but the few stealthy and marauding gangs which live in the mountains and subsist by indiscriminate plunder.

Gen. Blunt has done this work most completely. A series of successes have crowned his efforts, unparalleled in the history of this war. From a First Lieutenancy he has attained his present position. His promotion has not been the result of favor, but of real *field-earned merit*—he has proved himself a General in fact. That he possesses the real qualifications of a field General there can no longer be any doubt, and it may be all summed up in two words, *patriotism* and *energy*. Could he be made a Major General and confined strictly to the field, his talent would render the nation most ample service.

On the 23d inst. a command, consisting of the 1st Indian regiment, commanded by Major Ellithorpe, the 2d Indian regiment, and a portion of the 3d Indian regiment, with a detachment from the 6th Kansas, and four howitzers, commanded by Col. Philips, left Cane Hill camp for the Cherokee and Creek countries. The object was to penetrate these countries, and drive the enemy out, and at the same time assist the suffering Union families to remove to some place of security. This task has been well done. The command passed through the entire Cherokee country, by the way of Park Hill and Taliqua to Fort Gibson, surprising and capturing a small party of Col. McIntosh's command at the Fort. We then crossed the Arkansas river near the junction of Grand river, captured and burned Fort Davis, and destroyed what stores were there. The buildings were fired just at sunset. The dense columns of smoke from over fifteen buildings, and the lurid glare of the flames, were truly a grand sight. The vast prairie country rendered this beacon of destruction visible for many miles. These movements were made in conjunction; at the same time Fort Davis sent up its clouds of flames and smoke, our batteries, under the personal command of General Blunt, were raining iron hail and shell into the rebel ranks across the river, at Van Buren.

There is no mistaking the real consternation of the rebel troops at the bold and dashing advances of our forces. The command that burned Fort Davis made the distance of one hundred miles in 36 hours. This is the way our troops win laurels. Rapid movements are the prominent characteristics of this army (under the direction of Gen. Blunt), and all of his brigade commanders partake of the dash and daring of the General. Probably at no time during the war has there been a more daring and enthusiastic charge than our entrance into Van Buren. Nearly two thousand cavalry, with Col. Cloud, commanding the 3d brigade, at the head, charged in columns by fours for a distance of four miles, driving the enemy at a furious pace into and through the town.

The inhabitants of Van Buren were wholly unconscious of the approach of our forces until the streets were filled with them. The batteries followed upon the rear, and were quickly put in position, hurling shell into the camps of the enemy across the river. Our soldiers all partake of the enthusiasm and seem to never weary—prompt and cheerful, always ready to obey the bugle calls.

Our return from the Indian nations drew after us nearly 400 contrabands. They make their escape in all conceivable ways—some on foot, carrying their children upon their backs and in their arms; in ox teams, mule teams, upon the backs of ponies, donkeys, &c. Old and young—the infirm and crippled, of all shades of color—Creek, Cherokee, Seminole, Chickasaw and Choctaw, male and female—present a conglomeration of Southern chattels illustrative of the deep-seated curse that inevitably follows in the wake of a slaveholding policy. These poor creatures have somehow become impressed with the idea that the present war is solely on their account, and that the present is the long-looked-for time when their shackles shall fall and their race shall become free. They seem willing to endure any hardships. They cheerfully undergo hunger and unaccountable fatigue, storms, without shelter, long marches over the sharp flint roads, without shoes, pressing forward towards a strange land—for what? Simply that they may say *we are free.* The spirit of freedom is abroad, and it can never be suppressed. From the most intelligent to the most stupid of the enslaved race, all are equally determined and eager to be free.

We are now resting and foraging our stock for a few days. As soon as this is done we shall move. Wherever an enemy can be found, he must fight or run. You will soon hear of more important events from this quarter.

SEMINOLE.

[Published January 29, 1863.]

JOURNAL ENTRIES, JANUARY 2, 1863–JANUARY 4, 1863

January 2, 1863

This morning we were ordered to march in the direction of Elm Springs, for the purpose of forage. tonight we camp at __________ [blank included in original] Mills 10 miles from our morning camp. Nothing new has taken place[.]

January 3, 1863

This morning we started for Elm Springs. and arrived in camp at 4 Oclock—The day was fine—like a summer day—We came here for forage, but find there is but very little in the surrounding country.

Camp Elm Springs, January 4, 1863

We arrived in camp last evening at this point, we find no forage in the country around here of any consequence, but will be compelled to stop here until after the general review. Things looke dark as to the further success of this division. Col Weere is now in command of the division & he will ruin its success even to injure a single enemy (personal)[.] Drunkenness is one of his besetting sins. The result will show that he will do all in his power to defeat Genl Blunt, he is truly a modern Arnold[.][23]

Chicago Evening Journal Article

ANOTHER LETTER.
HEADQUARTERS ARMY OF THE FRONTIER,
CAMP WILLOW SPRINGS, Jan. 4, 1863.

Since my last, important events have occurred. How this campaign will be affected by the changes is yet to be seen. Gen. Blunt's campaign No. 1 may now be considered at an end. He is relieved, and Gen. J. M. Schofield assumes command.[24] The reasons for this change have not transpired to the army here. History will accord to Gen. Blunt the praise of planning and perfecting one of the most successful campaigns of the present war. He has surmounted the thousand little obstacles that, to many Generals, would have been sufficient excuses for delay. Quick to perceive, prompt to execute, and possessed with an indomitable energy, he has led his little army to glorious victories in every important engagement. All the country north of the Arkansas river is now free from any organized rebel forces.

The General retires only for a short time. He will turn up in a more important command. The good wishes of the whole army go with him. Upon his taking leave of his officers and soldiers, a silent tear found its way over the sun-burnt cheek of many a brave soldier. The *people* will remember and reward the man of real genuine merit.

The Kansas division of the army is undergoing a reorganization. Our new brigade is formed, called the "Indian Brigade," and under the command of Colonel Wm. A. Philips, Colonel of the 3d Indian regiment. Colonel Wm. Weere is placed in command of the Kansas division, for the reason, solely, that he is the ranking officer. It is hoped that he will conduct it with discretion.

General Schofield is a man of marked ability, and will show himself equal to any emergency that may arise. General Herron has fully proved himself competent, and hence the Army of the Frontier is still provided with a military talent that will warrant success, wherever it goes.

The marauding bushwhackers still infest the secret hiding-places in the mountains, and occasionally drop down upon some of our pickets and stragglers, robbing and plundering everybody they chance to meet. This will be one of the growing and continued evils that will curse this country until long after the war shall cease. Hundreds of desperadoes will band together and re-enact the bloody deeds that have always followed in the wake of protracted revolutions. When the rebellion is conquered, the brutal deeds of lawless bands will only have commenced, and a military power will be required, perhaps, for years. The adaptation of this country to guerrilla bands equals even the mountain ranges of Mexico.

The forage is nearly all exhausted, and our only anxiety now is to sustain our stock, for the enemy have fled beyond our reach, unless we are permitted to commence a campaign south of the Arkansas river. I am thoroughly convinced that the true policy is not to stop the advance of this army, but if necessaryr [*sic*] einforce [*sic*] it and sweep everything down to the Gulf. To do this it is only necessary that we control the Mississippi and its western tributaries; and there will never come a time when this policy could be so well executed as this winter. Why stop it? Why encourage the enemy, and dispirit our soldiers, by stopping the march of a victorious army? Surely those who are responsible for this halt and retrograde cannot understand the condition of affairs here; or, if they do, they must be recreant to the policy of offensive means for the suppression of this rebellion.

I had hoped, like every other Western man, that the ruling military powers would at least permit this isolated little army to go forward and wipe out the last vestige of treason west of the Mississippi; but we now fear that the rebels will be permitted to recuperate from the defeats they have recently sustained.

The result of the President's Emancipation Proclamation is now being evidenced throughout this country.[25] All appear to understand it in its literal sense. The slave and the master, the rebel and the loyal man, appear to be fully convinced that it was no idle message, but a stern reality. It is met with candor, and will be yielded to with considerate submission. The Union element rejoice over it as a triumph; the rebels view it as a military necessity, and offer no obstacles to its inevitable results.

That the slave is now free, in all that portion of this Western country where our arms have been victorious, is beyond a doubt; for they have forsaken the masters and flocked to our lines. Many of them pass on North; many find ready employment in our army. These will never again be returned to bondage. The prestige of popular liberty will guarantee freedom to all who come to our lines. The day is past when military commanders will willingly engage in executing the cursed provisions of the "Fugitive Slave Law."[26] The slave statute may yet doom and oppress the soil, but the chattels have taken to themselves "legs and flown." I never so fully realized the absolute dependency of the Southern man upon his slaves as since I have had occasion to witness the real condition of affairs around the domestic board of these once really independent people. I had occasion to call for dinner at the house of one of these formerly independent planters. They manifested a cheerful desire to render every accommodation in their power, but the household was in a state of wretched confusion. Everything appeared to be disjointed. The ladies, who were evidently as well schooled and refined as is usual in the best circles of Southern society, appeared to a great disadvantage in the performance of ordinary household duties. The coffee was unsettled; the biscuits were heavy; the corn cake was an original compound of meal and water; the meat was burned; the butter shed great white tears of milk, in grief for its unworked condition, (or perhaps for the absence of "Dinah"). The lady herself, mortified at the unskillful preparation, wept despairingly and said: "My servants have all gone, and I am not used to this kind of labor." This condition of affairs is applicable to almost every slave-holding family. The machinery of ease, luxury, and comfort is swept away from them; the great pillar of arrogant aristocracy is shattered, and the whole fabric of reliant independence is crumbling to atoms.

CREEK.

[Published January 29, 1863.]

JOURNAL ENTRIES, JANUARY 5, 1863–JANUARY 7, 1863

Elm Springs, January 5, 1863

We are still in camp & preparing for a general review—

I still have to fight the swindlers in this regiment. They are putting me to all the trouble in their power. I shall yet overwhelm them with shame[.]

Elm Springs January 6, 1863

The weather is fine, no news of any enemy except bushwhackers.

Tomorow is our grand review & we expect a good time. Yet I must confess that I do not take the least enjoyment in these ostentatious show parades. The only comfort I take is when I am in pursuit of an enemy or engaged in some strong active operations. I no longer take comfort in the company of the [illegible word]. I am fully aware that we shall have trouble in our division arising from the aspirations of the many office seeking & aspiring men in the army—Two days ago our Indian Brigade was organized & Col Philips put in command,

I think he will be shorne of all strength, that would tend to make the brigade efficient—We shall see—

Elm Springs, January 7, 1863

Today we were reviewed by Genl Schofield, everything passed off in the usual style to the satisfaction of nearly all parties concerned[.]

In the evening there will be a ball & supper,—Mornin—I attended the supper last evening & it was a grand affair as good as could be had at the best hotell in the Nation[.] About 20 of the Rebel Ladies came in & attended the ball[.] They seemed well pleased with the whole performance[.]

To Colonel Norton P. Chipman, January 7, 1863

Head Quarters 1st Ind Regt
Camp Elm Springs
Arkansas
Jan 7th 1863

Col N. P. Chipman
Chief [of] Staff Army Missouri

Sir—

Yours of the 10th inst was received—I thank you for your kindness in desiring to promote my interest.—The difficulties I spoke to you about in the regiment still continue however I have succeded in getting the returne of Lieut-Col Wattles, & the returne of the mony, amounting to near three thousand dollars. I was induced to withdraw the charges, on account of his extreme ill health, & his earnest desire to withdraw from the service. He has sent in his resignation, &

Genl Blunt forwarded it, accompanied by a medical certificate of disability—Immediately however he assumed command of the regt[.]

The charges are again prefered by one of the Lieutenants, & thus the matter stands. The resignation of Col Furnas was forwarded direct to the Secretary of War, & hence it did not probably pass through your hands. I am well satisfied that the Kansas clique will effect the appointment of some other man to the Colncy [Colonelcy] of the regt—The political influences are strong. I suceeded in adding 500 men to the Regt since my returne. Lane will be induced to use his influence for some Kansas man—Yet I cannot well conceive how the Sec of War under his custom can promote over me in regular line & be consistent.

I would not arogate any thing to myself more than is justly my due, & hence will only say that I think I have done vastly more to promote the interests of the regiment than any other officer in it[.]

Some five petitions have been circulated for as many diferent men, for Col of the regt—Genl Blunt tells me he has refused to sign any one of them. I have a petition signed by every Captain in the whole Rgt, but have thought it premature to forward it untill official notice was received of the vacancy. I will however herewith forward to you, & you may make such a disposal of it as shall seem to you most proper—I do not desire to commit the Genl & hence have not asked him to sign it. I could get any number of official signatures to it—but think it will have no weight with the Sec of War.—If any of these interested parties desire to perpetrate the injustice upon me, let them take the responsibility of it. My conduct in the regt I think has been beyond the aspersions of any one—I am in the field & cannot pull wires in Washington, & hence must abide the result even though it be ever so unjust—I can only retire whenever I believe myself degraded by the appointment of an inferior & incompetent man.

I have not yet received the cartridges from Col. Coffin.—my "Henry" has done its work well I emptied 32 shots from it at in the Battle of "Prarie Grove" at a very short range. I think the gun has done good service—

The Indian Brigade is formed under the Com of Col Wm. A. Phillips, he is a very good man. Col Weere of whom you have hird so much, is in Com during Blunts absence—I hope he may prove worthy of the trust imposed in him—

I would suggest that the Ind be confined strictly to the Indian Country this done they will be efficient & content[.]

All of those at Leroy have come down & if the Regt can ever be cleared of *thieves* & *rob[b]ers* it will be a brilliant success[.]

I would like the permission to recruit a battalion of sharp shooters, to operate against the Guerilla bands which will infest this country long after the War ceases[.]

You will see Genl Blunt & get all particulars. Accept my kind regards, & please post me[.]

With Respect I am your Obt
Servt
A. C. Ellithorpe

[*Source:* National Archives and Records Administration, Compiled Service Records of Union Volunteers from the State of Kansas, First Indian Home Guards, Record Group 94, A. C. Ellithorpe file.]

JOURNAL ENTRY

January 8, 1863 Elm Springs

Today we have done nothing but the ordinary camp duties. The Indian Regts were today Brigaded by the order of Genl Shofield, in conformity to an order or request of Genl Blunt—Col Philips, the former Major of this Rgt & now Col of the 3d Cherokee—is put in command of the brigade. He has not got this position because he has earned it for I have done much more labour in the Indian service than he has[.]

He takes the prefferance simply because he is a Kansas man, his abilities as a military man are of a very low order—his acquirements as a business man, are only medium. But every favored Kansas politician, of the Jim Lane school, & who will pledge a future support to Lane for U.S. Senator, can obtain promotions irrespective of personal qualifications. There is no help for this system of unjust & we might say criminal bargain & sale.

Promotions are farmed out, in patches to suit purchasers.

Chicago Evening Journal Article

FROM THE ARMY OF THE FRONTIER.

HEADQUARTERS ARMY OF THE FRONTIER,

CAMP ELM SPRINGS, ARKANSAS, January 8, 1863.
Correspondence of The Chicago Evening Journal.

The Devil is said to have once been an angel, but this is a question which has been the occasion of voluminous theological discussion. That some of these marauding rebels are devils is so conclusively evident that no argument or sophistry is necessary to prove the fact. While on my late trip to Fort Gibson, I learned of the brutal murder of two of our soldiers, who were taken last July, while we were in the Indian country. These two men were missing from the command, and, as it is now proved, were taken by the rebels, carried to Fort Gibson, taken into the old Government square, stripped of their clothing, and shot. Then a rope was fastened to their necks, and hitched to a wagon, and the bodies dragged some half a mile on the prairie and left there, unburied, to be devoured by the hogs. From some of the inhabitants along the line of the Arkansas river, I learn that many of our prisoners have been in this same manner brutally murdered. It makes one's blood boil with a holy vengeance, to think that these brutal demons are permitted to share the least kind consideration at our hands.

Only last week, two of the loyal white citizens who lived in the Cherokee country—Dr. Palmer and Judge Hildebrand, both prominent men[27]—were captured near Taliqua, and taken into the woods, stripped of their clothing, and the Judge was shot through the forehead. Dr. Palmer saw what his fate would be and, determined to sell his life, as dearly as possible, he seized the gun in the hands of one of the ruffians, wrenched it from him, and knocked him in the head, and then leaped into the brush, the remaining ruffians firing upon him. One shot took effect in his leg, but, nerved for a death struggle, he pushed forward, and finally made his escape. He found his way into our camp yesterday, exhausted, and almost famished. These desperadoes belong to the command of Gen. Cooper, and were Missourians and Texans.

This is the treatment our prisoners get at the hands of the "Southern chivalry," while we exercise the most diligent care for the comfort of their prisoners and wounded. We have over a thousand of their wounded in our lines at the present time, and they are provided with every comfort that the country produces. The policy of trying to conciliate these brutal demons with kind treatment is an exercise of Christian charity that history may record as commendable; but the blood of these murdered victims will rise up for vengeance, and I very much mistake the spirit of our people if they fail to mete out retribution tenfold. There is hardly a day passes but we hear of some such outrage. Two days ago a party of fugitive negroes, women and children, were overtaken by one of these marauding bands. Some of them were killed, some made their escape, and others were turned back and driven to Texas. The inhabitants of the country are filled with terror, and are fleeing in every direction for safety. A few of our sick, left at Rhea's Mills, only 22 miles from our present camp, were visited by some twenty of these guerrillas, night before last, and all their blankets, clothing and food taken away or destroyed. Our camp is filled with the families of both loyal and rebel, seeking safety from these organized robbers. The work of depopulating this State is going on rapidly, and it will soon be given over to rapine and plunder.

The course that the rebels are now pursuing will result in meting out to themselves a more certain and lasting destruction than the force of our arms against them. By their own lawless acts and reckless policy they insure the destruction of every agricultural and commercial interest, besides sundering every social and domestic tie that renders a people powerful. The whole South is fast becoming decimated. Many of its best people are seeking safety and quiet in the North, and thousands more will continue to come forward, until the best element of their country is entirely gone. Their slaves are every day becoming more petulant and seek every opportunity to escape. This unquiet of the slave population will shortly result in open insurrection; then will come the final demolition of the cursed altar upon which was attempted the sacrifice of a nation's liberty and independence.

The soldiers of the Western division are getting impatient at the tardy movements of the Eastern army.[28] And truly there seems to be some reason for the impatience. Is it still true that we yet have men in high positions who dare truckle to any policy that will give rest, comfort, or the faintest encouragement to the enemy? Are there yet any advocates of a stand-still, defensive policy, and opposed to the most offensive measures, that will not only destroy but wrench from its roots the main nerve that feeds and gives life to the rebellion? If so, let them be branded with infamy and shame; for upon them rests the responsibility of protracting the rebellion, and destroying the lives of thousands. It is this class of men who, if circumstances had located them elsewhere, would have been the first to sacrifice this great Republic upon the altar of treason. Nothing but pure, unselfish patriotism, and a holy love of our flag, will ever unite and preserve this nation from the wicked conspiracies that have long been plotted against it. The whole energy of a liberty-loving slavery-hating people must be put forth, until the cause of the treason is destroyed and the conspirators overwhelmed.

This afternoon we have a grand review of the whole army under Gen. Schofield. We anticipate a grand affair. A grand supper will be given in honor of the General. The general impression is that the army will be divided and distributed over different portions of the country. The Indian brigade will go to the Indian country, accompanied by at least one good battery. This will be quite sufficient to hold the Creek, Cherokee and Choctaw countries, no rebel forces being there, except the demoralized regiment of Col. McIntosh, and over one half of his men will come over to us upon the first good opportunity.

The Choctaws are tired of the war. Many of them have been killed; they are poorly paid, worse clothed, and still worse fed. The rebel Cherokee regiment, under Col. Standwaite, is in a state of dissolution, owing to the defeats sustained by Hindman and Marmaduke. The Texas troops have followed the fortunes of Hindman. The Missouri troops are bitten, and have no other course to pursue than to stick to the main army. There is no chance for them to return. They know too well what would be their fate; for the devilish deeds they are guilty of have rendered their stay in Missouri next to impossible.

If our gunboats can now control the Mississipi river, I see no possible chance for the rebel army west of the river to escape. Deserters from the rebel army continue to straggle in, heart-sick and repentant, making loud protestations that they have been duped into the army, and are now willing to atone for the offense by fighting for our cause.

We may do all that can be done in this department, even to the total destruction of the enemy, and yet it will avail but little unless our arms in the East are crowned with important and speedy victories. The centre must be broken, and his grand army shattered, and that, too, before the 1st of May, else we shall be in imminent danger of acceding to a compromise that will carry disgrace and shame to the hearth-stone of every Northern man. Three months more of inactivity and criminal inefficiency will not only crush the hope of nineteen millions of American people, but will grind to powder the hopes of the whole world in the success of republics.

CREEK.

[Published January 23, 1863.]

FIG. 1.

Wartime photograph of Albert Chapman Ellithorpe.
(Courtesy of Kansas State Historical Society.)

FIG. 2.

Senator James H. Lane was a controversial and colorful Kansas politician. (Photo courtesy of Wilson's Creek National Battlefield [WICR 31692].)

FIG. 3.

Ho-tul-ko-mi-ko (Silas Jefferson), an African Creek, served in Company I of the First Indian Home Guards. (Photo courtesy of National Anthropological Archives, Smithsonian Institution [BAE GN 01117 06230200.])

FIG. 4.

Engraving of Micco Hutka, a Muscogee Creek Indian, commanded a company in the First Indian Home Guards. (Photo courtesy of Research Division of the Oklahoma Historical Society.)

FIG. 5.

John Chupco, an assistant principal chief of the Seminoles, served in the First Indian Home Guards. (Photo courtesy of Research Division of the Oklahoma Historical Society.)

FIG. 6.

An unidentified soldier of the Indian Home Guards. (Photo courtesy of Wilson's Creek National Battlefield [WICR 30114].)

FIG. 7.

Flag captured at the Locust Grove skirmish by Lt. David Whittaker of the Tenth Kansas Infantry. (Photo courtesy of Wilson's Creek National Battlefield [WICR 30118].)

FIG. 8.

Maj. Gen. James G. Blunt developed a reputation as an aggressive military commander. (Photo courtesy of Wilson's Creek National Battlefield [WICR 31930].)

FIG. 9.

Col. William Addison Phillips became the commander of the Indian Brigade in 1862. (Photo courtesy of Research Division of the Oklahoma Historical Society.)

CHAPTER 6

GUERRILLA WARFARE, JANUARY-MARCH 1863

If he persists in his threat to stop in the hills, we shall shortly introduce his neck to the end of a few feet of hemp.

—ALBERT C. ELLITHORPE, *Chicago Evening Journal*, January 26, 1863

Six of Albert Ellithorpe's *Chicago Evening Journal* articles and several letters comprise the period from January 9 to March 17, 1863, with strong journal coverage for January and most of February; after that the entries become more scattered, with the last entry written on March 17. Ellithorpe's only surviving letter to his wife is presented in this chapter, along with two letters to Col. Norton P. Chipman and a short note in which Col. William A. Phillips praised Ellithorpe.

Historians Gary W. Gallagher and Kathryn Shively Meier have argued that the current emphasis on guerrilla warfare in the literature relates to interest in the war in Vietnam and more recent American actions in Iraq and Afghanistan. They dismiss guerrilla actions during the Civil War by labeling them as "ancillary, disruptive, and deemed unacceptable for nations attempting to conduct civilized, western warfare." Yet Ellithorpe's writings vividly depict the challenges of combating guerrillas and illustrate that by early 1863, for soldiers on the ground, guerrilla warfare had gone beyond being merely "ancillary" or "disruptive" and had become "almost exclusively" the main form of combat in northwestern Arkansas and southwestern Missouri. The great increase in guerrilla warfare was fueled in part by the Partisan Ranger Act passed in April 1862 by the Confederate Congress. The law allowed men to arm themselves as part of partisan (referred to here also as guerrilla) bands with the Confederate government providing funding for forage and food. Confederate leaders found the partisan groups difficult to control in part because they were often distant from regular Confederate troops. Guerrillas frequently traveled to Texas in the winter because they had lost the protection of tree foliage, and leaders often attempted to assert or reassert control there. As much as leaders in Richmond, Virginia, may have wanted to dictate guerrilla policy, it was actually controlled by those closer to the scene in the trans-Mississippi.[1]

The guerrillas whom Ellithorpe encountered had complex motivations for taking to the bush. Hatred of the enemy, along with "bitterness, anger, hope, desperation, and the seeking of excitement," often fueled guerrillas. The ability to serve close to their homes appealed strongly as well. The environment, particularly in Arkansas, proved to be well suited for guerrilla warfare, and guerrillas were often intimately familiar with the territory that they traversed. Southwestern Missouri, with its more open terrain, was not quite as suitable, and yet Ellithorpe found guerrilla operations there difficult to counter. Federal troops in the border region operated in a badly damaged area. By early 1863 soldiers in southwestern Missouri had to travel farther and farther from their camps even to obtain forage for their horses. Guerrillas often targeted these foraging parties, attacked supply lines, and occasionally raided "a town, garrison, or farmstead" in Missouri to acquire supplies for themselves. These activities forced Union troops to respond and "often dictated troop movements." Countering such an unpredictable and mobile enemy presented serious challenges.[2]

Guerrillas used horses for maximum mobility and often fought on horseback. The ambush was a favorite tactic. Resulting fights were usually brief, although running fights lasting a number of miles sometimes developed. Ellithorpe described one of them in his February 3, 1863, *Chicago Evening Journal* article. Revolvers were the weapon of choice, and the Colt Navy .36 caliber revolver used by Ellithorpe was one of the most popular weapons employed in this type of warfare. As partisans retreated, they scattered and generally rendezvoused at a predesignated site. If forced to retreat, Union soldiers made their way back to camp or to a garrison as best they could. Developing effective counterinsurgency measures took time, but by the period described in this chapter, Union troops had created some effective techniques by "using small units, burning popular hideouts, and organizing and fortifying armed colonies, [so that] Federal forces were finally able to gain an equal footing with their counterparts."[3]

Normally, guerrilla activity decreased significantly in the fall and winter months, but in January and February 1863 there was an unusual amount of fighting. Although counterinsurgency measures were difficult in the border region, Union troops at least benefited from the lack of tree foliage that normally concealed the enemy. How to deal strategically with the foe and its civilian sympathizers was a pressing question. In Missouri, and likely in other areas, two schools of thought emerged. Michael Fellman, one of the leading scholars of Missouri's guerrilla war, asserts that the "softs" were the reconciliationists, and the "hards" were the punishers, with some individuals falling between the two camps. Ellithorpe, in a position to put his views into action, demonstrated in his writings that he was a hard who believed that leniency had failed and harshness should be adopted.[4]

Ellithorpe saw himself as a formidable counterinsurgent. Writing in the third person in his January 26, 1863, *Chicago Evening Journal* article, he noted, "Major Ellithorpe . . . carried out the plans in a gallant manner . . . [and ended by] completely routing" the guerrillas. Indeed, he wrote, "his rapid movements make him a terror to these marauders." According to Fellman, few soldiers wrote in a straightforward way about executing prisoners, and yet Ellithorpe made clear that it occurred and that he approved. Ellithorpe's Indian soldiers were formidable counterinsurgents in his assessment. The environment that they operated in was similar to the eastern part of the Indian Territory, and these men were skilled at "tracking out and destroying the bushwhacker gangs of this brush and jungle country." Like many Union soldiers, Ellithorpe used "hunting imagery" when describing guerrilla warfare. He wrote of "fox chases after the numerous guerrilla bands" and reported that "to-day we brought down a couple of these birds" [bushwhackers]. In this way he dehumanized guerrillas, and for him, as for many others, the frustrating nature of guerrilla warfare "spawned a callous disregard for human life and suffering," making it easy to justify killing guerrillas.[5]

Members of Thomas Livingston's guerrilla band were the main opposition for Ellithorpe and his soldiers during this time. A miner in southwestern Missouri before the war, Livingston organized the "Cherokee Spikes" in February 1862. For one and a half years he and his men plagued Federal troops; in fact, they operated more successfully in the area for a longer period than any other guerrilla band. Their "trademark became the murder of most prisoners." Livingston wound up dying in an attack on July 11, 1863, in Stockton, Missouri, but in early 1863 he was a significant problem for Union forces. Besides dealing with Livingston and other guerrillas, Ellithorpe continued to grapple with challenges within his brigade.[6]

Lt. Col. Stephen H. Wattles infuriated Ellithorpe by continuing to serve in the First Indian Home Guards in spite of his promise to leave. As he had done in the past, Ellithorpe used Colonel Chipman as a sounding board, evident in a letter of February 4, 1863, in which he vented about the Wattles situation as well as another scandal in his regiment. In January, Ellithorpe preferred charges against two lieutenants in his regiment, although records for only one man were located. First Lt. George W. Dobler was charged while Wattles was on leave. Ellithorpe alleged that in October 1862 Dobler induced three Indians to answer as present to the names of three men who were either dead or absent without leave while pay was drawn. The Indians received a cut of the proceeds, but Dobler kept the bulk of it. Although Ellithorpe expressed doubt that the court would find Dobler guilty, he was cashiered from the service and ordered to refund ninety dollars. During this time friction developed between Ellithorpe and his brigade commander, Col. William A. Phillips, a former major in the First Indian Home Guards (fig. 9).[7]

Ellithorpe continued to press for permission to recruit a battalion of riflemen, and Phillips endorsed the idea to Maj. Gen. Samuel R. Curtis and wrote that Ellithorpe "has been the most efficient field officer in the 1st Indian Regt." Perhaps it was an effort to get Ellithorpe out of the brigade, however, as a month earlier Phillips had informed Curtis that the First was in the worst condition of any of the Indian regiments. Close to "utter demoralization," he claimed that they were poorly disciplined, had not been drilled much, and were "indifferently informed as to duties." Figuratively wringing his hands, Phillips expressed his embarrassment and admitted that "arresting all the officers of a regiment is not to be thought of." By the end of March, Phillips reported great improvement in the First as a result of increased drill and praised his old regiment, the Third, as being "as good as any regiment in the service." Writing about three weeks after Ellithorpe left for Fort Scott, Phillips informed Maj. Gen. James G. Blunt, "The discipline of the whole force has much improved since Colonel Wattles and Major Ellithorpe left." Ellithorpe wrote in his diary that Phillips was undermining him, attributing the colonel's actions to jealousy. He summed it up bluntly in his February 7 entry: "Col Philips still continues to make a great ass of himself." Soon thereafter Ellithorpe received a promotion, which separated him officially from his regiment.[8]

Near the end of 1862 Secretary of War Edwin M. Stanton authorized the creation of two more Indian Home Guards regiments. On Christmas day 1862 Ellithorpe received a commission as lieutenant colonel of the Fifth Indian Home Guards. He had pushed for a promotion in his own regiment and advocated creating the rifleman battalion; he did not want the promotion and exploded in outrage. Ellithorpe vented his anger in his diary, in a letter to Chipman, and even in the pages of the *Chicago Evening Journal*. He believed that there simply were not enough Indian recruits for the two new regiments. Furthermore, he believed that "the hungry political hounds of Kansas" had devised the scheme to siphon off experienced officers who were not Kansans into regiments that would never organize and replace the old officers with Kansans. By contrast, a soldier in the ranks, young Wiley Britton of the Sixth Kansas Cavalry, heard that the newly commissioned officers were "nearly all relatives or favorites of high officials of the Government, and perhaps not in a single instance has an appointment been made on account of merit, that is, on account of bravery displayed on the field, and ability to handle troops in action." In the spring of 1863 recruitment began at Fort Blunt (formerly Fort Gibson). The *Leavenworth Daily Conservative* reported that recruiting was brisk in April, and the paper was optimistic that the two new regiments would be filled if the Indian brigade stayed longer in the area.[9]

Ellithorpe wrote about many topics in the winter of 1863 besides guerrilla warfare and internal challenges. He described the destruction of the countryside by soldiers, the terrible winter weather, famine, the plight of civilians, his joy over the slaves' claim of freedom, and his viewpoints on strategy. Distressed by the abandonment of captured territory, Ellithorpe proposed occupying a line along the Arkansas River in both the Indian Territory and in Arkansas.

JOURNAL ENTRIES, JANUARY 9, 1863–JANUARY 14, 1863

Elm Springs, January 9, 1863

I am ordered to command a large scout of 500 men, starting tonight at 10 Oclock & go to Maysville, we have inteligence that a force is gathering at that place. I anticipate a brisk skirmish. I will close my Journal untill the scout is ended, & then I may have some incidents to relate.

January 10, 1863—on the march from Elm Springs to Maysville—

last night I cap[t]ured two bushwhackers, one of them named *Coffelt* had in his pocket a scalp taken from the head of some one of our soldiers. I find the country full of these *birds*—I use them rough & every day closes with less of these Dls [Devils] than it commenced[.]

January 11, 1863

This morning I started at day break from near the head of the Spavinaw Creeke & made a rapid march in the direction of Maysville. Thoroughly scouting every part of the mountains & hills as I passed through, throwing out upon either flank some two hundred of my men—taking the center myself with three hundred men & riding rapidly towards Maysville—when within five miles of the town we started up 15 or twenty of the enemy—then the race began, & we ran them into Maysville killing nine of them & taking 14 prisoners—I have thoroughly routed the whole gang my flank scouts have killed a great many[.]

January 12, 1863

in camp at at [*sic*] Maysville. The whole country is in a state of consternation at my rapid de[s]cent, & the enemy have fled in all directions[.] I have succeded beyond my expectations in scattering them[.] My scouts are returning with good success[.]

Camp Curtiss 1½ mile from Maysville—January 13, 1863

The prospect is that we shall lay here for some days.[10] The whole Brigade has come up, in good order & we shall now do nothing but scout for bushwhackers, & forage our stock.

January 14, 1863, Camp Curtiss

We are comfortably in camp & find forage tolerable plenty, we get news from the bushwhackers daily—Kill some—take some, & some come in & surrender[.]

Chicago Evening Journal Article

FROM THE ARMY OF THE FRONTIER.
Correspondence of The Chicago Evening Journal.
HEADQUARTERS OF THIRD BRIGADE,
Detachment of Army in the Field, I. T. MAYSVILLE, January 14.

The Army of the Frontier divided at Elm Springs, Arkansas, on the morning of the 10th inst. The 3d brigade took up its line of march for the Cherokee country, and the other several brigades will indicate their destination and location at the proper time. The 3d brigade is under the command of Col. W. A. Phipps, [Phillips] of Kansas, and is destined to hold the Indian country. The brigade was preceded by a detachment of 500 mounted men, under the command of Major Ellithorpe, who carried out the plans in a gallant manner. He made a rapid march of thirty miles during the night, surprising, killing and capturing a portion of the notorious bushwhacking gangs of Livingston, Quantrell and Standwaiter,[11] completely routing them in the greatest confusion. Upon one of the prisoners was found a scalp, taken from one of our murdered soldiers. The gang was armed with the improved Merrill's carbine and Colt's navies. It is unnecessary to say that the Major knows exactly how to treat these cases. His rapid movements make him a terror to these marauders.

We are now in the very midst of the guerrilla region. The mountainous character of the country, its extreme rocky surface, and vast forests of low, thick brush, with the thousands of by-paths winding in every direction, adapt it peculiarly to the operations of these murderous, scalping devils.

Every day, however, learns some of them a bitter lesson. Yesterday a small scouting party traced the tracks of horses to one of those deep, brushy hollows, some ten miles distant from camp, and struck a small gang of Livingston's band. During the day they had taken two of our men from a foraging party. The arrival of our scouts was opportune, for they had stripped the two prisoners, and were in the act of shooting them as our gallant boys dashed in. We killed four and took *no* prisoners, and saved the lines [*sic*] of our two men. The guerrillas had built a log house and collected two or three hundred bushels of corn. They had evidently made arrangements for winter quarters. The whole nest was routed and everything burned. Not a day passes without some little excitement of this kind.

There are many serious questions to be considered relating to the permanent occupation of this country—(I mean the Western part of Arkansas and the Indian Territories). Our large armies may pass through these countries in every direction, and drive the enemy before us wherever we go, yet they will follow our retrograde up to the very rear pickets, not in force, but in small marauding scouting bands, who render the country more impassable, and its condition more deplorable, if possible, than would its occupation by a large army. Our armies may advance and recede like the tide of the ocean, but every movement renders it more desolate and uninhabitable. Nothing short of a permanent occupancy of the whole lines of the Arkansas river will ever restore quiet and drive constant terror from the doors of the people. This is simply an advance of our base of operations to an accessible point.

Van Buren and Fort Smith should have been held when we were in possession of them, and the steamers loaded with stores should have been preserved for the use of our army instead of being destroyed. Who is accountable for the retrograde from Van Buren, will at the proper time be made known, and who accountable for the surrendering of the Army of the Frontier must yet assume the responsibility. Generals commanding departments are supposed to be thoroughly posted, and should have some definite plans to work from. What that plan is in this department I cannot divine.

One thing is certain, Gen. Blunt has conquered the country north of the Arkansas river. Now, why not hold it? The scattering and retrograde of our forces will only involve the necessity, perhaps, of fighting the same ground over again. It is just as easy to maintain our army on the banks of the Arkansas, as it is forty or fifty miles north of it, and probably could be done with much less expense to the Government, and less labor and exposure to the soldiers. The climate is much more genial, and the river is a natural barrier against the enemy equivalent to thousands of men. All the forage north of us would then be within our reach, and our foraging trains would do the double duty of hunting bushwhackers and collecting subsistence. This was the plan of Gen. Blunt, and with him at our head, we should not only hold the river, but advance our front to the southern lines of Arkansas, and into Texas; thus accomplishing the subjugation of the entire Southwest. But in military, as in all human affairs, individual aggrandizement is paramount to all other considerations. No sooner one man wins the applause of his patriotic countryman, than he is shelved, for fear that he may illuminate the nation. The President and Cabinet may make Generals and soldiers *in name,* but God makes patriots and General *in fact.*

Little Rock, Van Buren, Fort Smith, Fort Gibson, and the Creek Agency should be occupied by our forces. This would gradually drive out all bands in our rear, and save, perhaps, the country from depopulation and desolation.

The negro question is very effectually settled in these parts, for there is none left to give evidence that slavery ever existed here. The Proclamation of the President will only take effect upon the *statutes of the State.* "Sambo" anticipated the event and claimed the advantages of its provisions,[12] *and more too*—for in most cases he has confiscated his master's horse, mule, donkey, wagon, etc., simply as a matter of convenience to facilitate his compliance with Executive and official privileges. The novel confusion that this general stampede has caused is truly wonderful. Many truly laughable incidents occur in the general *melee* of the dusky exodus. That the present is the appointed time for deliverance is most sincerely believed by them all; nor are they tardy in accepting and improving the advantage of our presence.

News has just arrived that one of our scouting parties has killed seven more of the Livingston gang. You may rest assured that we shall give these devils warmer work than they have calculated on. The following is a note sent into our camp by one McCall; from it you will learn the *animus* of the gang:[13]

"In the Woods, January 12, 1863.

"General Blunt:

"Sir—I caught four of your d—d blue-coated Yankees the other day and killed them. I learn that you have shot some of our men, and I promise you that I will stay in these woods, and you can't drive me out. I will kill every man of yours I catch, and Gen. Blunt and all hell can't drive me out.

"McCALL,
"1st Lieut. Standwaiter's Regiment."

I will say that we have started this fellow on a "double quick" with his murderous gang, and if he persists in his threat to stop in the hills, we shall shortly introduce his neck to the end of a few feet of hemp.

We learn with regret of the many misfortunes that befall our arms on the line of the Potomac. What is the immediate cause of these constant disasters can be only known to those who participate in them. One thing may be relied upon as certain: that is, some one ought to be made an example of, and taught that to be a soldier and to play soldier are two different things.

In my next I will post you in all important matters that are proper to be made public.

CREEK.

[Published January 26, 1863.]

JOURNAL ENTRIES, JANUARY 15, 1863–JANUARY 16, 1863

January 15, 1863 Camp Curtiss

The weather is cool, snow is falling, & bids fair for real winter[.]

Camp Curtis, January 16, 1863

The day has been a very cold one the snow is flying in real northern winter style—Men are suffering in the camps no stores,—

To Colonel Norton P. Chipman, January 16, 1863

HDQRS. THIRD BRIGADE, ARMY OF THE FRONTIER
Camp Curtis, Maysville, January 16, 1863

Col. N. P. CHIPMAN, Chief of Staff:
MY DEAR COLONEL:

You will see by the date of this that my letter of the 7th instant is yet in my hands. I send it, as it contains all the facts of which I wished to write. The cartridges have come to hand all safe and very opportune, as my last loads were in the guns. Many thanks for your trouble and kindness. I will use them well.

I preceded the advance of our brigade from Elm Springs to this place in command of 500 mounted men. The distance of 25 miles I made during the night, and surprised a party of Livingston's gang. I killed 9 and captured 13 of the gentry. We have sent the prisoners on to Fort Scott. The country is full of these marauding devils, but we are clearing them out rapidly. This light snow for the past two days enables us to track them to a charm. They have turned their heads south, and are making for the river. We are hauling them in and putting them under every day. This country is in a terrible condition. Families, both Union and secesh, are fleeing for safety to our lines. Union, however, are scarce in these parts. One of the devils that I took had the scalp of one of our soldiers in his pocket.

This brigade, well equipped and filled, will hold the Indian countries, and I am of the firm opinion that the Indians can be used in no other locality to so good an advantage; in fact, I believe that to divert them to any other field of operations than the Indian countries will tend to demoralize them to dissolution. Lieutenant-Colonel Wattles' resignation is returned as informal. Although serious charges are preferred against him, he is yet in command. I think that a plenty of forage can be had to sustain this brigade during the winter between here and Neosho and in the vicinity of Cowskin Prairie.

I should still like to raise a battalion of sharpshooters and have the Henry rifle. I can make it equal to two regiments, and a terror to the enemy, yet I am here and cannot figure for the thing. The weather is cold and freezing very hard; real winter has come at last. Please use the petition inclosed as best you may, and gum it together, as I have not these little conveniences. I send it simply to show you the feeling amongst the Indian officers, not that I imagine it will have a feather's weight with the Secretary of War. "There must be a friend in court."

Well, excuse me for my tedious letter, and the next will be short and to the point.

I have the honor to be, your friend,

A. C. ELLITHORPE

[*Source:* United States War Department, *War of the Rebellion: A Compilation of the Official Records of the Union and Confederate Armies,* 128 vols. (1880–1901; repr., Harrisburg, Pa.: National Historical Society, 1971), ser. 1, 22, pt. 2, 48–49.]

JOURNAL ENTRIES, JANUARY 17, 1863–JANUARY 22, 1863

January 17, 1863, Camp Curtis

The day has been a little mild & it looks a little like rain or snow—

January 18, 1863 Camp C—

Rain falling this morning & continued during the taking off all the snow & making mud the "*King of terrors*"[.]

January 19, 1863 Camp C—

Rain continued all night—& we poor devils awoke this morning with about 4 inches of water in our tents—ditching & draining is the order—

January 20, 1863, Camp C—

Weather is still lowery & the mud intense[.]

Camp Curtis, Jan 21, 1863

The weather during today has been fair with high wind—which helps to dry up the mud—

Many things are transpiring which tend to make things in the regiment unpleasant. Col Wattles resumed command soon after his release from arrest—this he done in violation of his word of honor, he aver[r]ed that if the charges were withdrawn he would resign his position & qui[e]tly leave the service—this I permitted to be done at the instance of Genl Blunt—Charges are again prefered by Lieut hall & are now on the road to head quarters[14]—They will never be here withdrawn again, but must be settled by court martial—

The two Lieuts against whom I prefered charges, will be on tryal very soon, & disposed of—Untill these things are settled I cannot enjoy much peace or comfort, but these things will all come right in time although there is an apparen[t] desire & ingenious effort upon the part of Col Philips to suppress any further investigation. This he cannot do long for I will force every charge to an issue.

Camp Curtis

January 22, 1863

The weather a little damp & looks much like rain—The Officers are getting up a ball for tomorow evening[.]

I shall not be able to attend my shoulder pains me very much. I am unable for duty, & shall not venture to attend a party.

Our Brigade court Martial is in cession, & the cases of this Regt will probably soon be up for trial[.]

To Maria L. Ellithorpe, January 22, 1863

Head Quarters 1st Ind
Regt. Camp Curtis
January 22, 1863

Dear Maria

Again I drop you a line, that you may know where I am & how I am getting along. I think my last was written from this Camp only 3 or four days ago. I remain here hemmed in by oceans of mud—The roads are almost impassable, we are compelled to be as quiet as possible, & spend our time in hunting a few Bushwhackers & finding forage for our stock—No important movements will be made until the roads get better—unless the enemy see fit to come & attack us—I think they will hardly venture after us, since we have taught them so many severe lessons—The weather is the most disagreeable you can imagine, snow, sleet, rain, mud, mist, high winds, &c.

The camp is one pool of mud knee deep. it is next to impossible to be comfortable in our tents, when we can get straw to lay on the ground we can barely keep out of the water[.]

This kind of weather will continue yet for two months—Camp pneumonia is quite prevalent & fatal[15]—The only thing that will save the men from fearful camp diseases, will be to remove to high grounds. I take as good care of myself as possible under the circumstances.

I hope you are getting along well & that you are in good health—I have had no late news from home—

I feel quite anxious ~~that~~ about the family & the business—You are now in the midst of your winter & I presume have cold sound weather, which is far more pr-efferable than the weather we get here—The socks mother sent me I am wearing with great comfort & as also those you sent[16]—Thanks for them—Also to mother for the gold dollar—which I have no particular use for—My health is good I am 8 or ten lbs heavier than usual, this doing pretty well I think, when you concider that the fatigue I endure is very great—

I think the Army of the Potomace is proving very inefficient, & all through the bad policy of incompetent generals—

Our Army so far has had a bright record, but how long it will last is uncertain—Other men now direct it & politicians have got hold if it—

Give my love to all the children & tell them be good & prudent,—My love to mother E——& say to her that she must not worry, but in her old age live as quiet & enjoy herself all she can & not borow trouble—

I presume you have got the letters I sent by Genl Blunt & have perhaps seen him. I think Blunt is my friend, & unlike most of the Kansas men, seems willing to share the honors of the field—He may not come back to this department again, but I think there is no doubt but he will be made a Maj Genl[17]—He is a lucky man, as a man of great talents he can lay no claim to it—he is only medium, but luck makes him a great man—

As soon as I can honorably leave the army I shall do so—but the condition of affairs in our Rgt are such now that I cannot well resign—I shall write soon again & as ever your affectionate

Albert

[*Source:* Kansas Historical Society, Ellithorpe Family Papers. *Note:* On an envelope filed next to this document, Ellithorpe wrote, "One of My Army letters from 'Camp Curtis' Indian Territory (To My Wife)."]

JOURNAL ENTRY

Camp Curtis, January 23, 1863

The day has been very pleasant & the weather lookes like being settled—I hope so for we are in a suffering condition—The ball goes off tonight & bids fair to be a passable affair.

Chicago Evening Journal Article

FROM THE ARMY OF THE FRONTIER.

Correspondence of The Chicago Evening Journal.

HEADQUARTERS OF THE INDIAN BRIGADE,

IN THE FIELD, INDIAN TERRITORY,

January 23.

Since the organizing of the Indian regiments into a brigade by themselves, we have had a good opportunity to witness the workings of this peculiar branch of the service. Various ideas have been entertained in reference to the practicability [*sic*] of making soldiers of the Indians. The term "Indian" is applied to all conditions of that race, from the wild savage of full blood to the enlightened, civilized, educated, and almost white man.

It may be interesting to your readers to take an inside view of an Indian brigade, more especially as its workings will enter into the future history of this war, in many important particulars. Many of the hard-fought battles in the West will attest how well the Indian has earned the name of soldier. His services as guide, and upon scouts, and in the tracking out and destroying the bushwhacking gangs of this brush and jungle country, will furnish more instances of individual daring and cool bravery than can be evidenced from any other class of men. Many instances of great fatigue and narrow escapes will be the theme of many a tale.

In our brigade we have three regiments, numbering about 3,000 men. The 1st regiment is composed of Creeks and Seminoles, and most of them are what are termed "full-bloods," yet they are educated, and when in their own country pursue the civilized avocations of life. Many are large farmers and heavy stock raisers. They are educated in their own language; they have books printed in the Creek tongue and in a very neat style; their schools are conducted in good order.

The 2d and 3d regiments are composed of Cherokees. This nation of people have been undergoing a gradual change from barbarism to a civilized condition for over forty years. Nearly one half are as white as our own race, and speak the English language fluently. They are probably the most enlightened race of Indians upon the continent. The uninitiated would hardly think that he was conversing with an Indian, unless the fact was made known. It is an honorable mark here to boast of Cherokee blood. Many claim to be Cherokees who, in fact, have no Cherokee blood in their veins. The reason for this is very palpable, when we consider that the lands belonging to that nation are a heritage of wealth to every person of the tribe. The principal Chief, or Governor of the nation (John Ross) claims to be a Cherokee, but in the physique of the man it is not discernable. So with hundreds of others—the slightest trace of the Indian is not perceptible. From these facts you will readily see that, although we have an Indian brigade, yet its appearance of order, discipline, and soldierly bearing will compare favorably with white brigades.

The people of these Indian nations were divided upon the politics of the day, the same as the whites; and when we consider the geographical position of their country, their years of friendly intercourse with Southern people, and the seductive institution of slavery, incorporated into every element of their national existence, it is a wonder, even, that one man may be found with the moral courage to break loose from these ties and proclaim for liberty and the Union. But a large majority of all these tribes have taken up arms for the Government, and exhibit a real genuine patriotism that ought to flush the cheek of every pale-faced traitor with shame.

The Government would not have permitted the Indian to participate in the war had they not been divided amongst themselves. The rebel portion of the Indians were the first to take up arms and commence a series of outrages upon those who desired to stand neutral. Aided by the power of white rebel troops, the loyal portion were compelled to flee for safety. Thus the two parties have taken sides. The Indian territories have become almost depopulated, each in turn making raids through the country, and spreading desolation upon every hand.

There are five regiments of the rebel Indians, composed of the Cherokees, Creeks, Choctaws, and a few from the wild tribes. Since their rout and defeat at the battle of Fort Wayne, they have been in a scattered, confused, and disappointed condition. Many of them have gone home, and many deserted to our lines. A few of the families of both parties yet remain in the country, fleeing from their houses upon the approach of troops, and hiding in the bushes and mountains, until they are gone. Constant fear and alarm pervade the whole country.

The houses of almost every family have been robbed of their most valuable articles, leaving hardly sufficient to cloth or feed therefrom for any great length of time. The desolation is almost complete; a few months' time will accomplish the destruction.

We may now begin to speculate what will be the destiny of these Indian territories, if they will, upon the consummation of the war, maintain their former independent relations towards our Government, or if the Indian titles will be extinguished and new States formed from them. The eagle-eyed politicians have already discovered the new field of conquest, and bright dreams of Congressional and Senatorial seats flit across their brain.

I can give you no important news, more than our continued fox chases after the numerous guerrilla bands. These chases are exciting in the extreme. A buffalo, wolf, or fox chase is no comparison. Two days ago, while crossing Walker's Prairie, just at the eastern edge of the Cherokee nation, we started up six of the "Livingston gang." They were dressed throughout in the Federal uniform of blue, which they had pilfered from our murdered prisoners. They even wore the little *Union flag* in the side of the hat. Eight of us approached them until within about five hundred yards. One of the number advanced a few paces in front, and with his hands gave a series of signs, which of course were unintelligible to us. The signs not being answered, they, of course, knew us to be enemies. They instantly wheeled their horses and put in the spurs. A five mile prairie lay before us, and now the race commenced. Now and then they would look over their shoulders and send a navy bullet at us. Our boys were ordered to hold their fire and apply the whip and spur. With loud yells and Indian war-whoops we dashed on. For the first three miles the race was even, no apparent advantage being gained by either.

The pursued were running for life, and the pursuing for victory. Soon four of our best horses commenced to gain upon them until not over one hundred yards separated us. Now commenced the work. Our navies began to send the fatal little missiles. One reels and falls from his horse; another horse is hit, and plunges headlong, throwing his rider to the ground; a single shot holds him there. All are dashing forward, with hideous yells, and the quick reports of the pistol make the scene one to be long remembered. A third reels and tumbles to the ground, and a fourth horse is disabled and his rider helpless, and in another instant is writhing in the agonies of death. The other two owe their lives to the speed of their horses. The chase is ended, and our panting horses tell how severe it has been. Four lifeless marauders lay to bleach in the suns and rains of heaven.

These scenes are of almost daily occurrence, and will continue for a long time to come.

The weather is extremely wet, and the mud is almost intolerable. There is a great deficiency of tents, and if this inclement weather continues long, the camps will suffer from disease. Pneumonia is becoming quite prevalent.

I cannot refrain from repeating what I wrote in a former letter, in regard to the division and retrogade [*sic*] movement of the Army of the Frontier. Every day proves to me more conclusively that it is a bad stroke of policy. The Arkansas river should have been our line of operations, and the future will show this policy to be correct. We shall not only lose the prestige of the victories we have gained, but the most important field for subsistence is the whole Southwest. It may be strategy, and there may be some deep-laid scheme at the bottom, but "I can't see it."

Marmaduke, with a force of two or three thousand cavalry, is reported to be below Van Buren, and contemplating an advance this side of the mountains. This will be the natural result of our abandonment of the country we have conquered. We must expect that the enemy will again overrun the country, if for no other reason than for forage, and to wreak their vengeance upon the few remaining families of Union sentiment.

The Indian brigade will be fully competent to hold the Indian territories north of the river, unless there should be a concentration of more forces than they have above Fort Smith. I am firmly of the opinion that Hindman and Marmaduke will not concentrate any important force west of Little Rock, but have determined to unite their destiny with that of the main rebel army east of the Mississippi.

We had no news from the East for the past ten days, and we are very anxious to know how things are progressing on the Potomac.

THE JOURNAL is fast becoming an indispensable friend in the general dearth of news. It is the only Chicago paper I have chanced to meet in this army.

CREEK.

[Published February 3, 1863.]

JOURNAL ENTRIES, JANUARY 24, 1863–JANUARY 26, 1863

Camp Curtis, January 24, 1863

This morning the rain falling, which added to the already damp condition of the ground will make our camp almost insufferable—we shall be compelled to moove into the hills, or a fearful amount of sickness will surely result—The court martial is still in cession I have but little to expect from it. The President of the board is a man of little sense & less experience in fact a young drunken profligate who thinks more of a good time, & a supply of whiskey than he does of his country[18]—he takes pride in boasting how drunk he gets & how reckless he can be—hence I cannot, nor do I make an associate of him[;] he is the boon companion of the very men who are on tryal for drunkenness, & for theft from the Government. I imagine that Col Philips through a spirit of jealousy is secretly aiding in the promotion of the interest of every one opposed to me & for this purpose will wink at the suppression of any & even all the evidence in the cases.

Sunday, January 25, 1863

Rain is the order of the day, & mud is the ruling element.—I am today detailed as grand officer of the day[.][19] This duty falls on me almost every

~~day~~ other day. There are only three other officers in the Brigade upon whoom this duty can fall it cannot go below the rank of major—Lieut Col Wattles got very mad this morning because I opened an official document directed to the commanding officer of the Regt.

This I had a right to do,—let him *rip*—Col Philips has sent the charges against Col Wattles forward to Genl Curtis this is done for the purpose of procrastination & he thinks to worry the thing out by delay—I shall very soon send forward the statement of the whole matter directly to Genl Curtis—

Camp Curtis, January 26, 1863

Still in camp—& still it is raining.

The Court Martial is in cession & I learn from witnesses in the cases that the tryals are being conducted in a very partial & improper maner—The Judge advocate has no ability to investigate facts or draw evidence from witnesses[.]

The prospect is that the man *Dobler* who has made a writen confession of stealing one hundred dollars from the Govt will not be found guilty[20]—God have mercy upon such a tribunal[.] It is characteristic however of the way justice is meeted out to vilians in this western country[.] And any man who attempts to bring a rascal to justice here may as well engage passage on the next train, for the hounds will unite to grind him out, & the only safe cours is to stand by & wink approvingly while the balance plunder—but do not on any account attempt to get a share of the plunder for this is equaly fatal, & the every *devil* of *them* will halloe "stop thief" at the same time they have both hands in your pockets[.]

Chicago Evening Journal Article

FROM THE ARMY OF THE FRONTIER

Correspondence of The Chicago Evening Journal.

HEADQUARTERS 8TH AND 9TH DIVISIONS,

ARMY OF THE FRONTIER,

CAMP CURTIS, MAYSVILLE, Ark, Jan. 26.

A bright, warm sun, almost a cloudless sky, and the green grass springing up beneath your feet, on the 26th of January, would doubtless be a rarity to you cold-blooded Northerners. Don't take offense—for some one has said

"The cold in clime are cold in blood."[21]

The Dixieites most religiously believe this to be a fact. The real, genuine, Southern-raised, uneducated whites entertain an opinion of Northern people anything but complimentary to even the worst specimens of the human race.

I appreciated the compliment paid us the other day by one of the *softer* sex, in answer to "How she liked the looks of the Feds?" She replied, "Wall now, stranger, since you wanter know, I jist allow to tell yer. I was borned and raised a real Southern woman, and think that a nigger hadn't otter be on a level; but you trifling, pin-making, codfish-eating, abolition Yankees think they had; so, you see, I jist think, from the bottom of my heart, that if there is a difference 'twixt you and the nigger, the nigger has a right smart chance the advantage." "Bully for you!" said I, and then she took a pinch of snuff that would have sneezed an elephant for half an hour, without even winking at it. I passed on with the advance guard, but heard the poultry screaming terrifically in the rear, caused, probably, by the unusual sight of blue coats, or in derision of the Feds.

Hardly a day passes but our forage train is fired into by the bushwhackers. To-day we brought down a couple of these birds in the most approved style. They generally pay for their temerity severely. You would shudder to pass over this country and witness the horrid condition of affairs. "Bread!" is now the cry from all quarters, and hundreds are applying to our lines for something to eat. You will remember that in a former letter I predicted the approach of the "evil genius of war." He is here—*famine* is sitting upon the thresholds of almost every cabin in the country. All must flee before him, and where can they go but to our lines? Many of these deluded people have already emigrated a half a dozen times to get beyond our reach. We find them all the way from Northwestern Missouri, having moved from point to point, thinking to find a place of safety and rest; but, alas! our armies have hunted them to their last hiding places. Further retreat is hopeless, and they now come and ask us to help them to go North. Poverty-stricken, almost without clothes or food, we are compelled to give them rations and send them forward in our empty commissary trains. They go back a wiser, and, I hope, a better and more loyal people. Almost every day the Commander is in receipt of notes from those who have been in the "bushes" for months, asking if they may come and give themselves up and have their lives spared.

This shows the approaching dissolution of the rebel cause in this country, and thus will it terminate, throughout our whole lines if our Generals will only pull off their gloves and deal with rebellion and treason as if it were a crime endangering the existence of the nation. Two days ago we sent a heavy scouting party in the direction of Taliqua and Park Hill, in the Cherokee Nation, under the command of Lieut. Col. Downing, a Cherokee officer of fine ability.[22] We are compelled to send forward subsistence to many loyal families there, who are in a state of entire destitution. What few small bands there are now in the country are committing robberies upon all classes of people. They are dressed in our army clothes, and pass themselves as *Feds*, or Kansas Jayhawkers. The greater portion of Col. McIntosh's Cherokee and Creek regiment will come to us the first opportunity. Col. Standwaiter's regiment is in about the same condition. They have not over 350 men each, and those tired of the rebel service.

Hindman is said to be hovering along the Arkansas river, above Little Rock, afraid to make any demonstration north, and not able to take his forces much further east. His Missouri and Arkansas troops refuse to fight east of the Mississippi river. Marmaduke has two or three thousand cavalry in the vicinity of Clarksville, below Van Buren. We have just learned that a band of wild, marauding Indians, Kickapoos, Osages and Kecheis are in camp nearly west of this some 40 miles, on the Verdigris river, in the Creek Nation.[23] They will soon be routed. News just in from Fort Gibson and the Creek Agency say that the rebel forces have all fallen back to Red river and Boggy Depot.

The refugee Indian families now in Southern Kansas will probably go to their homes early in the spring. The total of their number must be about twelve thousand. These, at the present time, are being fed and partially clothed at the expense of the Government, but the amount will be taken from their annuity moneys, upon final settlement.

As soon as the grass starts in the spring, sufficient to subsist the ponies, the grand cavalcade will take up its line of march, and make the effort to raise a crop, upon their own lands. To this end, this division of the Army of the Frontier is working, and, unless the rebels can amass a much larger army than we now think, the object will be attained.

We have just learned of the heavy fighting in Tennessee and Kentucky.[24] No definite results have yet reached us. We are waiting anxiously for THE JOURNAL.

CREEK.

[Published February 11, 1863.]

JOURNAL ENTRIES, JANUARY 27, 1863–FEBRUARY 1, 1863

Camp Curtis, January 27, 1863

No court in Cession today. I have thrown a *bomb Shell* into the corrupt conclave & they have adjourned I think to concider & councill what is best to do. They begin to think they are in danger of censure & possibly they may yet try to do justice & make an effort to detect rascality. I shall not slacken my vigilence in these cases—I am today convinced of the desire of Col Philips to embaras me all he can—& if possible help Col Wattles to extricate himself from the charges against him—his object is for a double purpose 1st embaras me & keep me from being Col of the Regt—2d use Wattles as an instrument for a time & then cast him off—he has come to this conclusion after long counseling with the Kansas asperants—We will see how his plans worke—& if I succede in foiling him in his dishonorable motives—*Col Philips* resorts to every little thing that a comanding officer has the power to—to annoy me, every technicality of regulation he enforces on me while he lets others pass quietly & without these pittet [petty] anoyances—I will however show him that two can play at this game—& from today it commences—Mark the result—

Camp Curtis, January 28, 63

Dull in camp I am Guard officer of the day—no event transpired except the returne of our Scout after Bushwhackers. Several were killed & some taken prisoners[.] They are scattering with great fear.

Camp Curtis, January 29, 1863

The weather is gloomy & the mud is unbareable.

Phillips, still dose all he can do to anoy me, he is favoring every man that I have tryed to bring to justice. he is determined that he will not let any case come to tryal if he can help it[.]

Swindling appears to be the general material proclivity of every man from Kansas[.]

Nor will they suffer any one to be court Martialed.

January 30, 1863, Camp Curtis

Last night a young man who lives in this country of Rebel Parentage, & who was in our employ stole my pistol a horse saddle & bridle, & left made his way through the pickets out of our lines. I have sent after him with a party of thirty men & think I shall get the scamp if I do, his neck will *pull*[.]

Camp Curtis, January 31, 1863

My scout came in today & brought my pistol, the horse saddle & bridle, the young man *did not come in*—The way of the transgressor is hard[.]

Tomorrow we shall moove camp north west about 19 miles we are compelled to do that on account of forage. Yesterday we killed several bush whackers & took several prisoners.

Camp John Ross February 1, 1863

Today we mooved as calculated[;] we have a fine place to camp & a plenty of forage for two weeks[.]

Chicago Evening Journal Article

FROM THE ARMY OF THE FRONTIER.

Correspondence of the Chicago Evening Journal.

HEADQUARTERS 9TH AND 10TH DISTRICT.

ARMY OF THE FRONTIER, CAMP CURTIS, ARK.

February 1, 1863.

You have probably heard that we sent a small detachment of our forces over the mountains, for the purpose of calling upon some of our Van Buren friends, and to ascertain how the rebels were progressing along the line of the Arkansas. The scout was a very successful one. With only about two hundred mounted men and two mountain howitzers, under command of Lieut. Col. Stewart, we took over three hundred prisoners, burned one steamer loaded with corn, threw a few shells into an infantry camp the other side of the river, besides doing many other things to the great damage of rebeldom generally, and for the benefit of the cause at large.[25]

A more disheartened set of traitors never followed the filthy "rag" of treason than these same Southwestern rebels. They have lost all hope in their cause, and are now only at a loss to derive some safe method of escape from the ragamuffin army of Hindman. Most of them manifest a desire to join our army; but the trouble is, we don't like the breed, and the probability is that our ranks are better off without them. However, there are two regiments more raising out of this element. They wish to be denominated "State troops," for the defense of the State.[26] This will never do, and, if entered into, it will be regretted deeply. Missouri has furnished ample illustrations of this kind of blindfold sympathy with the rotten dogma of pro-slavery doctrines. The accounts with the rebel slave States were closed on the 1st of January last, and the balance sheet struck. Now let them pay up that balance, which is emancipation to every slave in the States, and a constitution guaranteeing eternal freedom to every human being upon her soil.

Our scout from Taliqua returned, performing its mission well. Several thousand pounds of flour was distributed to the destitute families, to their great joy and relief. To-day we leave Camp Curtis and proceed to Cowskin Prairie, about fifteen miles from here, in the Cherokee Nation.

To-morrow the Council of the Cherokee Nation will meet and proceed to pass such enactments and laws as will again place the county in communion with the Federal Government.[27] The ordinance of secession will be rescinded, and slavery be abolished, accepting the terms of the President's Proclamation. A large majority of the Council will be present. Chief John Ross will not be there, but the executive chair will doubtless be filled by some able official of the Nation.[28]

A small military post will be established at Maysville, for the better occupation of the country, and to afford protection to the inhabitants against the bushwhackers. For twenty miles around our present camp the forage is entirely cleaned out. In the vicinity of our next camp we shall be able to subsist for two or three weeks. So you see we are managing to wrench from this brushy, rocky country enough to subsist upon, until the spring shall send forth green grass, when our stock will be independent of forage.

The past week we turned 500 of the Creek Indians loose into the mountains, hills and gorges, with instructions to *hole* every bushwhacker in range. The work has been accomplished, and the only reports made of the matter have been the sharp crack of the rifle upon the hill tops, or in the dark, deep ravines. History will never record the many individual scenes and death struggles that have "frightened the air" but for a moment, and then died away in the solitudes of the wilderness. The father, the son, and the brother lie scattered among the leaves, without a record of their last moments—their whitening bones the only monument of their last resting place. Such is domestic war—such is treason.

As soon as the National Council concludes its session, I will give you the important features of it.

The weather is mild, rainy and muddy and much sickness prevails. The principal diseases are pneumonia, rheumatism and corn-bread.

CREEK.

[Published February 13, 1863.]

JOURNAL ENTRIES, FEBRUARY 2, 1863–FEBRUARY 4, 1863

February 2, 1863, Camp John Ross

We have got comfortably located again & feel more at home, for two days the weather has been very cold & the wind very severe.

Camp John Ross, February 3, 1863

Today we herd of the approach of our Comissary train—it comes in good time for our rations are very short—We hear of bush whackers north of us. they have made attack upon our scouts several times[.]

we shall have another fox hunt[.]

February 4, 1863

Train arrived & brot no mail matters from Ft Scott—The Q. M. got drunk & left all the mail. So it will be three weeks before we get it—A lot of commissions arived by a messenger, for the officers of new regiments. I have one as Lieut Col in the 5th Regt.

Jim Lane has done this to spite me, but I will pay him for it in the end. I am transfered from my old Regt in order that the corruptions of some of the officers there may go unpunished[.]

To Colonel Norton P. Chipman, February 4, 1863

Head Quarters 1st Ind Regt
Camp John Ross, Arkansas
Feb 4th 1863

Dear Chipman,

"God helps them who helps themselves." Hence the necesity of every man puting himself in a position to help himself—for the last few months my hands have been tied, *in the field*. I have been a large portion of the time in command of the Regt & so thoroughly engaged that I have had little chance to take care of my own interests—Well this means that the Kansas "hounds" have accomplished what they desired—viz—They "cut & carved" unjointed & *linked* together again, the officers of the Indian Regiments, to suit their own private notions of political preferment. For instance, in my Regt they have "*jumped me,*" & appointed a *Lieutenant from another Regt* a *Lieut Col* in my regt *over me*—They have promoted Lieut Col Wattles to Col in the "*face & eyes*" of charges for the most heinous offenses of fraudulently cheating the men of the Regt—& of drawing money from the Division Q. M. upon fictitious & vouchers, as alsoe causing fraudulent vouchers to be isued to men who had never rendered any kind of service to the govt—And thus it has gone—In order to smooth me down & keep my mouth shut, they have sent me an appointment from the President as Lieut Col in the "*fifth Regt of the Indian Brigade*" a mythical institution only found in the brain of "Kansas Politicians[.]" A regiment that never can be raised from Indians only in imagination—Should I accept it, as they intend, it would fill the bill, of launching me out upon the *ethereal blue*—upon a Quixotick expedition ~~that~~ that I have no particular penchant ~~for~~ to embark in—No less than three sets of charges have been forwarded against Lieut Col Wattles, & still no action.

I dont know as it is possible for me to ever get a hearing through the "proper chanels" & perhaps it is impossible, in this out of the way place, to ever get a hearing upon any charges however serious they may be—

Yet I have still faith in the virtue & integrity of the heads of the Department & shall not cease my exertions untill I have completely exhausted my energies,—which, I think, I have a large supply on hand.

I lay these facts before you in an unofficial forme, but cannot say how soon I shall be obliged to approach Department Head Quarters, direct with a petition for *relief*—I acquainted Doctor Gillpatrick a secret agent of the Govt of all these frauds & speculations upon his departure for Washington. It has done no good & has terminated as I expected—He has seen fit to make a *door* through which I could *go out*, & leave these fraudulent acts to themselves—*I shan't go*. The military powers, *must* either take notice of them, or dispose of me in less *polite* maner.

These things have never reached the Heads of power, if they have, May God have mercy upon our country if such things go unnoticed—& when I become satisfied that the Govt will not take notice of such complaints then I am ready to leave the service & pray for a deliverance from our *enemies at home*—I care but little for my own promotion but I have a pride that inferior officers shall not be promoted over me—unless they possess merit or have done the Govt signal service[.]

In fact—I think I showed you a petition to the Pres & Sec of War, asking for my promotion to the rank of Maj [?] for meritorious & galant conduct upon the battle field—This was signed by Genl Blunt and all the officers of my own Regt as well as several Cols from other Regiments—But a man who owed [?] me [?] *envy* has been to Washington & probably by fraud & misrepresentation has accomplished this dirty work—

I may see you soon & will then open the whole scheme to you[.]

until then God Bless You
A. C. Ellithorpe

[*Source:* National Archives and Records Administration, Compiled Service Records of Union Volunteers from the State of Kansas, First Indian Home Guards, Record Group 94, A. C. Ellithorpe file.]

JOURNAL ENTRIES, FEBRUARY 5, 1863–FEBRUARY 6, 1863

Camp John Ross, February 5, 1863

I shall now figure to go north & try & put my self right by applying to the war department direct.

Otherwise I shall resign.

February 6, 1863

Every thing is running smoothe; we have been out hunting the enemy for two days. Killed some taken some prisoners[.]

Chicago Evening Journal Article

FROM THE ARMY OF THE FRONTIER.

Correspondence of The Chicago Evening Journal.

HEADQUARTERS ARMY OF THE FRONTIER,
CAMP JOHN ROSS, February 6.

Our present camp is on the east bank of the Cowskin river—one of the finest streams for pure water in the State of Missouri. We are close to the Cherokee line, and almost in the extreme southwestern corner of Missouri. To-day the snow is six inches deep on the level, and still falling very fast.

We are in the vicinity of quite a large amount of forage, enough, perhaps, to last our command two or three weeks. We have left a small post at Maysville, and there is also a post at Neosho, twenty-two miles north of this, at which point the refugee Cherokee Indians are assembling, preparatory to moving into their country in the spring. The Executive Council of the Cherokee Nation is in session about four miles from here, in the Nation. No business has yet been transacted.

Our commissary train arrived yesterday from Fort Scott, with twenty days' supply. Our mail matter for the whole brigade was left at Fort Scott, through the drunken negligence of an incompetent. This is refreshing to us, who seldom hear from home, to be cheated out of our mail matter by perhaps one bottle of very bad whisky. Some news, however, arrived in the shape of a batch of new commissions from the President of the United States. The arrival of these commissions show the finger-marks of the hungry political hounds of Kansas, who are determined to rule or ruin this branch of the Frontier Army. To give you an illustration of the gross injustice and unprincipled villainy of these men I will cite a few examples. First, they conceived the brilliant idea of creating two more "Indian regiments" as a "back door exit" for such officers as they wished to retire, in order to make room for a few more Kansas men yet unprovided for. All who have any knowledge of the Indian Nations well know that no more can be raised, unless we go south of the Arkansas river to recruit them, and then we are compelled to conquer or coax them from the ranks of the Southern Confederacy. The Osages and Delawares were mustered out of the service as worthless. Moreover, it would be an unwise policy to put any more Indians into the service, especially those from the wild tribes. Again, the officers, many of them, who raised the three regiments that are in the field, have acquitted themselves with great credit. Yet, here comes a batch of commissions, taking a Lieutenant, *jumping* him over Captains, Majors, etc., and converting him into a Lieutenant-Colonel, and for those whom they have "jumped over" they forward commissions of promotion in these new, mythical regiments, that exist only in the minds of these tricksters.

This is the "back door" through which they very *politely* ask the old officers to walk and give room for the favorite new comers. These men, many of them, have been in the field in active service for the last year, and have helped to win for this department the glory that excites the admiration of all; and, to make the thing still more bare-faced and disgraceful, they have not retired, through this newly made "back door," a single Kansas man—only the boys from foreign States are permitted to pass out. It cannot be that the President or the Secretary of War have any idea of the outrage that is being perpetrated. Such abuse to a tried and field-worn officer is enough to make him burn with indignation—such a reward for long and gallant service is an indignity that will not go unchecked.

Every man promoted to a desirable position is either a *Kansas man* or a relative of the "Heads of the Interior Department," at Washington.

Again, we find the very men engaged in this kind of disgraceful chicanery to whom the Government pays large wages as its secret agents. They make use of their position to the detriment of the service and the injury of those who will not clique with them.

The Government has been openly defrauded of money, and this *agent* has been apprised of it; yet he takes no heed, and still works for the promotion of the guilty party. It is almost impossible to gain access to the powers at Washington, unless one has a friend seated there in one of the soft official chairs. You may start your complaint, but its chance of getting through is very uncertain. I would sooner insure the life of our "blue-coated boys," in traveling the entire extent of this bushwhacking country, than the safe arrival of a paper in Washington containing charges against a Kansas man.

There are one or two cases of officers with the rank of Major, who, if they had been in any other field but a department controlled exclusively by political demagogues, would have been honored and promoted for efficient service and noble conduct. As it is, in both instances, a Lieutenant and a Kansas civilian receive appointments over their heads to the rank of Lieutenant Colonels. These old officers were the first to embark in the experiment of organizing the Indians into the service, and have led them in many hard fought engagements, with honor and credit.

They now stand aside to make room for new and untried men, who are willing to commit themselves to the service of a Kansas man who trembles for his re-election to the U.S. Senate in 1865. Merit is no recommendation for promotion, when the primitive promoting power is in the hands of a selfish demagogue, who considers it legitimate to misrepresent facts to the President and the Secretary of War. I speak of these wrongs and abuses, with no intention of reflecting upon any of the *sober,* worthy officers of this department, for there are many of them, with Blunt at the head of the list; but I refer to the *wire pullers* outside of the military circle; those who sit close to the heads of power in Washington and abuse their ears with advice that heaps disgrace and outrage upon many a well-tried and war-worn officer.

Who so fit to judge of the merits of a subordinate officer as his superior in command? Is it possible that the War Department will consent to degrade an officer by the promotion of an inferior over him without good and sufficient cause, or at least without the recommendation of the officer commanding? Or will they listen to the wily schemes of a *home-guard* political aspirant who thinks the security of his own civil, official position paramount to the general good of his country? If so, then merit will go begging, and incentives to patriotism will be at a discount.

Enclosed please find some of the promotions and appointments, as taken from a Kansas paper.

CREEK.

[Published February 26, 1863.]

JOURNAL ENTRIES, FEBRUARY 7, 1863–FEBRUARY 10, 1863

February 7, 1863 Sunday—

I am again detailed for officer of the day—a duty I dislike to performe—The weather is mild looks much like rain—There is a large meeting today in an old distillery close to our camp, preaching in Creek & Cherokee—

No news of any importance has come to Camp—Col Philips still continues to make a great ass of himself—

Camp John Ross, February 8,1863

Several of our scouts have returned no news of the enemy except in small goings.

The weather has moderated very much—Col Philips proposes to give me orders to report to Genl Blunt—This I would do any way, upon the order of the Sec of War—I think I will start north in two days—

Camp John Ross, February 9, 1863

I have my matters all arranged to go tomorow—

Mrs Moody runs the Brigade—I am heartily disgusted with the tomfoolery of Philips I think the man is crazy.

Forage has nearly been exhausted here—the cav will be obliged to moove soon—

February 10, 1863, Camp on the route to Ft. Scott 14 miles north of camp John Ross

We have had a very hard days travel. The roads are very bad & forage scarce[.]

We hear that Livingstons band of Bush Whackers are ahead of us—we may have some fun with them before we get through—Tonight I am camped in an old log secesh house full of fleas & lice I guess. Every house we meet with so far ~~has~~ is deserted not a soul can we see, the desolation is complete.

Treason has done its worke teribly—

To Major General Samuel R. Curtis, from Colonel William A. Phillips, February 10, 1863

Headquarters 8th and 9th Dis
Dept. Mo.—In the Field
Camp John Ross Feb 10. 63

Major Gen. Curtis,

Understanding that Lt Col. Ellithorpe, of the (new) 5th Regt. proposes to secure if possible a battalion of Riflemen with Henry breech loading rifles, I think it would redound to the interests of the service here that he proceed[.]

I do not hesitate to say that he has been the most efficient field officer in the 1st. Indian Regt[.]

Wm A. Phillips
Col. Commanding

[*Source:* Kansas Historical Society, Ellithorpe Family Papers.]

JOURNAL ENTRIES, FEBRUARY 11, 1863–MARCH 13, 1863

Camp on the route, February 11, 1863

We have lain in camp all day & the rain has poured down in torrents, we have found forage enough to feed our stock—mostly wheat—Tonight the rain is pouring down—thunder & light[n]ing is *brisk*—I fear the creekes & rivers will be up to such a heighth as to prevent our crossing for several days[.]

The numerous families mooving out are suffering very much—most of them have no kind of shelter to ward off the storm—children ar[e] crying with wet hunger & cold—the rain is so terrific that fires cannot be built to cooke—Rumors are still rife as to the premeditated attack of Livingston & his gang—I have little fears of any demonstration upon his part—We contemplated marching in the morning but the rain may prevent us—We shall only go a few miles, it will take us 8 or ten days to get to Fort Scott[.]

Camp Sparlin, February 12, 1863

Today we mooved 8 miles to this point for the purpose of getting forage—I find we are in the same neighborhood of Barlins Mills—the place where I was shot at from the brush last June by by one Jo Price & Fay Price—The people here all recognize me, here I found my old guide a Mr Crabtree who is a brave & good union man[.]

The country is dessolated.

Camp Sparlin, February 13, 1863

W[e] have laid here all day for forage & that the train from Fayetteville with the wounded might overtake us, & alsoe that we may get supplies from Neosh[o]—a distance of 12 miles—we expect to remain here tomorrow—& then shall push along if the train comes up—

Camp Sparlin, February 14, 63

Remained here all day the wagons sent to Neosho came in with only two days rations. No news from the Fayetteville train. We shall move tomorrow some twelve miles to Shoal Creeke or "Reddings Mills[.]"

Camp at Reddings Mills, Sunday February 15, 1863

We made a very easy days march to this point today—weather fine—much like spring—we find a good mill here & in operation it will grind about 15 bbls [barrels] flour per day. We hear that Livingston with his gang is close by here with 150 men—This is a larger force than we have with us but we can whip him—

Camp Redding, February 16, 1863

All day in camp—Livingston came within two miles of our camp last night[;] we sent a scout after him today—he has about 75 men constantly with him, & is constantly commiting depredations upon all our stragling soldiers & forage trains. I think we will have a fight with him before two days.

February 17, 1863

We lay in camp all day in waiting for the train which we hear will be up tomorrow—Nothing new has transpired[.]

February 18, 1863 (Camp Diamond Grove)

Today we mooved forward to Diamond Grove a distance of 10 miles. our scouts report Livingston & his gang ahead. They expect to attack the train at the Spring River crossing.

We shall be prepared for them, & if the[y] desire a little fun we will accommodate them to their heart's content[.]

Camp on the Prarie, February 19, 1863

As I anticipated we today found Livingston & his gang in ambuscade. We had but 35 men in our scout, & as we were scouring the woods, on Spring river in search of him, we had a full volly of some 75 guns fired at us from the brush Killing instantly Lieut Spencer & two privates all from the Kansas 9th[29]—We immediately dismounted & commenced the battle after several rounds, the enemy fled—but ralying again they made a desperate charge upon us & we were compelled to fall back in turn some 30 rods—here, we gained a good position & made a desperate stand with our little brave band. They came charging on untill within 50 steps. we poured a volly into their ranks. That put them to flight in the greatest confusion[.]

Again they ralyed & at this moment our ammunition failed & we were compelled to fall back to our horses. here again we made a stand & repulsed them. Our failure of ammunition compelled us to take our horses & make a retreat to camp. We lost 6 killed & six wounded. The loss of the Rebels we could not ascertain[.]

February 20, 1863, Camp at Fort Scott

We today arived at the Fort[;] the last 24 hours has been very stormy, rain hail & snow. I have been out in the storm since last night & have not a dry thread about me. I have suffered very much. I shall remain here untill Genl Blunt comes around, which I expect will be sometime this week. When I have an interview with the Genl I will determine if I resign or longer continue in the service[.] Unless I can be assured that I shall have the full credit of my own service, I will not remain in the service[.]

March 5, 1863

Still I am in Fort Scott & yet the Genl has not arived—The weather has been very bad & the roads from here to Leavenworth has been almost impassible[;] the streams are impassible & so I must wait. I would like much to be at home but I must bide my time[.]

March 10, 1863

This morning I left Fort Scott on my route for Leavenworth[.]

Leavenworth, March 13, 1863

Arived in this place this day—I shall have to remain here untile the arival of Genl Blunt

When I shall procede to St Louis or Chicago[.]

Chicago Evening Journal Article

FROM THE ARMY OF THE WESTERN FRONTIER.

About Guerrillas, Indians and Copperheads.

LETTER FROM OUR OWN CORRESPONDENT.

CHEROKEE NATION.

HEADQUARTERS 8TH AND 9TH DIV.,

ARMY OF THE FRONTIER, March 15, 1863.

Talk about the "sloughs of Illinois," and the quagmires of "Mud Lake." They are *nowhere*, when you compare them to the unfathomable mud-pits of this deluged and water-soaked brush-and-jungle country. The whole extent of this rebel region is converted into one vast quagmire. The bottom-lands, the table-lands, the side-hills, tops of the mountains, every place, are pitfalls for man or beast. You toil and labor to reach the top of some contiguous ridge, hoping to extricate yourself from the mire of the low-lands, but alas, the stony ridges prove an *ignis fatuus* and you only reach their tops to involve yourself in a more *mireous* difficulty.

I told you in my last that the Army of the Frontier would remain hereabouts until spring, moving from point to point, solely for the purpose of subsistence. This occupation, alone, has kept us very busy. The corn patches are small and the *cribs* are scarce; hence we can only remain in one camp to exceed three or four days. Then to remove is a job almost equal to crossing the Alps. If we make seven or eight miles in one day we have done bravely.

The guerrillas are the only enemy in striking distance, and almost every day we have a little fun with these lawless vagabonds. They generally pay for any impudence or temerity that they may be guilty of. The suppression of the guerrilla warfare will very soon engage the serious attention of our Government. I am fully satisfied from experience (and I have now had twelve months' fighting them), that the present method will not prove effectual, and, moreover, it is incurring an enormous expense upon the Government.

Our forces are generally too large and encumbered with too much transportation. The policy of the guerrillas is to organize in small bands of from three to fifty men and prey upon our scouts, messengers, forage trains, and stragglers. If they are pursued, they separate, and now, when you are upon the trail of fifty horses, in a half an hour you are following the track of a single horse. Each one has his hiding place, and a home in some secret sympathizer's little cabin, where he goes to rest and feed. If you chance to overtake him here, his horse is unsaddled and horse in the brush; his arms are hidden under some log; his blue Government overcoat is secreted in another place; and he will look you innocently in the face and swear that he is quietly stopping at home, and that he at heart is a good Union man. All the women and children of the house will attest the same, and in many instances he will show you a protection paper given by some Government officer. This is the character of seven-eighths of them. They are the residents of the country, reinforced by all the natural horse thieves, highway robbers, and evil-minded, lawless vagabonds in the country. And these villains are harbored by the women who are left at home and in many instances receiving rations and support from our Government. Again, some of our officers treat these outlaws with too much consideration, by extending to them all the etiquette due to persons engaged in honorable warfare—such as exchange of prisoners, flags of truce, communications for the establishing of *cartels*, &c., &c. This method compels us to treat them as prisoners of war, and hence we surrender the very rascals who carry on this secret and murderous system. Only a few days ago, while our train was on its way up from the command to Fort Scott, our men were ambushed by Tom Livingston and his gang, and five of them killed, and this within 30 miles of Fort Scott, where Livingston makes his headquarters. Still we cannot catch him, simply because we move in too large bodies, and so openly that spies always precede us with intelligence of our strength and plan of operations. Any good officer, with three hundred well-mounted and well-equipped men, left entirely to mature and put in execution his plans, can drive these men out of the country or exterminate them in thirty days. Livingston remarked, the other day, to an exchanged prisoner, that "as soon as grass came he would keep an army of five thousand busy chasing him."

Now, that the enemy are driven out of all the country north of the Arkansas river, what remains for the Army of the Frontier to do? Occupy their time in hunting a few lawless gangs? Or will there be a grand concentrated movement across the river and on towards the Gulf? These are questions that the Government will undoubtedly weigh maturely. I take this to be true: that a hundred little battles, and all of them victorious, west of the Mississippi, will avail us but little, if we cannot gain some signal victory nearer the heart of the enemy. We are now fighting their paralyzed extremities, and going a great distance with land transportation to reach them.

Vicksburg must fall, and the entire possession of the Mississippi must be maintained. The Arkansas river must be a new base of operations; then our army can push forward and in a short time complete the work in the Southwest.

The Cherokee Council has adjourned, after abrogating the secession ordinance and passing an emancipation act. They have sent delegates to Washington, to confer with the President upon important matters connected with the contemplated return of their families to the country.

In a few days we shall have some important items of news to give you.

As I am an Illinois man, and there are a great many of us out here, I, perhaps, may be permitted to drop a hint to the Copperheads at home. I find this whole country down here full of just such Union men as they are. These are the devils that bushwhack, and *stay at home to do it.* They are for the Union, but—they are for whipping the rebels, but—&c. The way we treat them here is: first give them the contents of the gun, and then the butt.

Please say to them, for me, that unless they mend their ways they will shortly hear it *thunder.*

CREEK.

[Published March 21, 1863.]

JOURNAL ENTRY

March 17, 1863

The Genl came today[;] I shall start for Chicago in the morning[.]

I have succeeded in getting all the papers from the Genl that I could ask[.]

I close this Journal untill I take the field again[.]

CHAPTER 7

CLOSING WAR SCENES, APRIL 1863–OCTOBER 1864

How many times must we conquer this country, and how many times fall back without any apparent cause?
—ALBERT C. ELLITHORPE, *Chicago Evening Journal*, May 20, 1863

Albert Ellithorpe's diary entries ceased as he transitioned to the next stage of his military service, an attempt to recruit the Fifth Indian Home Guards. As Ellithorpe predicted, the two new Indian Home Guards regiments never organized, but Ellithorpe continued on duty until he was discharged with the other officers on August 29, 1863. Whether his commission was part of a plot or not, the result was the same—Ellithorpe was out of the military. Seven *Chicago Evening Journal* articles and one brief article about Price's expedition published in the *Leavenworth Daily Conservative* documented the last part of his service. His final article, written under a pseudonym, was published on October 13, 1864, ending a run of twenty-three articles in the *Chicago Evening Journal*.[1]

Ellithorpe apparently did not campaign actively from April to August 1863, with the exception of the march that culminated with the reoccupation of Fort Blunt (the former Fort Gibson) on April 13, 1863, and the return of the Indian refugees. Ellithorpe traveled through northwestern Arkansas and then on to St. Louis in May, but the purpose of the journey is now unknown. He returned to Fort Blunt in early June, just in time to observe the latest unfolding of a feud between Maj. Gen. John M. Schofield and Maj. Gen. James G. Blunt that helped lead to another campaign. Blunt's and Maj. Gen. Francis J. Herron's victory at Prairie Grove caused a jealous rage in Schofield. Just weeks after the battle, Schofield tartly informed his department commander, Maj. Gen. Samuel R. Curtis: "The operations of the army, since I left it, have been a series of blunders, from which it narrowly escaped disaster where it should have met with complete success. At Prairie Grove Blunt and Herron were badly beaten in detail, and owed their escape to a false report of my arrival with re-enforcements." It did not help his attitude when officials rewarded Blunt and Herron with promotions to major general. Blunt, volatile anyway, was angered by Schofield's attempts to undermine him and tried to damage his foe. Fortunately, he never read Schofield's damning postwar comment that Blunt was "probably the lowest specimen of humanity that ever disgraced a general's stars in this or perhaps any other country." Schofield, in alliance with Kansas governor Thomas Carney and Brig. Gen. Thomas Ewing, divided Blunt's District of Kansas, with Blunt receiving the new District of the Frontier and Ewing appointed to the new District of the Border. Blunt maintained control of a district, thanks to his alliance with Senator James H. Lane, but both men feared that Blunt would be forced from the service.[2]

Claiming that Confederate forces were organizing for an attack on Fort Blunt, Major General Blunt returned to the field in early July. This politically driven campaign was nothing less than an attempt by Blunt to save his military career, and it resulted in a significant Union victory at Honey Springs on July 17. Ellithorpe's former regiment, the First Indian Home Guards, fought in the battle and, along with other units, performed superbly a difficult maneuver from column into battle line. Ellithorpe's newspaper account of the battle provided few details and suggested that he had remained at Fort Blunt during the battle.[3]

Following his discharge in August, Ellithorpe probably returned to Chicago to visit his family. The draw of the frontier was strong, however, and he returned to the Indian Territory and accompanied an expedition led by Col. William A. Phillips in February 1864. Starting from Fort Blunt, the force drove deep into the Choctaw Nation, burning structures and even killing prisoners. Along the route the men distributed an amnesty proclamation from President Abraham Lincoln translated into the major Indian languages of the region. The combination of strong-arm tactics with the offer of amnesty did not sway the tribes from their loyalty to the Confederacy, but the destruction and killings horrified many in the area.[4]

In August or September 1864 Ellithorpe became the editor of the *Leavenworth Daily Conservative* and used his editor's pen to write in support of the reelection of Senator Lane and the election to the governor's post of the relatively unknown Samuel Crawford, the colonel of the Second Kansas Colored Infantry. It was in his capacity as a journalist that Ellithorpe became an eyewitness to Price's Missouri expedition. Gen. Edmund Kirby Smith, the commander of the Trans-Mississippi Department, and Maj. Gen. Sterling Price planned a cavalry expedition into Missouri. The campaign goals were to capture St. Louis, recruit more men, and hopefully increase dissatisfaction with President Lincoln just months before his reelection bid. Commanding three divisions of cavalrymen, Price led his twelve thousand troops into his home state on September 19. Foiled from capturing St. Louis, Price's men moved slowly along the Missouri River, where they gained recruits but angered residents, whose property had been plundered by guerrillas and undisciplined Confederate recruits. Meanwhile, Federal troops attempted to trap Price's force by using converging columns. The commander of one of them was Blunt, the general whom Ellithorpe most admired. Although Ellithorpe claimed after the war that he had served on Blunt's staff during the campaign, there is no evidence of any official status for him. Ellithorpe did serve in some capacity, however, and a postwar biographical piece stated that he "was in the saddle and on the march almost constantly for over two weeks . . . not taking any of his clothes off in all that time."[5]

On October 23 Price's army retreated after actions at Brush Creek and Byram's Ford near Kansas City. The next day Ellithorpe joined Lt. George T. Robinson, a chief engineer from the Eleventh Kansas Cavalry, Robinson's assistants, and Richard J. Hinton, a prominent journalist and one of Blunt's aides. The group traveled from Kansas City to Little Santa Fe, nineteen miles south. There they happened to link up with Maj. Gen. William S. Rosecrans, the commander of the District of the Missouri. Robinson's district commander, Maj. Gen. Samuel R. Curtis, had hoped to make contact with Rosecrans, so the meeting of the two groups was fortunate. At the request of the assistant adjutant general of the District of Kansas, Lieutenant Robinson wrote a report of his two days with Rosecrans, whose staff he had once served on, reporting verbatim on several conversations with the opinionated general. According to Hinton and Robinson, the unsuspecting Rosecrans expressed several negative opinions about Curtis, who had deployed militiamen and other troops near the border; Hinton wrote later that the comments were expressed "in the hearing of Colonel Ellithorpe." Rosecrans complained about "Old Curtis," and his strategy, and then returned to St. Louis.[6]

Federal troops hastened south, where they dealt a devastating blow to Price's men at Mine Creek (also known as Marais des Cygnes) on October 25. The campaign continued southward, and three days later a sharp action occurred in southwestern Missouri, at Newtonia, with Blunt's men emerging as the victors. The expedition's survivors retreated through Arkansas, the Indian Territory, and finally into Texas. About a month after Newtonia, Blunt and Maj. Gen. Francis J. Herron arrived in Leavenworth. An artillery salute greeted them, and Ellithorpe "made a short, appropriate speech of welcome in behalf of the citizens of Leavenworth and Kansas, referring to the Generals as mutual heroes of Prairie Grove." Later in the week Ellithorpe sent a note to the printers and other employees of his newspaper to join him at Mr. Slyman's restaurant. There the men were treated to wine and an oyster supper (styled as "Original" by the attendees), "and a season of enjoyment followed . . . Toasts were drank, stories told, and everything passed off pleasantly." The major fighting was over in the border region, and Ellithorpe observed no other campaigns. Political campaigns, however, remained a focus. Republican candidates won a number of races, with Samuel Crawford winning decisively on November 8 as the next governor of Kansas. On January 12, 1865, Jim Lane was reelected to the U.S. Senate by the Kansas State Legislature. With elections now at an end, Ellithorpe returned to Chicago in early 1865.[7]

Yet there was one last piece of military business. In 1865 the former officers of the two unsuccessfully organized Indian regiments claimed pay for the services they rendered while trying to recruit the units. Following an investigation, the officers were required to take an oath, state their duties, and provide documentation of their service.[8]

Chicago Evening Journal Article

FROM THE ARMY OF THE FRONTIER. The Situation and Prospects in That Region.
Correspondence of The Chicago Evening Journal:
CHEROKEE NATION, PARK HILL, I. T.,
April 24, 1863.

Great changes have taken place in this region of country since last fall. Up to the time that Gen. Blunt advanced with his small but brave army, to Boonsborough and Cane Hill, the rebels had held undisputed control over this whole section. The defeat of Cooper at Old Fort Wayne, of Marmaduke at Cane Hill, and then, again, the overwhelming defeat of the whole combined force of Hindman, Marmaduke, Cooper, McDonald & Co., at Prairie Grove, changed the complexion of rebel hopes and of their sanguine expectations. With these defeats, the cause of treason has sunk in the Southwestern country beyond the hope of recovery.[9]

The Missouri troops have not realized that speedy deliverance of their homes from the grasp of our Government that was promised them. The Arkansas conscripts joined the ranks of Hindman, some reluctantly and many willingly, as a last effort to repulse our army. The Texas troops joined him, confident that the combination of 30,000 soldiers could drive us back to the Free States, and thus leave the States of Missouri and Arkansas, and the Indian Territory, free from the presence of a Federal foe.

The whole mission of Hindman was a failure, and the plans of the Confederate Government were thwarted on every hand. With their defeats, disaffection arose.[10] The Texas troops became demoralized, and hundreds of them returned home in confusion, cursing the impotency of Hindman. The conscript troops of Arkansas became disgusted, and deserted by hundreds—many came to our lines and asked to be enrolled—others sought their families, and are gradually making their way North—the rebel Indians became terrified and were suffered, as a necessity, to disperse to their homes upon a furlough. Thus the grand army of Hindman melted away, covered with ignominious defeat.

When we look back and see how much has been accomplished by a few regiments of determined troops, although poorly equipped, led by a man of untiring energy and unyielding will, we have no fears for the future of the South-west, with such a general to lead. It must be borne in mind that the whole work of last summer's and fall's campaign was done by the Division under Gen. J. G. Blunt. The battle of Fort Waine [*sic*] and Cane Hill was fought by his troops entirely. At the battle of Prairie Grove, Schofield's Division, under the direction of Gen. Blunt, did noble service, led by the gallant Herron. But Gen. Blunt was the architect and moving spirit that planned and brought about the series of events that culminated in his great victory of "Prairie Grove"; in fact, Herron did not even know that a battle was imminent, but, like a true officer, bent his entire energies to execute his orders, holding himself in readiness to meet the enemy at any moment.

You must not imagine that this country is permanently conquered, without further effort, and even with the presence of a powerful army. The enemy are only dispersed, not conquered. The whole of this rebel region is a smouldering Vesuvius of treason and treachery, that will belch forth with fury whenever opportunity offers. Even now, while I write, we have reliable information, that the hundreds of little bands are preparing to assemble under the banners of Price. The whole length of the Arkansas river, upon the south side, is alive to his appeals to rally.[11] I imagine they do not intend to make any strong demonstration this side of the river, but to resist our advance south of it. They would be well contended [*sic*] to give up everything north of the river if they can only hold the great stock and grain country south of it; for between it and Texas they hope to draw abundant supplies to subsist a large army. General Price boastingly declares that he will leave his body upon the southern banks of the Arkansas river—(this is probably his "last ditch")—before we shall cross. South of this river is where all the slaves and stock from Missouri, Northern Arkansas and the Indian Territory are assembled; here is their store-house of human and brute chattels, and their last hope is involved in the defense of it. Here, too, is where we may add twenty thousand *chattels* to our army—enough to sweep everything like a whirlwind to the gulf.

Then how important it is, that our army of the Southwest should be put in motion, and let us close out the straggling rebel army, which, if left to recuperate, may give us vastly more trouble than we imagine.

The refugee Indians have mostly returned to their homes, and are busy putting in a crop. They are determined to never leave their country again, and woe be to the rebel army that shall attempt to invade their homes.

Small scouting gangs of robbers, dart through the borders occasionally, but dare not tarry long; sure death awaits them if they are discovered.

The milk-and-water process is (to use a vulgarism) "played out" with us, and a furlough of death speedily given to all bushwhackers. We have never known a single instance where this furlough has been broken.

The weather is beautiful and feed for stock abundant. The health of the troops is good.

CHEROKEE.

[Published May 4, 1863.]

Chicago Evening Journal Article

FROM THE ARMY OF THE FRONTIER.

Correspondence of The Chicago Evening Journal.

HEADQUARTERS 3D BRIGADE

ARMY OF THE FRONTIER

FORT GIBSON, May 1, 1863.

Not having anything new to write, I have not afflicted you with any communication of late, but presuming that your readers would like to know what this brigade is doing, I will proceed to give you a few items.

Since my last, we have been moving gradually, by slow marches, down into the Cherokee country, to this point, which will constitute our base of operation for this summer. Col. Philips, who is in command of the brigade, has established several posts, around in the Nation, and marked out districts for the settlers to occupy, so that they can be protected from marauders and bushwhackers, and also get their supplies from the different posts. Bushwhackers are not entirely cleaned out of this country, but they are getting very scarce. The Indians have accomplished wonders in that line. They have done as much as double their number of white troops could have done, in ridding the country of these barbarians, because they can beat them at their own game, when it it [*sic*] is commenced by them. The night we camped at Park Hill, a few days before we came to this place, Col. Philips sent a party to scout through this place. They got in about daylight, in this place, and surprised and captured a number of the gentry in butternut that were in town, from the other side of the river.

A few days ago, a spy was taken, dressed in *petticoats* and other things corresponding, of which cotton was a large ingredient, being used quite freely to fill up vacancies, which would lead to the belief that it was not very scarce where he came from. From what we have gathered, we conclude that the rebels are in a bad way. Below us, they are almost naked. They have used their old tents for clothes, which is sufficiently proved by the apparel of the refugees that are coming in daily from that region, and they are almost starving in some places.

The officers of the 4th and 5th regiments are here, or nearly all of them, and are at work in good earnest. Forming their new regiments will be a short job, if they continue as they have begun; they have them nicely started now.

Col. Philips is having this point fortified,[12] so that in a few days we will not be afraid of twenty-five thousand of the enemy, should that many make their appearance, which is not at all probable, as that is more than they can possibly concentrate at that point. It is one of the finest places in the country to fortify. It commands all of the surrounding country and has plenty of good water, and roads leading out in every direction, which make it a central point.

On the 24th of last month, a large scouting party went out, commanded by Col. Philips in person. Its destination was Weber's Falls, some twenty-five miles below, on the other side of the Arkansas river. We came on the rebels about daylight, put them all to rout, captured all they had there, including camps, provisions, horses, saddles, &c. It will prove a severe blow to them. We also killed and captured a large number.[13]

There was no loss on our side during the engagement, but it proved to be dearly bought in the end. Through rebel treachery, we have to mourn the loss of Doctor Gillpatrick, one of the finest men this western country afforded. In him, the Government has lost a valuable and trusty leader. Bold, courageous, and afraid of nothing, he traveled between Fort Scott and this army all winter, without escort, bearing dispatches. The circumstances of his murder are these: After the place was taken, some ladies came in and said they would like to be protected, as they were afraid of the Indians, and also requested to have a doctor go with them, as there was a wounded man at their home, which was only some half a mile away. The Doctor immediately volunteered to go, and we, not supposing there was any danger, did not send any escort with him, as he did not ask it. When within a few rods of the house, a party of rebels came out of a thicket, upon which he commenced to retreat, but they assured him he would not be hurt, as he was a doctor, and should be protected. Upon this assurance he went forward, but when within a few feet of them, the whole party fired, and he fell, completely riddled with bullets.[14] What punishment is great enough for such treacherous devils? We brought his body to this place, and, after due ceremonies, we consigned his body to the dust with military honors.

Now is the time for Gen. Blunt to push ahead, and with six or seven thousand men he could go right through to Texas and clean out everything, without trouble. There is no force below us to do any damage whatever, and, in fact, I think Colonel Philips could go with this brigade, if he could only leave this country; and I am in hopes of seeing a movement of some kind soon. Col. Philips is striking whenever and wherever he gets a chance. There is a large scouting party out now, but what it will accomplish cannot be told.

SEMINOLE.

[Published May 15, 1863.]

Chicago Evening Journal Article

FROM THE ARMY OF THE FRONTIER.

Correspondence of The Chicago Evening Journal.

St. Louis, Mo., May 16, 1863.

Having just returned from the country where Major General Blunt so brilliantly closed the last fall's campaign of the Army of the Frontier, I can but lament over the present condition of the many good and loyal families in that section, and I tremble for the horrors that await them. The rebels of that country well know every family that received our Union army with hope and cheer, and with joy that the hour of deliverance from the terrible oppressions of rebel rule had at last come. These people, at our approach, threw off the mantle of deception, which they were forced to wear for self-preservation, and avowed themselves what they really were, under the solemn assurance of our authorities that we had come to permanently occupy the country and protect the people from their traitorous persecutors.[15] True to themselves and their country, they cheerfully did all in their power to aid our arms and put down the unholy rebellion. Thus they have openly committed themselves to our cause, and that, too, with their homes surrounded by traitors, who seek their lives at every step. It seems so strange that after our army had conquered and put to flight the combined forces of the enemy, driving them all to the other side of the Arkansas river, in a state of confusion and powerless to do evil, we should quietly fall back, and, like some powerful beast that has gorged himself upon the flesh of his prey, sluggishly seek his lair until the gnawing of hunger again drive him forth. Is it possible that for any personal, local cause our brave soldiers of the Frontier Army are kept from holding and occupying the country they have already twice conquered, and affording protection to loyal citizens who have unmasked themselves in the face of their bitter foes for our cause?

How many times must we conquer this country, and how many times fall back without any apparent cause? All who have any knowledge of the operations of the Army of the Southwest well know that allthat [*sic*] has been accomplished was done under the personal direction and management of Major General Blunt. Whilst everything tended to discourage and dishearten him, he pressed forward; and, even after the expedition was pronounced a failure by the ranking officer in the field, and General Curtis was importuned to recall the troops and abandon the whole project, General Blunt, saw the critical condition of affairs. Feeling that the campaign would end ingloriously, unless prompt steps were taken, he resolved to fight Gen. Hindman's army of 25,000 men, even though he did it with his own division of less than 7,000.

The result of the battle of Prairie Grove is well known, and from this date the rebel host fled in confusion. General Schofield, being the ranking officer, immediately returned from St. Louis, and assumed the command. General Blunt, of course, retired to his own district, and from this hour the conquered country has been gradually surrendered to the guerrillas and marauding gangs who prey upon the Union people in the most fiendish and brutal manner.

Our army certainly was not withdrawn on account of provisions, for the country is filled with wheat, beef, pork and corn, with as many good flouring mills as any country can boast of.[16] Nor was it because a powerful enemy menaced us, for they were whipped; nor was it on account of any disaffection among the troops, for they were healthy and in the best of spirits, and eager to make their camp fires even south of the Arkansas river. Then what was the reason that Gen. Schofield gradually evacuated the country, and again handed it over to the tender mercies of the rebels? I have asked the question, but I dare not, if I could, answer it.

First, I will tell you how things are running, around the section of country we occupied in the fall and most of the winter, and then something else. The rebel portion of the inhabitants are jubilant, and avail themselves of every opportunity to wreak their vengeance upon the Union people, who will have to leave or lose their lives. Constant raids from Marmaduke's and Price's accumulating forces keep the country in a state of confusion. Outrages of all descriptions are of frequent occurrence, and treason and terror are again predominant, where but a short time ago they were crushed out.

The Indian country is yet held by our troops, but God only knows how long it will remain so. I almost fear that these unfortunate loyal people will again be refugees.

Since my arrival in St. Louis, the news comes that Brigadier Gen. Schofield takes command, in place of Major General Curtis.[17] Although it is generally believed here, I look upon it with much doubt, and shall only believe it when I am forced to. If this be so, I ask in the name of energy, zeal, patriotism, and every other good qualification that is essential to put down the rebellion, what incentive there is for zealous field-worn officers to toil amid the dangers of the battle-field for the preservation of our country under the dictation of thrice-proven incompetent Generals? I well know the sentiments of the Army of the Frontier and the Army of the Southwest. I also know the power of an order from the War Department, and while any order will be promptly obeyed by our loyal officers and soldiers, yet a deep murmur will rise from almost every lip, to see their old battle-tried and victorious Generals thrust aside to make room for those they have no confidence it. It may be well; the reasons may be good; some deep scheme of strategy, some master stroke of policy, may underlie this strange movement. Let us hope it is so; but I fear that it is the work of incendiary spirits, who would tear down the temple, and chain the Goddess of Liberty at the feet of Slavery.

CREEK.

[Published May 20, 1863.]

Chicago Evening Journal Article

FROM THE ARMY OF THE FRONTIER.

Reinforcements Needed—The Rebels Re-Occupying the Indian Country.

Correspondence of The Chicago Evening Journal.

FORT BLUNT, CHEROKEE NATION,

June 19, 1863.

For the last twenty days we have had quite exciting times. Scarcely a day passes but we have a chase and a skirmish with the rebels.

I presume I shall not be giving information contraband, when I say that our force here is small—much too small to successfully hold this vast area of country and afford anything like protection to the inhabitants.[18] The three Indian regiments are here, and, as usual render good service. Fort Blunt is now in a condition to resist almost any force the enemy can bring to bear upon us. You are aware that this was formerly called Fort Gibson.

The enemy are concentrating above and below us, on the Arkansas river, and intend to cut off our line of communication with Fort Scott, which they may possibly do, unless we get reinforcements soon.

Does it not seem very strange that after Gen. Blunt has effectually conquered this country once, and driven the rebel forces out, it should be left open to the pillage of the enemy. After a series of brilliant victories, and the restoration of the Creek and Cherokee families to their homes, with the assurance that the Government would afford ample protection, we now find them once more open to the brutal outrages of a lawless, bandit foe. Col. Philips, who is in command here, is doing all in his power to protect the loyal citizens, but his force is wholly inadequate for the emergency. He can simply defend himself within our lines of fortifications, waiting anxiously for the arrival of reinforcements. A rumor came to camp to-day that Gen. Blunt was on his way to give us aid.

We were much amused at the coolness of a telegram emanating from St. Louis, a few days ago, intimately connected with Gen. Schofield's order assigning Gen. Blunt to the command of this district, which concluded by saying that "Gen. Blunt would take the field and endeavor to win for himself a department." Now, was not that rather icy? The hero of every important battle fought by the Army of the Frontier, sent out simply to give him a chance to make his mark. How generous, and how thankful the little General must be for such thoughtful and considerate kindness. History will make the immortal the perpetrators of such unenvious deeds.

We are all of one mind here; if they will not give us more regiments, give us Blunt, and we will whip the enemy. I fear that the loyal Indians will again be refugees, and the ten thousand helpless women, children and old men will have to seek an asylum for another winter in Southern Kansas. This, perhaps, is the programme, for the contractors who fatted from the Department of the Interior are now nearly out of a job. I presume that you are aware that all Indian refugees are provided for directly by that Department. This is a side show, outside of the War Department.

The Arkansas river is high—the weather hot—bushwhackers plenty—contrabands jovial and praying for the real millennium of emancipation—while our Indian soldiers and chiefs hope that the Great Father at Washington may see clearly through the dense fog that surrounds him.

CREEK.

[Published July 8, 1863.]

Chicago Evening Journal Article

FROM THE ARMY OF THE FRONTIER.
Its Operations in the Indian Territory.
Correspondence of The Chicago Evening Journal.
FORT GIBSON, IND. TERR, July 20.

I have delayed writing you for some days past hoping to have cheerful news to give you. As to [illegible word] I can only offer you congratulations in view of the bright prospects before us. Since Gen. Blunt left here for the lower country, we have all felt satisfied that stirring times would commence. True to his tendencies, he has been "pitching in" again and although he had but a few hundred men the whole entire rebel gang of marauding thieves has scattered as though some fearful calamity were about to overwhelm it. At Cabin Creek they were handsomely whipped,[19] and again the hordes that held Col. Phillips and his forces inside the rifle pits of Fort Gibson, with almost certain prospects of capturing the entire force, fled as soon as the little General hove in sight with his little guard.[20] His appearance among the troops gave new life to everything. The timid shivering policy of Col. Phillips gave way to a general rally, and a forward move across the Arkansas river. A few hours, and the rebels were attacked in their fortified position at Elk Creek, and completely routed and scattered in every direction.

The rebel forces consisted of a portion of the old Hindman army, mostly Texans and Arkansas troops, with two regiments of Choctaw and Cherokee Indians.[21] General dispatches will give you a full account of the affair. All your readers wish to know is, that we have whipped them.

To say that the Department of the Missouri is badly managed, gives one but a faint idea of the real condition of things. Every screw appears to be loose from St. Louis to Helena, and from there up the Arkansas river to Fort Smith. We have small squads of soldiers scattered over the whole country, under command of no one knows who, but apparently "going it on their own hook." There is no concert of action, and a general feeling of disgust at the neglected condition of the department.

The soldiers, however, are in good spirits, and have the utmost confidence in the power of our Government to whip the rebels, even though they do it by piecemeal. Uncle Sam, thus far, has fought the enemy with both hands in his pockets. The strong cords of political parties have almost bound him to the post of policy; occasionally, he would kick out of the traces and deal the monster a telling blow on the head, in the shape of an order, that would send hope bounding through the heart of every patriot. You may think that we, away down here, never think of the why and wherefores of this or that line of policy, or that we ever pretend to scrutinize the past, present, or inevitable future acts of the Government; but we do—in our backwoods and homely way. You will pardon me here for calling things by common names when you remember that we are very close to the stamping ground of that rough old patriot, Da[v]y Crockett;[22] that we are a rough set of fellows, in a rough country, living on rough fare, fighting as rough a set of traitorous devils as ever drew breath upon a Western frontier. We eat our "hard tack" and hunt bushwhackers with a cheerfulness that would surprise you.

Sometimes, things go swimmingly along. The merry laugh rings through the camp and a tear of joy glides down the sun-burnt cheek at the happy thought of seeing the dear ones at home, and of enjoying the pleasures of the family circle, where the terrors of war are only recounted, but no more endured. But, alas! when we have the monster by the throat, holding him down to his last death-struggle, our strong arms are paralyzed, through the agency of some complicated chicanery, and the devil lives again to fight another day. Well, this is but a recurrence of the history of all past wars, especially where some gigantic evil was to be rooted out. We must defeat, and be defeated, toil in adversity, and rejoice in prosperity, rise and fall like the waves of the ocean, shifting sail to the caprice of every vicious blast, until the strong arm of right and power shall overwhelm the hosts of treason, the enemies of our common humanity. How natural it is for common soldiers to discuss, by the dim and smouldering embers of the camp fire, *great questions.* They even go so far, sometimes, as to criticise the acts of superior officers, and I have heard them express opinions, even about the policy pursued by the President and his Cabinet. They all have the utmost confidence in their wisdom and patriotism, but their impatience leads them to think that the blows of progression fall too slowly. Even the slaveholding citizens here express the firm conviction that peace will never be restored until slavery finds its grave.

The force here is not sufficient to go far south of the Arkansas, as the scattering forces of the enemy are again concentrating, and there is little use of starting upon an expedition that we will fail in. Our stock is worn out, the weather is hot, and supplies scarce.

During the battle of Elk Creek the General was very sick, but the first gun found him in his saddle, and wherever the fight was thickest he was sure to be.[23] Not much more can be done until we get an army. We can hold the country up to the river any length of time.

SEMINOLE.

[Published August 7, 1863.]

Chicago Evening Journal Article

FROM THE WESTERN FRONTIER.

General Blunt's Command—What Colonel Phillips' Expedition towards Texas Accomplished—Anticipated Movement Southward.

Correspondence of The Chicago Evening Journal.

FORT BLUNT, CHEROKEE NATION, March 10.

The expedition from this place into the Choctaw country has perhaps accomplished as much as was contemplated by the officer in command, Colonel Phillips: as far as it went, beneficial results will accrue. The command was not in condition to accomplish any great feats, from the fact of its being in a woeful condition for service. It consisted of portions of the three Indian regiments, the 1st colored, and small detachments of two white regiments and a portion of two batteries.[24] The country was penetrated in the direction of the Northern Texas border, about one hundred and fifty miles. Small squads of completely demoralized Indians (rebel) were frequently found, who were ready to join our lines with the hope of obtaining either clothes, bread or whisky. The latter article we did not have, and it was quite apparent that they were sadly disappointed, at not finding it.

The greater portion of the Indians belonging to the rebels have become disgusted with the effects of the war; it has cut off their whisky, beads, calico, gold and silver, and the many other trinkets of ornament and luxury that they were in the habit of annually receiving, prior to the war, at the hands of the Government. One of the old Choctaw chiefs gave his views of the "Southern Confederacy" in a very laconic and expressive manner when he said, "Jeff. Davis humbug—big heap, heap." The missionary stations throughout the Nation are mostly abandoned. Plunder and theft have taken the place of their agricultural pursuits, and they are fast becoming a prey to one another. Hardships and abuse have been the reward for their fidelity to the South. A little kindness, and they will return to their allegiance, and take vengeance upon their deceivers.

About one hundred rebels were killed, and several hundred willing prisoners taken during the expedition.[25] Their commissary stores and war appliances amount to nothing.

Until we are reinforced, and until General Blunt takes command, no extensive movement will be made. We expect General Blunt daily.

We ascertained that there were thousands of negroes one hundred miles beyond the point to which our expedition went, all of whom will help to swell our lines when we reach them.

Texas and Arkansas contain within their own bounds ample elements to conquer themselves. All we have to do is to reach, arm and control them.

The small pox has made fearful ravages amongst the Indians and negroes.[26] Many of our white men have fallen victims to it. The noted Billy Bowlegs, the great Seminole chief and warrior, died with it.[27]

There will be no fighting until we get beyond Red river, then we expect to meet the combined forces of the enemy. The grass is now sufficient to sustain the stock, but the dust, hot weather, and scarcity of water will cause great suffering to our troops as they proceed South. You will be posted as we progress, and know our whereabouts and conditions—but the watchword is "The Gulf."

CREEK.

[Published March 18, 1864.]

Chicago Evening Journal Notice

MAJOR GENERAL BLUNT TO ARRIVE HERE ON TUESDAY.
Special Dispatch for The Chicago Evening Journal.
LEAVENWORTH, May 24.

Major General Blunt will arrive at the Tremont House, in your city, on Thursday.

A. C. E.

[Published May 24, 1864.]

Chicago Evening Journal Article

LETTER FROM KANSAS.
The Recent Indian Hostilities—Rebel Agents at the Bottom of the Trouble—General Blunt—Price's Army of Invasion Expected in Kansas—Political Affairs, Etc., Etc.
Correspondence of The Chicago Evening Journal.

LEAVENWORTH, Kansas.
October 8, 1864.

A recent trip to the Western border and the scene of the Indian troubles, has given me an opportunity to ascertain the true state of affairs in that quarter. It may now all be summed up about as follows:

There are a large number of the various tribes unquestionably hostile to our Government and people, made so by the presence and interposition of regular agents of the rebels. The fact is now beyond dispute that these agents have been at work for several months among these friendly tribes, making presents, furnishing arms, and using arguments to excite them to hostility. One of the arguments used has been that the Government was trying to free all the negroes and give them the lands now occupied by them (the Indians) and drive the Indians on to lands farther west.[28] This has been one of the arguments used, and it has been a powerful one, taken in connection with the fact that our Government has been constantly treating for the Indian lands. But, I am happy to say, this false doctrine has been exposed, and many of them again avow their allegiance and promise peace.

General Blunt has done more to put things in shape during the short time he has been upon the border, than even a large army could have done. With only a small handful of men he has penetrated their country, and set them to thinking in the right direction.

The General is ordered to the command of the Southern border—he takes the place of General Sikes.[29] This is done to protect the exposed portion of Kansas which is now threatened by Price's invasion of Missouri. It is generally thought here that when Price retreats from Missouri, he will aim to take a trip through Kansas, and make his way south by Fort Scott, and thence down Grand river to Fort Blunt, and across the Arkansas at "Frozen Rock Ford," about eighty miles above Fort Smith. Should this be his plan, you may expect lively times in these quarters. Let him come; he will run against something "Blunt" before he gets out.

The various routes to Santa Fe, California, Denver, etc., are now open, and will probably not be molested much more.

You may put Kansas down for Lincoln and Johnson, unanimously.[30] The Little Mackerels are very scarce here. This State will not give McClellan a corporal's guard—in fact the only men in Kansas who are for him are those who tried to make this a slave State, under "Old Bucks" reign. They are what was then termed the "Border Ruffians"—a set of Northern rascals with Southern faces. Most of them could be convicted of horse-stealing, or some other crime equally bad.

On Saturday evening we had in Leavenworth the largest meeting ever held in the place, to rejoice over the recent victories, and fully ratify the Baltimore nominations and the regular Republican State nominations. The Rev. Dr. King, formerly of the First Universalist Church in Chicago, made one of the most scathing speeches upon copperhead Democracy I ever listened to. The Reverend Doctor, in company with other able gentlemen, is now canvassing the State. Politics run high (locally), but J. H. Lane, the present United States Senator, will be returned by an overwhelming vote. A few of the weak-kneed, milk and water Republicans have united with the copperhead Democracy to elect a man of doubtful character upon the great radical question—slavery. Bolters, copperheads, and traitors will find a common grave with their chieftain, "Little Mac."

CHEROKEE.

[Published October 13, 1864.]

Leavenworth Daily Conservative Article

BY TELEGRAPH.

MORNING REPORT.

FROM THE FRONT!

PRICE IN FULL RETREAT!

HE IS HOTLY PURSUED! Curtis, Blunt & McNeil after Him!

Gen. Smith at Hand with 10,000 Fresh Men!

COL. CRAWFORD LEADS THE CHARGE THAT CAPTURED PRICE'S BATTERY!

HE IS AT HIS OLD TRICKS!

PRICE DESTROYS 200 WAGONS!

A Continual Victory!

GEN. LANE AT THE FRONT!

[Special to the *Leavenworth Daily Conservative.*]

We have received the following dispatch from Col. Ellithorpe, the latest intelligence we have from our army.[31] Everything works gloriously:

FORT SCOTT, Oct. 27, 1864.

TO CONSERVATIVE: The battle of the 25th, commencing at the Trading Post,[32] resulted in a complete success. Price lost eleven pieces of cannon, 1,000 muskets, 600 prisoners, and many officers. Maj. Gen. Marmaduke and Brig. Gen. Cabell are prisoners here.[33] We cannot estimate the enemy's killed and wounded. Ours small.

Cols. Crawford and Blair,[34] Major Hunt, and others, staff officers of Curtis, led the charge that captured the enemy's battery.

Curtis, Blunt and McNeil are close upon Price's rear, between Lamar and Carthage. They will probably fight to-night or in the morning.

Price destroyed about two hundred of his wagons yesterday.[35]

Gen. Pleasanton is here, and for reasons unknown, does not follow the enemy.[36]

Gens. Curtis, Blunt and McNeil will have to terminate the fight.

Rosecrans is east of here but a few miles. 10,000 infantry, the 16th army corps, commanded by Gen. Smith, are close to Rosecrans.

Gen. Lane is at the front with Gen. Curtis.[37]

A. C. ELLITHORPE.

CHAPTER 8

LIFE AFTER THE WAR

Perhaps no prominent man in Chicago has had so varied a career as has Albert Chapman Ellithorpe.
—*Chicago Sunday Chronicle,* February 28, 1897

When Ellithorpe returned to Chicago in 1865, he moved into the family's new abode on 11 North Morgan Street. Ellithorpe reentered city politics by campaigning for an alderman's seat in 1866 but was denied it by the voters. Always searching for business ventures, he became a "real estate agent," which consisted in part of collecting rents, rather than reentering the carriage business. It was in his rent collecting capacity that Ellithorpe became involved in a scandal that absorbed the city for many months. Joseph Medill, one of the owners of the *Chicago Tribune,* hearing of a "woman scrape" that allegedly involved Ellithorpe, an old acquaintance and neighbor, ordered his employees not to publish an article about it. Through a mistake, however, the October 3, 1867, issue contained an article titled "Scandal and Turmoil" that described "a scandalous affair" that "was yesterday partially ventilated in the Police Court." The article explained that Ellithorpe had become acquainted with Mrs. Frances Wilkinson, a widow, while collecting rents. She leased a part of 277 Randolph Street, one of the buildings that he was responsible for. "His acquaintance ripened into intimacy," the article read, and a suspicious Mrs. Maria Ellithorpe followed her husband one evening to Wilkinson's rooms, where "she beheld her husband in the arms of another woman. Mrs. Ellithorpe rushed into the room, and in a frenzy of rage seized the woman, to whom she administered a severe beating." A policeman arrived on the scene and took all three into custody for "disorderly conduct." Mrs. Wilkinson's ensuing lawsuit for libel against the *Tribune* led to a packed courtroom for the seven days of the trial, which occurred during the 1868 Christmas holiday season. The issues raised by the suit attracted "many prominent lawyers," and other attendees were presumably attracted by the high visibility of the defendant and the delicious scandal of it all.[1]

The trial started on December 22, 1868, with Wirt Dexter and Sidney Smith representing the defendants. Dexter, one of Chicago's leading attorneys, would go on to chair the board of the Chicago Relief and Aid Society, which bore responsibility for relief efforts after the Great Fire in 1871. Smith became one of the first members of the Chicago Bar Association and subsequently became a judge on the superior court. John Lyle King represented the plaintiff with the assistance of Mr. R. W. Evans. The *Tribune* reporter on the trial's first day penned scathing descriptions of Ellithorpe and Wilkinson: "[Ellithorpe's] mouth, partially hidden by the strong, wiry hair, has lines that are eloquent of tales that need not be told. Of noses, he got a large one when they were going. It has a hump in the middle like a camel's back. On either side are the eyes of a fishy gray color, deep set and protected by shaggy eyebrows. The cheek bones stand out at an obtuse angle to the perpendicular; the forehead is round, and the thick, brown hair, brushed back, makes the head somewhat like a mop. Mr. Ellithorpe has the look of one who is overflowing with gallantry and devotion to the weaker sex."

Wilkinson, wrote the reporter, "wore a sneer upon her face. It did not, however, hide her inward emotions and the nervous twitchings of her mouth, and the tattoo played by her hands upon the table bespoke uneasiness and anxiety." While testifying, Ellithorpe used his "silver-mounted cane . . . to great advantage during the examination. With it he chastised both his legs, giving them about an equal amount of punishment. He was nervous, ill at ease, and tried to expend his anxiety upon his legs . . . He tried to show a calm demeanor and unruffled front, but could not do it. He chewed tobacco, and expectorated vigorously. When closely pressed he bandied words with the counsel, but always came out second best. Toward the close he lost his temper, and did not recover it until he was sent off the stand." Ellithorpe testified that while out on the evening of October 2, 1867, Wilkinson saw him on the street and asked him to go by and see to "a clothes-line difficulty." He went to 277 West Randolph, very close to his own home at 11 North Morgan, and while he and Mrs. Wilkinson visited, Mrs. Ellithorpe went in and attacked him. She then went to the window and yelled "Fire" and "Murder" to attract the attention of a policeman.[2]

Maria Ellithorpe's testimony varied from that of her husband. While she was sewing on the evening of October 2, 1867, her husband "brushed his hair and his whiskers, and stood up before the glass." After he left the house, she visited a nearby bakery and in the early evening hours saw her husband "sitting with Mrs.

Wilkinson in her house." Gaining access to Wilkinson's house, Maria put her arms around her husband and cried, "I think I have caught you now," and asked him to return home. Albert responded, she testified, by pushing her to the floor and holding her by the throat. She got up, grabbed his cane, and then "tried to pull him to the door . . . [but he] wretched it out of my hands." Further damning testimony followed, with Maria stating that Albert had often been away at night and that "his conduct with other women" had been a problem previously in their marriage. Witnesses stated that Wilkinson was known as "Ellithorpe's Woman" and, as one headline suggestively read, "The Lady Often Seen with Gentlemen at Late Hours of the Night."[3]

Under cross-examination Albert explained that beginning about June 1, 1867, he worked at the Illinois and Michigan Canal, and that from one to three nights a week he was not at home but twenty-five miles away. He assured the court that he "lodged always at home when I was in town, without exception." Still, his wife's testimony that he carried in his trouser pocket a photograph of an "immodestly attired" lady and about the alleged discovery of medicine used to treat venereal disease in Mrs. Wilkinson's bedroom was riveting. No wonder "a large audience of attentive spectators" continued to gather even though the trial took place during the Christmas season. The end came on December 31, 1868, when the twelve jurors met for an hour, found the *Tribune* guilty of libel, and awarded seventy-five hundred dollars in damages to Wilkinson. Albert wrote in a scathing pamphlet: "The calumny and ignominy the '*Tribune*' has heaped upon my name and character outside of this city, I cannot expect to remove, but must continue to suffer from its effects until the memory of those who read it shall fade out with age and infirmity. I have been a resident of the city of Chicago for nearly thirty-one years, and I shall be content to refer to those who have known me during these past years most intimately, and in a business capacity, for my character as a citizen."

After the trial Albert and his wife were estranged from each other. In 1873 she resided with her oldest son, who had accompanied her to Wilkinson's rooms, and Albert lived with their youngest son, Frederick. Although there is no surviving record of it, the couple divorced, but in a remarkable feat of reconciliation, they remarried on August 12, 1875, with the marriage enduring until Maria's death in 1891. Other than the temporary destruction of his marriage, Albert appears to have survived the scandal with no other major effects and soon embarked on the most creative period of his life.[4]

Besides engaging in real estate pursuits, Ellithorpe worked as a contractor and a loan broker from the late 1860s to the mid-1870s. Although unsuccessful at winning political office, Ellithorpe actively participated in Republican Party events. Listed as one of the city's "Prominent Republicans" in a November 1875 issue of the *Tribune*, the outcome of the 1876 political races absorbed Ellithorpe and many other Americans. The Republican Party nominated Union veteran and former Ohio governor Rutherford B. Hayes, and the Democratic Party settled on Samuel Tilden, the governor of New York. Ellithorpe asserted that the Republicans would be unsuccessful on Election Day unless "something were done to conciliate the foreign elements, which had been ostracized by the too Puritanical measures of the party." A third party, the Greenback, called for the issuance of more paper money. Ellithorpe joined the Greenback Party for a time but resigned in September 1876. In a letter to the *Tribune* he explained that the Greenback Party seemed to be helping the Democratic candidates, "an unholy alliance" he could not abide: "I am fully convinced that our party is being used in the interest of the Democratic party . . . Was the Democratic party organized and made up from the average intelligent and loyal portion of the people at large, I might think differently, but when I reflect that its composition embraces eight-tenths of the worst and most vicious elements of society, united with almost every former Southern Rebel, and again taking into its folds every Northern Copperhead, augmented again by seven-eighths of the non-reading and ignorant classes, I become alarmed at the situation . . . It is very unfortunate for the really good men belonging to the Democratic party that all of these vicious elements hang, like an incubus, to its skirts, driving from it all hopes of success."

Ellithorpe went on the campaign trail in support of Hayes, and in Indiana, while "making one of his characteristic speeches . . . he asserted that all the loafers, thieves, pimps, and bunko-steerers were voting with the Democratic party." A person in the audience shouted heatedly, "It is a lie." "'Excuse me,' retorted the Colonel, 'You're the first loafer I've seen who is going to vote for Hayes and Wheeler.'" Ellithorpe then concluded his speech with no further interruptions. Ellithorpe finished out the decade of the 1870s by participation in the Boys in Blue veterans organization and was honored with many others as one of Chicago's Old Settlers at a posh reception at the Calumet Club. In the midst of political business and other activities, Ellithorpe worked on several creative projects, some of them spurred by a disaster in Chicago.[5]

By early October 1871 Chicago, a city mostly constructed in wood and full of flammable items, had experienced a drought for several months. The city was a huge tinderbox, and when a fire started on October 8, it spread quickly, destroying 17,450 buildings in its path and killing at least 120 people. Suddenly Chicago had "almost 100,000 persons . . . left homeless" and $190 million in property damage. The Ellithorpe family resided several blocks west of the Chicago River, in an area not directly impacted by the fire. The remainder of the 1870s was devoted to reconstruction, but "no city in the world grew faster in the 1880s or was more chaotically alive than Chicago, a place people went to see the shape of the future." Prominent architects and builders such as Daniel Hudson Burnham, John Wellborn Root, and Louis H. Sullivan strived to reimagine and then construct Chicago's new "skyline" with buildings that were safely fireproof and whose roofs seemed to touch the big sky.[6]

In 1858 Ellithorpe and Ives Scoville received a patent for a machine to crack stone. After more than a ten year hiatus, Ellithorpe received two patents four months before the Great Fire: an "Improvement in Dredging Scoops" and an "Improvement in Mortar Mixing Machines." The following year he received patent 131088 for an "Improvement in Oil-Burning Steam-Generators" and, perhaps related to the aftermath of the Great Chicago Fire, a patent for an improved fire extinguisher and "escape tower." His most interesting inventions, however, concerned elevators, first known as vertical railways. These were initially used extensively in European cities in the late 1860s and early 1870s, but Ellithorpe found himself in the perfect city for modernization of the elevator.[7]

Elevators were a necessity for the skyscrapers, and Ellithorpe, along with other inventors, developed ideas to improve their safety. From 1879 to 1896 he was granted eight patents for elevator improvements, with most dealing with safety enhancements. Mixed in was another patent for a fire escape, perhaps showing that Ellithorpe was unconvinced by the fireproof claim attached to much new construction. In the early 1890s two patents related to elevators, one an improvement in piston packing and the other an improved lubricator, were also obtained. In July 1883 the Ellithorpe Air-Brake Company started business "with a capital stock of $100,000," with Ellithorpe listed as superintendent, Henry Beidler, a former lumber dealer, as president, and Ellithorpe's son, Albert Benjamin, as secretary. The company manufactured elevators for both passenger and freight service and built safety devises. The most notable safety feature marketed by the company was the air cushion (also known as the air brake).[8]

Albert Betteley of Boston received a patent for an air reservoir in 1859. Betteley had examined the wreckage of an elevator, carrying "seven boxes of sugar" that had plunged down an elevator shaft into a cellar. Expecting to find a great deal of damage, instead he was surprised to find "the boxes of sugar scarcely injured!" Eventually, he concluded "that, as the cellar was nearly air-tight, the rapidity of the descent of the platform had compressed the air so as to form an *air-cushion*, which had broken the violence of the fall." Betteley promptly patented the idea of the air cushion, which Otis Tufts, a prominent inventor, called "patenting a hole in the ground." The trick was to develop a sufficiently large and air tight reservoir at the shaft's bottom and develop ways to slow the fall of an elevator car. Ellithorpe's inventions were designed to tackle and resolve these issues. The result was a series of dramatic tests, not all of them successful, and the death of his son, Albert, in an accident.[9]

Two months after Ellithorpe received his first elevator patent, a test was made of the air cushion on October 7, 1879, at the famed Parker House in Boston. Eight people entered the elevator car, and "when the rope was cut at the seventh story the car fell with an awful crash," blowing out "the whole front of the lower portion of the shaft." Although three passengers were injured, the air cushion worked until the shaft blew out; it was generally agreed that the air cushion had saved the passengers from any severe injuries. In a letter published in several newspapers Ellithorpe explained: "I perhaps misjudged as to the strength of the hall-front. The massive construction of it was peculiarly calculated to deceive even the most expert mechanic. I must confess I was deceived as to its strength." A more satisfying test occurred on October 29 "on the large elevator in the carriage warerooms of C. P. Kimball & Co., on Wabash avenue" in Chicago. Two people rode in the elevator along with eggs in a basket and wineglasses. The elevator was dropped down the shaft, but "the two passengers came out smiling," and the eggs and wineglasses were unharmed. Several weeks later a test was undertaken at the American Express building in Chicago that resulted in plaster coming off part of the shaft's wall. One hundred people watched as the elevator plunged 110 feet down a shaft. The only passengers were eggs in a basket and four goblets, with the only victims being several eggs crushed by a goblet that fell on them. A more dramatic test was tried at the Exposition Building in 1880. Attracted by a newspaper announcement that an elevator would fall "with living freight," twenty thousand people gathered to watch. The crowd stared as six men, including Ellithorpe, a son-in-law, and his two sons entered an elevator car. At 4:00 p.m. the ropes were cut, and the twenty-eight thousand–pound car plummeted 109 feet down the shaft, where its descent was safely slowed by the air cushion. As the passengers emerged smiling, "the crowd cheered with wild enthusiasm" and "rushed forward to feel of the men and see if they were not rubber automata."[10]

The rest of the century brought orders for the installation and occasionally the remodeling of elevators in Chicago and in federal buildings in New Orleans and Washington, D.C. The mid-1880s was punctuated by a suit brought by Charles S. Crane against Henry Beidler, Ellithorpe, and the air brake and air cushion companies. The case ground its way through the legal system until it reached the Illinois Superior Court in 1886. The proceedings seemed to focus on Beidler, who had been given company stock and patents to be used allegedly to pay off loans. Crane and other creditors successfully argued that he had done so to keep assets out of their hands. Creditors wanted Ellithorpe and Beidler to pay thirteen thousand dollars owed to them, and the judge ordered Beidler to surrender the stock. Although Beidler was the focus, the implication was that Ellithorpe had also been involved in shady dealings.[11]

In 1888 Ellithorpe took the time to write to an old comrade about Maj. Gen. James G. Blunt, Ellithorpe's hero from the war. In the late 1870s Blunt's mental condition had rapidly deteriorated, and he was committed to an insane asylum, where he died on July 27, 1881. Speculation centered on the possibility that Blunt's mental decline had been caused by the venereal disease syphilis. In 1888 Ellithorpe learned that an effort was being made to obtain a pension for Blunt's widow, Nancy, and Ellithorpe wrote to his old comrade James H. Gillpatrick, Blunt's son-in-law and a distant blood relation of the general. Ellithorpe made no mention of the possibility that syphilis had caused Blunt's mental problems but instead suggested that the general had been psychologically traumatized by a wartime event: the Baxter Springs Massacre on October 6, 1863. Blunt and his escort had wandered unknowingly into an attack in progress by the notorious William Clarke Quantrill and his guerrilla force on the federal outpost at Baxter Springs, Kansas. Just weeks earlier, these exceptionally dangerous guerrillas had raided Lawrence, Kansas, and killed "approximately one hundred and fifty men and boys" there. Blunt attempted to rally his men at Baxter Spring but eventually fled the scene on a mule. He was lucky to escape with his life, as eighty of his men, most of his escort, were killed, many after attempting to surrender. Among the dead was Maj. Henry Z. Curtis, Maj. Gen. Samuel R. Curtis's son and a favorite of Blunt.[12]

To James H. Gillpatrick, April 18, 1888

Chicago, April 18, 1888
Col. J. H. Gillpatrick,
Leavenworth, Kan.

My Dear Colonel:—

I understand that an effort is being made to obtain a pension for Mrs. James

G. Blunt.[13] I have frequently wondered why an application for a pension has not been made before this. I am, and have been personally conversant and closely related to the General in all of his Western military campaigns. Perhaps I am revealing to you what you may have heretofore only suspicioned, but which are to me conclusive facts. My relations with Gen. Blunt from the time that he was a Colonel have been as you well know intimate. I was the bearer of dispatches from the Secretary of War, and carried to him his Commission as a Brigadier General. After his return from Missouri to Leavenworth, my intimate and close relations commenced with him. At that time I was with him in the field, where we were both, as well as all of the command, often baptized in blood. As you are well aware I was with him at the battle of Old Fort Wayne, Boonesboro, or Cane Hill, and at Prairie Grove. I always regarded him as one of the most cool headed, dashing and brave commanders in our Western army; possessed of a strong and powerful brain, kind almost to a fault with his men, yet exacting, close, rigid in his discipline. I never imagined that a man of so strong and positive a brain could ever have it turned or dethroned by any military adversity; but it seems that I, in my judgment, was mistaken, for while in the very heighth of his success, and while all his previous efforts in the field had been crowned with victory, I find after a certain event to be a changed man. From his buoyant and jovial disposition he became taciturn, and despondent at times, while many of his hours appeared to be spent in a moody, or absent minded reflection. I often asked myself, what can be the cause of this great change in the generals appearance, his habits, social, and military, all changed. I soon however, discovered what seemed to me to be the cause,

While on his march from Leavenworth to take command of the army assigned to him in Southern Missouri and the Indian Territory, his little escort was attacked at Baxter Springs and you know the result of that massacre, for it was nothing else but a cold-blooded and wanton sacrifice of life by the Quantrell and Livingston Bands of marauders[.] He with only a few of his guard escaped. The records and history in the War Department have full particulars of this event. From this hour forward I found the General a changed man; moody, very reflective, while all of that former buoyancy of spirit, and dash appeared to have left him. I frequently asked what trouble, or what anxieties depressed him; his answer invariably was "The Baxter Springs Massacre; I cannot throw it from my mind," said he; "It haunts me night and day, however much I try to throw it off, I can not, and I sometimes feel that I was to blame, and that the Government will blame me." Said he; "I sometimes think that it was one of those events liable to occur in the fortunes of war, & that all the care or caution of any man, could not prevent; then again, I feel, that, perhaps I did not exercise the care or caution which I ought to have exercised." This tradgedy or massacre, was the one great thing in my opinion, that commenced to affect, and finally resulted in ~~the~~ dethroning [of the] brain of our much loved General. From that time, he appeared changed his despondent hours grew upon him, and became more frequent; and from the close of the war to his death this, with other things, such as feeling that the Government Officials were against him, and that he was not properly appreciated for his acts and his services, all contributed to worry, depress, and and [*sic*] unnerve the man. It sapped his vital energies, he lapsed into a condition of moodiness which slowly but surely ended in paralysis of the brain[.]

I do not know if you, or his other companions have taken the same view of the causes that resulted in his death that I have, but I am most positive and sure, that this, one event; with other things, which were perhaps trifling in themselves, contributed, largely to dethrone his reason and end his days prematurely[.]

I think that every old companion of his, officer or soldier, who [k]new him intimately would all accord to him bravery, and in fact every qualification that goes to make up a gallant soldier. An officer who held not only the esteem, but the love of all in his command. I can only hope that his wife may be treated as kindly, and with as much consideration as the wives of other brave and noble officers who helped to fight the great battles of the Rebellion, and who have died by reason of hardships, excess of thought and energy for the cause in which we were all banded together to win.

If there is anything I can do by referring to papers or refreshing my recollections of other events, or causes, to show why the wife of as gallant a man as General Blunt should be treated as kindly, and with as much consideration as the wife of any man who ever fought a battle for the cause of human liberties and the perpetuity of this Union, I will cheerfully make the research and contribute what I can, and without prejudice, to accomplish such an end.

I leave here for Memphis Tenn., and will be there for one week, and should you desire to communicate with me, please do so at the Peabody Hotel.

With kind regards to yourself and family, I am,

Yours very respectfully,
A C Ellithorpe

[*Source:* Ellithorpe Family Papers, Kansas State Historical Society. On letterhead of Office of the Ellithorpe Air-Brake Co., Manufacturers of Steam and Hydraulic Elevators, 54 to 64 Waldo Place, Chicago. *Note: Copy* is handwritten to the left of Ellithorpe's signature.]

From James H. Gillpatrick, April 27, 1888

Leavenworth, Kan., April 27, 1888
Col. A. C. Ellithorpe
Chicago

My Dear Colonel:

Your letter of the 18th. Inst. at hand and I hasten to acknowledge ~~ist~~ it's reciept and thank you for the interest you manifest in the premises.[14]

And again, as I supposed, you give a very good suggestion as to the possible, or presumable cause of the Generals' mental decay. I had always thought that the placing of Genl. Schofield in command over Genl. Blunt had very much to do with his despondency and final break up. But I agree with you that the startling and tragic affair at Baxters Springs, May well have made his mind diseased.

I think you will be sure to do the best possible thing for Mrs. blunt in your affidavit, Let me call your attention to this—his morbid idea of writing a history of his campaigns and the war—He worked at it day and night in Washington just and Long before his break down. I thought he was off but as you say never dreamed that a man so made up could be off his base, until the crash came. However, I think I can do nothing to aid you in doing what you can do so much better without steering.

Yours:
J. H. Gillpatrick

[*Source:* Ellithorpe Family Papers, Kansas State Historical Society. On letterhead of J. H. Gillpatrick, Attorney at Law, Leavenworth, Kans.]

After a long and complex relationship with her husband, Maria died at their home on March 28, 1891. Her children "were at her bedside ministering to their mother" when she passed away of pneumonia. During her death Albert was in a Washington, D.C., hotel, severely ill, and was unable to travel for quite some time. Maria, according to an obituary, had a "warm motherly heart and [her] hand was extended at various times to a large number who fondly looked upon her as a parent." She left her estate, valued at twenty-six thousand dollars, to her four children. Now sixty-seven years old, Albert Ellithorpe never remarried, increasingly turned his business over to his sons, but remained active in politics and other favorite ventures.[15]

Many years earlier Ellithorpe had briefly joined the Greenback Party; in August 1896 he traveled to Joliet, Illinois, as part of a one hundred–man reception committee that welcomed the dynamic presidential candidate William Jennings Bryan, who had been nominated by both the Democratic Party and the Populist Party. It was the first time that Ellithorpe had supported a Democratic candidate. Ellithorpe apparently commanded a fair amount of curiosity and perhaps notoriety, as he was the subject of a lengthy biographical piece in the February 28, 1897, issue of the *Chicago Sunday Chronicle.* Strikingly avoiding any mention of the scandalous *Chicago Tribune* trial or the more recent lawsuit brought by Charles Crane, the article was nostalgic. The reporter wrote: "Perhaps no prominent man in Chicago has had so varied a career as has Albert Chapman Ellithorpe . . . He has never risen to high conspicuousity, but neither has he ever been . . . for long, in absolute obscurity . . . it may be said of him, that if his mind had always been as tenacious as it has certainly been active, he would have soared high among his fellow citizens in more than one line." The author observed that Ellithorpe had an "intelligent, eager countenance . . . and he is to day an entertaining conversationalist." Now he often stayed at home, where he enjoyed reading his books. The reporter was given the story of Ellithorpe's life with occasional departures from the truth, some self-criticisms, and much self-promotion. In the section about his Civil War career, Ellithorpe engaged in some "old soldier" stories in which he exaggerated his record. He enlarged his role so that he claimed primary responsibility for having organized his regiment and the Cherokee legislature that had "rescinded" secession. Ellithorpe asserted that when Opothele Yahola died, he had closed the old warrior's eyes and then buried him. He claimed to have been severely wounded at Prairie Grove, which cannot be confirmed in any of his wartime writings or contemporary records, although he mentioned two gunshot scars in his pension application. Although parts of the article were clearly overstated, it is apparent that he was proud of his wartime service. As the nineteenth century passed by and the twentieth century began, Ellithorpe experienced increasing health problems as well as a family tragedy.[16]

Sometime in the 1890s, Ellithorpe moved into his daughter Mary's home. Her husband, Charles Hathaway, had been a passenger in at least one of the elevator tests and in 1900 marketed artisan water. The Hathaways' two sons and a daughter also resided in the house at 939 N. 64th Avenue, along with Ruben Bristol, a young boarder from Kentucky. In April 1901 Ellithorpe applied for an invalid pension due to "failing sight & senility" and received the maximum twelve dollars per month pension. His son Albert Benjamin worked as manager of the family's elevator business, and his younger son, Frederick Tuttle, also assisted. Albert Benjamin apparently inherited some of his father's hotheadedness. In October 1900 Daniel D. Healy, the superintendent of public service, informed a city committee that the Ellithorpe company had not finished installing four elevators in the County Building. The contract stated that all four elevators would be installed by July 1, 1900, but only one had been fully installed, and it was unsatisfactory. At the October meeting Albert Benjamin promised that all of the elevators would be installed soon, and alterations would be made to the one deemed unsatisfactory. Problems continued, however, and Healy reported at the January 1901 meeting that the elevators were in unsatisfactory condition. Albert Benjamin attacked Healy after the meeting, and Healy knocked down his assailant, and commissioners intervened to stop the struggle.[17]

The saga continued when Albert Benjamin installed a new safety device involving "a pair of compressed air pipes on either side of the car" in one of the new County Building elevators. On September 7, 1901, he entered a test elevator there. Seating himself on a wooden chair with a basket of eggs and a glass of water nearby, the elevator was dropped down the shaft. In a freak accident the chair rocked, breaking a chair leg and piercing "the fleshy part of his right thigh to the bone." He was semiconscious from loss of blood when he was removed from the elevator. The eggs and the glass of water were unharmed. Sixteen days later, at the age of forty-eight, Albert Benjamin died from his injuries and was buried at Rosehill Cemetery.[18]

Six years later, on February 19, 1907, Ellithorpe "passed away peacefully" with his children by his bedside and, assured the *Chicago Chronicle*, "in possession of all his faculties." In an obituary summarizing many of his activities, the paper concluded that "his was a kaleidoscopic and useful career." A group of "Old Settlers" carried his coffin to his grave at Rosehill Cemetery on February 21, 1907. He had witnessed the United States becoming a transcontinental nation and had seen Chicago rise from a village to one of the nation's largest cities. Not content to sit on the sidelines, he had participated actively in the growth of his nation as a miner, a businessman, a journalist, an inventor, a politician, and a soldier. Although his military experience was confined to what traditionally has been thought of as an unimportant backwater of the war, Ellithorpe was part of a unit that uniquely and successfully allied three races in the task of defeating the Confederacy. Throughout his life Ellithorpe was proud of having shared "in all the rough and tumble experience of those terrible years on the frontier—a kind of experience which was so entirely different from that of the Armies in other parts of the country—so much more wild, exciting and critical that none but those actually under Blunt's command can appreciate its character. If the detailed history of that Army of the Frontier could be fully and faithfully written, it would be one of the most thrilling narratives of peril, bravery, self-sacrificing endurance under hardship, bloody encounters and bold and dashing deeds, that mark the annals of modern warfare."[19]

Appendix

ARTICLES PUBLISHED IN THE *CHICAGO EVENING JOURNAL*

Date published	Date of letter	Signature
November 25, 1862	November 12, 1862	CREEK
December 1, 1862	November 19, 1862	C
December 4, 1862	November 24, 1862	CHEROKEE
December 11, 1862	December 1, 1862	BOONEVILLE
December 23, 1862	December 7, 1862	CHEROKEE
December 26, 1862	December 14, 1862	CREEK
January 8, 1863	December 23, 1862	CREEK
January 23, 1863	January 8, 1863	CREEK
January 26, 1863	January 14, 1863	CREEK
January 29, 1863	January 1, 1863*	SEMINOLE
January 29, 1863	January 4, 1863**	CREEK
February 3, 1863	January 23, 1863	CREEK
February 11, 1863	January 26, 1863	CREEK
February 13, 1863	February 1, 1863	CREEK
February 26, 1863	February 6, 1863	CREEK
March 21, 1863	March 15, 1863	CREEK
May 4, 1863	April 24, 1863	CHEROKEE
May 15, 1863	May 1, 1863	SEMINOLE
May 20, 1863	May 16, 1863	CREEK
July 8, 1863	June 19, 1863	CREEK
August 7, 1863	July 20, 1863	SEMINOLE
March 18, 1864	March 10, 1864	CREEK
May 24, 1864	May 24, 1864	A. C. E.
October 13, 1864	October 8, 1864	CHEROKEE

* This article appears under the title "Delayed Letters to The Journal," which accounts for the date being out of order.

** This letter appears in the same edition, under the title "Another Letter," which accounts for the date being out of order.

NOTES

PREFACE

1. Stephen Berry, ed., *Weirding the War: Stories from the Civil War's Ragged Edges,* UnCivil War Series (Athens: University of Georgia Press, 2011), 3–4.

2. Frederick H. Dyer, comp., *A Compendium of the War of the Rebellion,* 2 vols. (1908; repr., Dayton, Ohio: Press of Morningside Bookshop, 1979), 1:582; Lawrence L. Hewitt, Arthur W. Bergeron Jr., and Thomas E. Schott, eds., *Confederate Generals in the Trans-Mississippi, vol. 1: Essays on America's Civil War* (Knoxville: University of Tennessee Press, 2013).

3. *Chicago Evening Journal,* February 3, 1863.

CHAPTER 1. LIFE BEFORE MILITARY SERVICE

1. Albert C. Ellithorpe, "Brief Record of the Life of A. C. Ellithorpe" (MS, ca. 1902), 2–3, 7, Ellithorpe Family Papers, Kansas Historical Society; "Jo Minert's Family Tree," accessed September 3, 2014, trees.ancestry.com/tree/23988265/person/1528091690?ssrc=.

2. Ellithorpe, "Brief Record," 3–5, 7–8, 11.

3. Ibid., 9–10.

4. *Canadian Encyclopedia,* s.v. "Rebellions of 1837," accessed September 2, 2014, www.thecanadianencyclopedia.ca/en/article/rebellions-of-1837; Ellithorpe, "Brief Record," 11–14; *Canadian Encyclopedia,* s.v. "Hunters' Lodges," accessed September 2, 2014, www.thecanadianencyclopedia.ca/en/article/hunters-lodges/.

5. Ellithorpe, "Brief Record," 14; Kenneth J. Winkle, *The Young Eagle: The Rise of Abraham Lincoln* (Dallas: Taylor Trade Publishing, 2001), 121, 123; Bessie Louise Pierce, *A History of Chicago,* vol. 1: *The Beginning of a City, 1673–1848* (New York: Knopf, 1937), 48; Robert Fergus, comp., *Fergus' Directory of the City of Chicago, 1839* (Chicago: Fergus Printing Co., 1876), 13; *Encyclopedia of Chicago,* s.v. "Demography," accessed September 2, 2014, www.encyclopedia.chicagohistory.org/pages/962.html; *Encyclopedia of Chicago,* s.v. "A Cosmopolitan Frontier," accessed September 2, 2014, www.encyclopedia.chicagohistory.org/pages/410136.html; Donald L. Miller, *City of the Century: The Epic of Chicago and the Making of America* (New York: Simon & Schuster, 1996), 70–71; *Encyclopedia of Chicago,* s.v. "Illinois and Michigan Canal," accessed September 22, 2014, www.encyclopedia.chicagohistory.org/pages/626.html; Bessie Louise Pierce, *A History of Chicago,* vol. 2: *From Town to City, 1848–1871* (New York: Knopf, 1940), 5; Bessie Louise Pierce, *A History of Chicago,* vol. 3: *The Rise of a Modern City, 1871–1893* (New York: Knopf, 1957), 20.

6. Ellithorpe, "Brief Record," 14–19; Richard Palmer, "Remember the Old Fanning Mill?" accessed August 26, 2014, www.crookedlakereview.com/articles/101_135/126winter2003/126palmer3.html.

7. Ellithorpe, "Brief Record," 17, 19–20, 24, 27; Pierce, *History of Chicago,* 1:134.

8. Ellithorpe, "Brief Record," 27–30, 33; Pierce, *History of Chicago*, 1:256–57, 259, 260–62; John Carbutt, *Biographical Sketches of the Leading Men of Chicago* (Chicago: Wilson, Peirce, & Co., 1876), 256; Miller, *City of the Century*, 76.

9. Carbutt, *Biographical Sketches*, 256; Pierce, *History of Chicago*, 1:262; Ellithorpe, "Brief Record," 33; *Catalogue of the Corporation, Officers and Students of Knox Manual Labor College, Galesburg, Knox County, Ill., for the Year Ending July 2, 1845* (Peoria, Ill.: S. H. Davis, Printer, 1845); *Catalogue of the Corporation, Officers and Students of Knox College, Galesburg, Ill., for the Year Ending June 24th, 1846* (Peoria, Ill.: S. H. Davis, Printer, 1846), 8–9.

10. *Cook County, Illinois Marriage and Death Indexes, 1833–1889* (Provo, Utah: Ancestry.com Operations, 2011), Ancestry.com; *Chicago Tribune*, March 29, 1891, Fold3.com; Carbutt, *Biographical Sketches*, 256; A. T. Andreas, *History of Chicago*, vol. 3: *From the Fire of 1871 until 1885* (Chicago: A. T. Andreas Co., 1886), 499; "Biography of Col. A. C. Ellithorpe, from Chicago Sunday Chronicle, Feb. 28th, 1897," typescript, 6, Ellithorpe Family Papers, Kansas Historical Society.

11. "Biography," 6; Carbutt, *Biographical Sketches*, 256; *Seventh Census of the United* States, 1850, Cook County, Ill., 313; *New Orleans, Passenger Lists, 1813–1945* (Provo, Utah: Ancestry.com Operations, 2006), Ancestry.com.

12. Carbutt, *Biographical Sketches*, 256; *The Rail-Roads, History and Commerce of Chicago* (Chicago: Democratic Press Job & Book Steam Printing Office, 1854), 54.

13. "Biography," 7; *Chicagology*, s.v. "Second Presbyterian Church," accessed September 4, 2014, chicagology.com/pre-fire-chicago/prefire01/prefire079/; Miller, *City of the Century*, 90.

14. *Halpin's Eighth Annual Edition Chicago City Directory, 1865–66* (Chicago: T. M. Halpin, Compiler & Publisher, 1865), v; "Biography," 7–8; *Chicago Tribune*, March 3, 1895, Fold3.com; A. C. Ellithorpe and Ives Scoville, Machine for Cracking Stone for Ballasting Railroads, &c, U.S. Patent 22113, issued November 23, 1858, *U.S. Patent and Trademark Office Patents, 1790–1909* (Provo, Utah: Ancestry.com Operations, 2008), Ancestry.com.

15. *Chicago Tribune*, October 24, 1861, Fold3.com; "Biography," 8; Miller, *City of the Century*, 124–25.

16. "Biography," 8; *Chicago Tribune*, April 3, 1860, Fold3.com; *Rocky Mountain News Weekly*, March 7, 1860; *Western Mountaineer*, November 1, 1860, both at www.coloradohistoricnewspapers.org/.

17. Jewett, a southern sympathizer, would go on to help organize the 1864 Niagara Falls Peace Conference, a meeting between newspaper editor Horace Greeley and several Confederate commissioners that was designed to bring a negotiated end to the Civil War. Clark C. Spence and Robin W. Winks, "William 'Colorado' Jewett of the Niagara Falls Conference," *Historian: A Journal of History* 23, no. 1 (1960): 23, 28–29; "Biography," 8–9; *Rocky Mountain News*, October 4, 13, December 15, 18, 1860, www.coloradohistoricnewspapers.org; *Daily Rocky Mountain News*, October 3, 1860, www.coloradohistoricnewspapers.org/.

18. "Biography," 9–10; David Fridtjof Halaas, *Boom Town Newspapers: Journalism on the Rocky Mountain Mining Frontier, 1859–1881* (Albuquerque: University of New Mexico Press, 1981), 15–16; Carbutt, *Biographical Sketches*, 257.

19. *Western Mountaineer*, November 1, 1860, www.coloradohistoricnewspapers.org/; *Chicago Evening Star*, September 25, October 2, 1861; Patricia L. Faust, *Historical Times Illustrated Encyclopedia of the Civil War* (New York: Harper & Row, 1986), 291.

20. Joseph W. Bell turned out to be an inefficient officer plagued by hemorrhoids. He left his regiment in August 1862 without permission because he did not receive a medical leave. Finally, he re-

signed in May 1863 but amazingly became a brevet brigadier general in 1867 for "gallant service in the war." Thomas P. Lowry, *Tarnished Eagles: The Courts-Martial of Fifty Union Colonels and Lieutenant Colonels* (Mechanicsburg, Pa.: Stackpole Books, 1997), 127–29; "Biography," 11; *Chicago Tribune*, January 16, 1862, Fold3.com; *Illinois in the Civil War*, s.v. "13th Illinois Cavalry Regiment," accessed September 9, 2014, civilwarillinoisgenweb.org/reg_html/cav_013.html.

CHAPTER 2. THE INDIAN EXPEDITION

1. David A. Nichols, *Lincoln and the Indians: Civil War Policy and Politics* (1978; repr., St. Paul: Minnesota Historical Society Press, 2012), 25–28; *Encyclopedia of Oklahoma History & Culture*, s.v. "Civil War Era," accessed September 11, 2014, digital.library.okstate.edu/encyclopedia/entries/C/CI011.html; Mary Jane Warde, *When the Wolf Came: The Civil War and the Indian Territory* (Fayetteville: University of Arkansas Press, 2013), 44–45, 52; Edmund J. Danziger Jr., "The Office of Indian Affairs and the Problem of Civil War Indian Refugees in Kansas," *Kansas Historical Quarterly* 35, no. 3 (1969): 259–60.

2. Warde, *When the Wolf Came*, 46, 51, 57; *Encyclopedia of Oklahoma History & Culture*, s.v. "Civil War Era"; *Encyclopedia of Oklahoma History & Culture*, s.v. "Seminole," accessed September 11, 2014, digital.library.okstate.edu/encyclopedia/entries/S/SE011.html.

3. *Encyclopedia of Oklahoma History & Culture*, s.v. "Creek (Mvskoke)," accessed September 11, 2014, digital.library.okstate.edu/encyclopedia/entries/C/CR006.html; Gary Zellar, *African Creeks: Estelvste and the Creek Nation* (Norman: University of Oklahoma Press, 2007), 25; Warde, *When the Wolf Came*, 53–55; *Encyclopedia of Oklahoma History & Culture*, s.v. "Opothleyahola," accessed September 11, 2014, digital.library.okstate.edu/encyclopedia/entries/O/OP003.html; *Encyclopedia of Oklahoma History & Culture*, s.v. "Civil War Era."

4. Warde, *When the Wolf Came*, 66, 68; Nichols, *Lincoln and the Indians*, 29; Zellar, *African Creeks*, 23, 39, 45; United States, Office of Indian Affairs, *Report of the Commissioner of Indian Affairs for the Year 1862* (Washington, D.C.: Government Printing Office, 1863), 142.

5. Zellar, *African Creeks*, 3, 32–36, 42; Gary Zellar, "Occupying the Middle Ground: African Creeks in the First Indian Home Guard, 1862–1865," *Chronicles of Oklahoma* 76, no. 1 (1998): 49–50.

6. Zellar, *African Creeks*, 36, 39–40; Warde, *When the Wolf Came*, 45.

7. Warde, *When the Wolf Came*, 66, 68–70.

8. Ibid., 70, 83, 85, 92; *Report of the Commissioner of Indian Affairs*, 136–37, 139.

9. Chris Rein, "The U.S. Army, Indian Agency, and the Path to Assimilation: The First Indian Home Guards in the American Civil War," *Kansas History: A Journal of the Central Plains* 36 (Spring 2013): 3, 6; Nichols, *Lincoln and the Indians*, 34, 40, 48–49; Michael E. Banasik, *Embattled Arkansas: The Prairie Grove Campaign of 1862* (Wilmington, N.C.: Broadfoot Publishing Co., 1996), 59–61; Gary N. Heath, "The First Federal Invasion of Indian Territory," *Chronicles of Oklahoma* 44 (Winter 1966–67): 409; United States War Department, *War of the Rebellion: A Compilation of the Official Records of the Union and Confederate Armies*, 128 vols. (1880–1901; repr., Harrisburg, Pa.: National Historical Society, 1971), ser. 1, 8:624–25.

10. Banasik, *Embattled Arkansas*, 62, 65–66, 69; Nichols, *Lincoln and the Indians*, 35; *Official Records*, ser. 1, 8:534.

11. Mark A. Lause, *Race and Radicalism in the Union Army* (Urbana: University of Illinois Press, 2009), 67; Nichols, *Lincoln and the Indians*, 48; *Official Records*, ser. 1, 13:456; *Report of the Commis-*

sioner of Indian Affairs, 148; Heath, "First Federal Invasion," 409–10; James G. Blunt, "General Blunt's Account of His Civil War Experiences," *Kansas Historical Quarterly* 1 (May 1932):223; James G. Blunt to Caleb B. Smith, November 21, 1862, reel 834, M234, Letters Received by the Office of Indian Affairs, 1824–1881, National Archives.

12. J. Medill to Adjutant General Fuller, January 7, 1862, J. H. Lane to Brig. Gen. R. B. Mitchell, April 9, 1862, William P. Dole to A. C. Ellithorpe, April 5, 1862, Ellithorpe Family Papers, Kansas Historical Society; Carbutt, *Biographical Sketches*, 256–57; "Biography," 11; Ellithorpe Compiled Service Record, National Archives; *Leavenworth Daily Conservative*, April 20, 1862.

13. Robert Furnas to W. P. Dole, May 4, 1862, reel 834, Letters Received by the Office of Indian Affairs; Lause, *Race and Radicalism*, 72; Robert C. Farb, "The Military Career of Robert W. Furnas," *Nebraska History* 32 (March 1951): 18–20; Rein, "U.S. Army," 6; Wattles Compiled Service Record, National Archives.

14. "Biography," 8; Zellar, "Occupying the Middle Ground," 54; Lause, *Race and Radicalism*, 3–4; *Territorial Kansas Online*, s.v. "William A. Phillips, 1824–1893," accessed September 17, 2014, www.territorialkansasonline.org/~imlskto/cgi-bin/index.php?SCREEN=bio_sketches/phillips_william_a; Linda A. Kerber, "The Abolitionist Perception of the Indian," *Journal of American History* 62 (September 1975): 279, 282, 288–89.

15. *Leavenworth Daily Conservative*, May 8, 1862; Nichols, *Lincoln and the Indians*, 41; Zellar, "Occupying the Middle Ground," 54; Warde, *When the Wolf Came*, 44, 71; Kenneth W. Porter, "Billy Bowlegs (Holuta Micco) in the Civil War, pt. II," *Florida Historical Quarterly* 45 (April 1967): 401.

16. Rein, "U.S. Army," 7; A. C. Ellithorpe to William P. Dole, June 9, 1862, reel 834, Letters Received by the Office of Indian Affairs; Edwin Cassander Manning, *Biographical Historical and Miscellaneous* (Cedar Rapids, Iowa: privately printed, 1911), 49; Gary Zellar, "First to Fight for Freedom: African Creek Soldiers Enter the Civil War," *Journal of the Indian Wars* 1, no. 4 (2000): 12–13; Zellar, *African Creeks*, 41, 55–56; Zellar, "Occupying the Middle Ground," 48–49, 54.

17. Heath, "First Federal Invasion," 410–11; Ellithorpe Compiled Service Record, National Archives; *Leavenworth Daily Conservative*, May 8, 1862; Muster Rolls, First Indian Home Guards, RG 94, Records of the Adjutant General's Office, United States War Department, National Archives; Robert Furnas to W. P. Dole, May 4, 1862, reel 834, Letters Received by the Office of Indian Affairs; Rein, "U.S. Army," 7.

18. President Abraham Lincoln appointed William P. Dole as commissioner of Indian affairs. The two men were acquainted from the time when "Lincoln rode the Eighth Judicial Circuit in Illinois"; Dole had no experience in Indian issues when he was appointed. Edmund Jefferson Danziger Jr., *Indians and Bureaucrats: Administering the Reservation Policy during the Civil War* (Urbana: University of Illinois Press, 1974), 15.

19. John Ritchey commanded the Second Indian Home Guards. On November 21, 1862, Brig. Gen. James G. Blunt wrote that "Col. Ritchey, was entirely incompetent as an officer. He is now under arrest, and, should be discharged from the service." James G. Blunt to Caleb B. Smith, November 21, 1862, reel 834, Letters Received by the Office of Indian Affairs.

20. First Lt. George Dole served as adjutant of the Second Indian Home Guards. Soldiers and Sailors Database, accessed October 31, 2014, www.nps.gov/civilwar/search-soldiers-detail.htm?soldierId=5C73E796-DC7A-DF11-BF36-B8AC6F5D926A.

21. Dr. William Kile of Illinois served for a time on Senator James H. Lane's staff in his Kansas bri-

gade. Kile became the senior physician that attended the Indian refugees during the winter of 1861–62. Another physician attending the Indians was S. D. Coffin, a relative of Superintendent William G. Coffin. Dr. Kile complained about his colleague's frequent absences, and this "marked the beginning of a serious estrangement between him and Superintendent Coffin." Kile resigned in September 1862. *Report of the Commissioner of Indian Affairs*, 148; Annie Heloise Abel, *The American Indian in the Civil War, 1862–1865* (1919; repr., Lincoln: University of Nebraska Press, 1992), 208.

22. Michael E. Banasik, ed., *Reluctant Cannoneer: The Diary of Robert T. McMahan of the Twenty-Fifth Independent Ohio Light Artillery*, Unwritten Chapters of the Civil War West of the River series (Iowa City: Camp Pope Bookshop, 2000), 38; Mark K. Christ, ed., *"This Day We Marched Again": A Union Soldier's Account of War in Arkansas and the Trans-Mississippi* (Little Rock: Butler Center for Arkansas Studies, 2014), 27, 30; W. G. Coffin to W. P. Dole, June 4, 1862, June 15, 1862, reel 834, Letters Received by the Office of Indian Affairs; William Weer, Special Orders No. 4, June 11, 1862, reel 1, Robert Furnas Papers, Nebraska Historical Society.

23. William Weer, Special Orders No. 4, June 11, 1862, reel 1, Robert Furnas Papers; W. G. Coffin to W. P. Dole, June 15, 1862, reel 834, Letters Received by the Office of Indian Affairs; *Leavenworth Daily Conservative*, June 21, July 8, 1862; John D. Spencer, *The American Civil War in the Indian Territory* (Long Island, N.Y.: Osprey Publishing, 2009), 20–21; Francis A. Lord, *Civil War Collector's Encyclopedia: Arms, Uniforms, and Equipment of the Union and Confederacy* (Secaucus, N.J.: Castle, 1982), 243.

24. *Leavenworth Daily Conservative*, June 21, 1862; *Official Records*, ser. 1, 13:441; W. G. Coffin to W. P. Dole, June 25, 1862, W. G. Coffin to E. H. Carruth, June 16, 1862, reel 834, Letters Received by the Office of Indian Affairs; Heath, "First Federal Invasion," 414.

25. *Leavenworth Daily Conservative*, May 31, June 21, 1862; W. G. Coffin to William P. Dole, June 25, 1862, reel 834, Letters Received by the Office of Indian Affairs; Banasik, *Reluctant Cannoneer*, 44.

26. Isaac Gause, *Four Years with Five Armies: Army of the Frontier, Army of the Potomac, Army of the Missouri, Army of the Ohio, Army of the Shenandoah* (New York: Neale Publishing Co., 1908), 96–97; Banasik, *Embattled Arkansas*, 76–80, 85–86.

27. Banasik, *Embattled Arkansas*, 86–91; Janet B. Hewett, Noah Andre Trudeau, and Bryce A. Suderow, eds., *Supplement to the Official Records of the Union and Confederate Armies*, 100 vols. (Wilmington, N.C.: Broadfoot Publishing Co., 1994), pt. 1, 3:36; Wiley Britton, *Memoirs of the Rebellion on the Border, 1863* (1882; repr., Lincoln: University of Nebraska Press, 1993), 233.

28. *Community & Conflict: The Impact of the Civil War in the Ozarks*, s.v. "George Falconer and Albert Ellithorpe," accessed September 22, 2014, www.ozarkscivilwar.org/archives/1166.

29. Prior to these entries by Falconer, he wrote brief entries for June 18 to June 21. These have been deleted from the text because the information was replicated in his longer entries. Also deleted were two pages in Falconer's hand of lyrics to a song titled "Down the River."

Established in 1817 on the Arkansas River near the border between Arkansas and the Indian Territory, Confederate forces controlled Fort Smith until Union forces captured it in August 1863. Faust, *Historical Times Illustrated Encyclopedia*, 278.

30. Referred to "as the Athens of the American Southwest," Park Hill was located south of Tahlequah, the capital of the Cherokee Nation. Charles Robert Goins and Danney Goble, *Historical Atlas of Oklahoma*, 4th ed. (Norman: University of Oklahoma Press, 2006), 82.

31. Grand Saline was a salt spring located near present-day Salina, Okla., in Mayes County. Extensive equipment and a number of buildings occupied this site where salt had been manufactured for a num-

ber of years. Grant Foreman, ed., *A Traveler in Indian Territory: The Journal of Ethan Allen Hitchcock, Late Major-General in the United States Army* (1930; repr. Norman: University of Oklahoma Press, 1996), 89.

32. Col. Stand Watie had a sawmill on Cowskin Prairie close to the Grand River and near present-day Grove, Okla. W. Craig Gaines, *The Confederate Cherokees: John Drew's Regiment of Mounted Rifles* (Baton Rouge: Louisiana State University Press, 1989), 95; *Encyclopedia of Oklahoma History & Culture*, s.v. "Cowskin Prairie Council (1863)," accessed November 3, 2014, digital.library.okstate.edu/encyclopedia/entries/C/CO181.html.

33. Falconer served in Gordon's Arkansas Cavalry following his exchange. He married in 1874 and farmed in Marion, Ark. He died at age forty-seven, on November 1, 1890. *Community & Conflict: The Impact of the Civil War in the Ozarks*, s.v. "George Falconer and Albert Ellithorpe," accessed September 22, 2014,www.ozarkscivilwar.org/archives/1166; Hewitt, *Supplement to the Official Records*, pt. 1, 3:36; Gaines, *Confederate Cherokees*, 104, 107, 111; Warde, *When the Wolf Came*, 57–58, 108–9, 113; Abel, *American Indian in the Civil War*, 137–38.

34. The Ninth Kansas Cavalry campaigned actively in the trans-Mississippi from its organization in March 1862 to the close of the war. The Tenth Kansas Infantry campaigned in the trans-Mississippi until November 1864, when it was transferred to the western theater. Capt. Norman Allen commanded the First Kansas Light Artillery until his death from disease in July 1863. His battery served in the trans-Mississippi until the late summer of 1863 when they were transferred to the western theater. Dyer, comp., *A Compendium of the War of the Rebellion*, 2 vols. (1908; repr., Dayton, Ohio: Press of Morningside Bookshop, 1979), 2:1183–85, 1188; W. S. Burke, *Official Military History of Kansas Regiments during the War for the Suppression of the Great Rebellion* (1870; repr., Ottawa: Kansas Heritage Press, 1995), 437.

35. Col. James J. Clarkson was born in Kentucky and migrated to Missouri in the 1840s. During the prewar border troubles, he commanded the notorious "Kickapoo Rangers," a proslavery force that participated in the 1856 attack on Lawrence. He fought at Wilson's Creek on August 10, 1861, and in March 1862 raised Clarkson's Independent Ranger Battalion. While held as a prisoner, he was charged with treason for a time but then exchanged. Four months after the Locust Grove skirmish, the battalion was ordered to unite with four companies of recruits to form the Ninth Missouri (Clark's) Infantry regiment. Clarkson was killed (possibly murdered) in the fall of 1864. Nancy Bunker Bowen, "An Uncivil Warrior: Missouri's Col. James J. Clarkson," accessed November 4, 2014,www.chrisanddavid.com/wilsonscreek/JamesClarkson.htm; James E. McGhee, *Guide to Missouri Confederate Units, 1861–1865* (Fayetteville: University of Arkansas Press, 2008), 215; William Garrett Piston and Thomas P. Sweeney, M.D., *Portraits of Conflict: A Photographic History of Missouri in the Civil War* (Fayetteville: University of Arkansas Press, 2009), 265.

36. Ellithorpe's assessment of Col. William Weer was one echoed by many other men in the Indian Expedition. A Kansas attorney when the war started, Weer had close ties to Senator James Lane and Brig. Gen. James G. Blunt. A number of Missourians disliked him for his role in burning Osceola, Mo., in September 1861, but he became commander of the Tenth Kansas Infantry on June 1, 1862. Banasik, *Reluctant Cannoneer*, 294.

37. Col. William R. Judson was born in New York in 1810 and worked at a variety of occupations in the prewar period. A Mexican War veteran, in September 1861 he became commander of the Sixth Kansas Cavalry and was brevetted brigadier general in March 1865. His sons, Charles and William Jr., served as officers in his regiment. *History of Tioga, Chemung, Tompkins, and Schuyler Counties, New York*

with Illustrations and Biographical Sketches of Some of Its Prominent Men and Pioneers (Philadelphia: Everts & Ensign, 1879), 251–52.

38. The site that Ellithorpe refers to is unclear. Hudson's Crossing was a well-known ford of the Neosho River just north of the Indian Territory–Kansas border. Ellithorpe remained near Locust Grove after the skirmish. Banasik, *Embattled Arkansas,* 88.

39. Established in 1842 in eastern Kansas, Fort Scott served as "a staging area for Union troops operating into Missouri, Arkansas, and Indian Territory[,] . . . an important gathering point for refugees," and a major supply center for Union troops operating in the area. Leo E. Oliva, *Fort Scott: Courage and Conflict on the Border* (Topeka: Kansas State Historical Society, 2008), 1, 67.

40. Confederate colonel Daniel N. McIntosh commanded the First Creek Regiment, and his brother, Chilly, served as lieutenant colonel of the unit. Gaines, *Confederate Cherokees,* 24.

41. Not specifically documented elsewhere, the scout was one of several sent out in the vicinity of Fort Gibson. *Official Records,* ser. 1, 13:160–62; Whit Edwards, *"The Prairie Was on Fire": Eyewitness Accounts of the Civil War in the Indian Territory* (Oklahoma City: Oklahoma Historical Society, 2001), 21–22.

42. Following the Locust Grove skirmish most of John Drew's Regiment of Mounted Rifles (Cherokee) defected from the Confederate cause with these men forming an important part of the Third Indian Home Guards. Gaines, *Confederate Cherokees,* 113–14.

43. Following the victory at Pea Ridge, Maj. Gen. Samuel R. Curtis led his army on a long and logistically challenging march through northeastern Arkansas. The first elements of his army reached Helena on July 12, 1862. William L. Shea and Earl J. Hess, *Pea Ridge: Civil War Campaign in the West* (Chapel Hill: University of North Carolina Press, 1992), 303.

44. Frederick Salomon and his three brothers emigrated from Prussia during the revolutions of 1848. He resided in Manitowoc, Wisc., and fought at the battle of Wilson's Creek as part of the Fifth Missouri Infantry. In November 1861 he was commissioned as colonel of the Ninth Wisconsin Infantry. He served throughout the war in the trans-Mississippi.

Although the expedition had achieved success, the hot weather, lack of adequate drinking water, and a lack of supplies led to increasing discontentment among the soldiers and Colonel Weer's subordinates. In a startling act of mutiny, Colonel Salomon arrested Weer on July 18 and ordered a retreat. The First and Second Indian Home Guards, however, remained in the Indian Territory for about ten more days. Salomon was never disciplined for his actions, perhaps because his brother was then serving as governor of Wisconsin. Colonel Weer continued in the service with both he and Salomon commanding brigades in the same division during the Prairie Grove campaign. Eventually, in April 1864 Weer's alcoholism led to a dishonorable discharge, although it was overturned the following year. Ezra J. Warner, *Generals in Blue: Lives of the Union Commanders* (Baton Rouge: Louisiana State University Press, 1992), 417–18; Banasik, *Embattled Arkansas,* 109, 486; Banasik, *Reluctant Cannoneer,* 295; William L. Shea, *Fields of Blood: The Prairie Grove Campaign* (Chapel Hill: University of North Carolina Press, 2009), 289.

45. Lt. Col. David B. Corwin served as ranking officer in the Second Indian Home Guards at this time. Abel, *American Indian in the Civil War,* 144.

46. Established in 1827, Fort Leavenworth (Kans.) was the supply deport for all military posts in the West during the Civil War. It was sited about 118 miles north of Fort Scott. Dr. Andrew Holladay joined the First Indian Home Guards with his friend and patient, Robert W. Furnas, from the Nebraska Territory. Holladay did not receive a surgeon's commission in the regiment because he performed

poorly on the examination for the position. Marvin H. Garfield, "The Military Post as a Factor in the Frontier Defense of Kansas, 1865–1869," *Kansas Historical Quarterly* 1 (November 1931): 53; Rein, "U.S. Army," 9; Zellar, *African Creeks*, 55–56.

47. Acting assistant adjutant-general.

48. Possibly refers to Maj. H. H. Williams, the commander of the Tenth Kansas Infantry at that time. Burke, *Official Military History*, 290.

49. Lt. Col. Lewis R. Jewell of the Sixth Kansas Cavalry was mortally wounded during the running skirmish near Cane Hill, Ark., on November 28, 1862.

Salomon's commission as brigadier general dated from July 16, 1862. Shea, *Fields of Blood*, 102; Warner, *Generals in Blue*, 418.

50. Fort Gibson was established in 1824 along the Grand River and near its confluence with the Arkansas and Verdigris Rivers; more popularly, this part of the Indian Territory was called the "Three Forks." Goins, *Historical Atlas of Oklahoma*, 48–49.

51. Refers to Tahlequah, the capital of the Cherokee Nation.

CHAPTER 3. BUSHWHACKING IN ARKANSAS

1. W. G. Coffin to Charles E. Mix, September 13, 1862, reel 834, M234, Letters Received by the Office of Indian Affairs, 1824–81, National Archives; Abel, *American Indian in the Civil War*, 209.

2. James G. Blunt to Caleb B. Smith, November 21, 1862, reel 834, Letters Received by the Office of Indian Affairs; Warner, *Generals in Blue*, 37–38.

3. James G. Blunt to Caleb B. Smith, November 21, 1862, reel 834, Letters Received by the Office of Indian Affairs; Danziger "Office of Indian Affairs," 266, 268–69.

4. Initially listed as killed by friendly fire at Locust Grove, Dr. Andrew Holladay had been accidentally wounded by a soldier in the Ninth Kansas Cavalry. United States War Department, *War of the Rebellion*, ser. 1, 13:137–38; Robert W. Furnas to A. C. Ellithorpe, July 13, July 25, August 18, 1862, Frederick Salomon to A. C. Ellithorpe, July 28, 1862, James G. Blunt to President Abraham Lincoln, September 2, 1862, James G. Blunt to Richard Yates, September 2, 1862, O. F. Winchester to A. C. Ellithorpe, September 11, 1862, J. H. Lane to H. S. Lane, September 7, 1862, Ellithorpe Family Papers, Kansas Historical Society; James G. Blunt, Special Orders No. 110, September 2, 1862, Ellithorpe Compiled Service Record, National Archives; A. C. Ellithorpe to W. G. Coffin, September 12, 1862, reel 834, Letters Received by the Office of Indian Affairs.

5. N. P. Chipman to Major Hunt, October 7, 1862, A. C. Ellithorpe to J. H. Gillpatrick, April 18, 1888, Ellithorpe Family Papers; *Leavenworth Daily Conservative*, October 3, 12, 21, 1862; Robert W. Furnas to E. M. Stanton, September 17, 1862, reel 11, Robert Furnas Papers, Nebraska Historical Society; Rein, "U.S. Army," 17; Ian Michael Spurgeon, *Soldiers in the Army of Freedom: The 1st Kansas Colored, the Civil War's First African American Combat Unit* (Norman: University of Oklahoma Press, 2014), 79.

6. Carbutt, *Biographical Sketches*, 257.

7. Daniel E. Sutherland, "Guerrillas: The Real War in Arkansas," in *Civil War Arkansas: Beyond Battles and Leaders*, ed. Anne J. Bailey and Daniel E. Sutherland (Fayetteville: University of Arkansas Press, 2000), 133, 135, 138.

8. *Official Records*, ser. 1, 13:765; Michael A. Hughes, "Wartime Gristmill Destruction in Northwest Arkansas and Military Farm Colonies," in *Civil War Arkansas*, 32, 34–35, 38; Mark K. Christ and Patrick

G. Williams, eds., *I Do Wish This Cruel War Was Over: First-Person Accounts of Civil War Arkansas from the Arkansas Historical Quarterly* (Fayetteville: University of Arkansas Press, 2014), 50; Edwin Cassander Manning, *Biographical Historical and Miscellaneous Selections* (Cedar Rapids, Iowa: privately printed, 1911), 48.

9. Robert W. Furnas to E. M. Stanton, September 17, 1862, reel 11, Robert Furnas Papers.

10. E. C. Amsden, Sworn Statement, February 27, 1863, H. A. Davison, Sworn Statement, September 5, 1862, Wattles Compiled Service Record, National Archives.

11. Invented by B. Tyler Henry and manufactured by Oliver Fisher Winchester, the Henry rifle was one of the best repeaters used during the war. With a sixteen-shot magazine and .44 caliber bullets, the gun was particularly popular among western soldiers. Although the federal government only purchased 1,730 Henry rifles, an estimated 10,000 were used during the war. Ellithorpe obtained a Henry rifle and used it effectively during the battle of Prairie Grove. William B. Edwards, *Civil War Guns: The Complete Story of Federal and Confederate Small Arms* (Secaucus, N.J.: Castle Books, 1978), 158; Faust, *Historical Times Illustrated Encyclopedia*, 358.

12. Ellithorpe's estimate may be a bit high. Michael E. Banasik estimated that "5000+" Union soldiers participated in the expedition. Banasik, *Embattled Arkansas*, 502.

13. After most of his regiment defected to the Union side, Confederate authorities distrusted Col. John Drew, and he played no significant military role in the fall 1862 campaigns. He manufactured salt for the Confederacy and later made "overtures of peace" to Col. Williams A. Phillips in 1863. Drew died on August 25, 1865. Gaines, *Confederate Cherokees*, 120–21.

14. James S. Rains held the rank of brigadier general in the Missouri State Guard. Although courageous and patriotic, Rains drank too much and was a poor disciplinarian and soldier. Maj. Gen. Thomas "Hindman relieved him in October 1862, alleging incompetence and insobriety." Bruce S. Allardice, *More Generals in Gray* (Baton Rouge: Louisiana State University Press, 1995), 190–91.

15. Maj. Gen. Franz Sigel immigrated to the United States after the failed 1848 revolution in Germany. Residing in St. Louis, Mo., when the war started, Sigel helped unify German immigrants in support of the Union cause. His finest military contributions occurred during the Pea Ridge campaign in February and March 1862. Warner, *Generals in Blue*, 447–48.

Soldiers from Brig. Gen. Alexander S. Asboth's division burned Bentonville, Ark., on February 18, 1862, in retaliation for the murder of a soldier from the Fifth Missouri Cavalry. Shea and Hess, *Pea Ridge*, 46.

16. Benton County, along with other counties in northwestern Arkansas, was strongly Unionist. Alfred Dinsmore, the county's representative at the convention to consider secession, was opposed to disunion and attempted to submit the matter to the people for a vote in May 1861. James M. Woods, *Rebellion and Realignment: Arkansas' Road to Secession* (Fayetteville: University of Arkansas Press, 1987), 151, 159.

17. Col. Thomas M. Bowen commanded the Thirteenth Kansas Infantry in Col. William Weer's brigade. Shea, *Fields of Blood*, 289.

18. Brig. Gen. Frederick Salomon commanded the First Brigade in the Kansas Division consisting of the Ninth Wisconsin Infantry, the Sixth Kansas Cavalry and Battery, the Ninth Kansas Cavalry and Battery, the Second Ohio Cavalry, the Third Wisconsin Cavalry, the Second Indian Home Guards, the Second Kansas Battery, and Stockton's Ohio Battery.

Col. William F. Cloud, a Kansas businessman and Methodist minister, began his military career in the Second Kansas Infantry, a three-month regiment. Next, he helped organize the Second Kansas Cavalry and became its commander. Maj. Gen. James G. Blunt had a high regard for Cloud's military abilities, and during the Prairie Grove campaign Cloud commanded the Third Brigade in Blunt's Kansas division consisting of the Eleventh Kansas Infantry, the Second Kansas Cavalry and Battery, the First Indian Home Guards, Rabb's Indiana Battery, and Hopkins's Kansas Battery.

Col. William Weer's Second Brigade of the Kansas Division consisted of the Tenth Kansas Infantry, the Thirteenth Kansas Infantry, the Third Indian Home Guards, and the First Kansas Battery. Ibid., 67, 289–90.

19. An 1853 graduate of the U.S. Military Academy, Brig. Gen. John M. Schofield commanded the Army of the Frontier at this time. Schofield's force prevented Hindman from gaining control of the roadways near Fayetteville as a result of the successful White River skirmish on October 28. Schofield met with Blunt at Elkhorn Tavern on November 3 "for a telegraphic conference" with Maj. Gen. Samuel R. Curtis, the commander of the Department of Missouri. Warner, *Generals in Blue*, 108, 425; Shea, *Fields of Blood*, 56–59, 63.

20. No other source has been found that corroborates this scout, but Ellithorpe wrote that it returned on November 14, and he described it in his December 1 *Chicago Evening Journal* account.

21. James H. Gillpatrick (or Gilpatrick) was born in Maine in about 1840. He married Sarah Blunt, a daughter of James G. Blunt and his wife, Nancy, about 1872. In other words, James G. Blunt became his father-in-law after the war, but the two men were probably distantly related. James H. Gillpatrick became major of the Second Kansas Colored Infantry in October 1863 and was the regiment's lieutenant colonel by the time he was discharged in November 1865. Gillpatrick worked as an attorney in Leavenworth, Kans., after the war. *Tenth Census of the United* States, 1880, Leavenworth County, Kans., 286; *Twelfth Census of the United* States, 1900, Leavenworth County, Kans., 229.

22. Col. William F. Cloud commanded a force of five hundred men from the Second Kansas Cavalry, the Sixth Kansas Cavalry, the Second Ohio Cavalry, the First Indian Home Guards, and the Second Kansas Cavalry's battery. They went to the Cane Hill, Ark., region, where Confederate cavalrymen were foraging and successfully drove them away. Shea, *Fields of Blood*, 67–68.

23. Ellithorpe incorrectly labeled his November 9, 10, and 11 entries as occurring in September. The dates have been corrected for the reader's convenience.

24. Ellithorpe was probably referring to Cloud's movement into the Cane Hill region, where they encountered the Missouri Cavalry Battalion commanded by Col. Emmett MacDonald. Cloud's men reportedly returned to Spavinaw Creek on November 11, however, rather than on November 9, as Ellithorpe wrote.

25. Col. Thomas Ewing Jr. commanded the Eleventh Kansas Infantry in Col. William F. Cloud's brigade. Shea, *Fields of Blood*, 290.

26. The Army of the Frontier had an effective strength of about ninety-five hundred at the battle of Prairie Grove on December 7, with another six hundred men serving as a wagon train guard. Ellithorpe's November 14 diary entry has a more accurate estimate of the army's strength. Banasik, *Embattled Arkansas*, 534.

27. Col. Douglas H. Cooper served in the First Mississippi Rifles during the Mexican War. In 1853 he became the Choctaw Indian agent and, maintaining his close ties with that tribe, became the colonel of the First Choctaw and Chickasaw Mounted Rifles when the war started. Cooper commanded Confederate forces in the Indian Territory at this time and gathered soldiers in mid-October at Old

Fort Wayne, not far from the Arkansas border. The skirmish near Old Fort Wayne occurred on October 22, lasted only a few minutes, and was indeed a "skedaddle," as Ellithorpe reported. Ezra J. Warner, *Generals in Gray: Lives of the Confederate Commanders* (Baton Rouge: Louisiana State University Press, 1999), 61–62; Manning, *Biographical Historical and Miscellaneous,* 25; Banasik, *Embattled Arkansas,* 245.

28. Union losses were four killed and three wounded in the Second Kansas Cavalry. The Confederates lost sixty-three total casualties and four artillery pieces. Banasik, *Embattled Arkansas,* 245.

29. Fort Davis, a log structure, was located across the river from Fort Gibson. Grant Foreman, "Fort Davis," *Chronicles of Oklahoma* 17 (June 1939): 148.

30. Confederate troopers were on the move, but James S. Rains had been relieved of duty in October. About two thousand Confederate cavalrymen marched into the Cane Hill, Ark., region in mid-November 1862 on a foraging operation. Shea, *Fields of Blood,* 70.

31. Camp Babcock was named for a beef contractor. Christ, "*This Day We Marched Again,*" 45 n. 91.

32. The Flint Creek camp was located about twenty-two miles northwest of Cane Hill. Shea, *Fields of Blood,* 91.

33. Hindman's army totaled approximately twelve thousand at the battle of Prairie Grove on December 7. Banasik, *Embattled Arkansas,* 517.

34. William H. Rhea was a Confederate sympathizer judging from the fact that he charged Union soldiers twice as much for his flour than Confederates were charged. Shea, *Fields of Blood,* 94; Hughes, "Wartime Gristmill Destruction," 36.

35. Lt. George W. Dobler of the First Indian Home Guards would be cashiered from the service for defrauding the government. This situation is explained in more detail in chapter 6.

36. Gen. George B. McClellan was removed from command of the Army of the Potomac on November 7, 1862, ending his controversial tenure in that post. Warner, *Generals in Blue,* 292.

37. Possibly refers to L. H. Hapgood, a thirty-four-year-old merchant residing in Franklin County, Vt., the county where Ellithorpe was born. *Eighth Census of the United* States, Franklin County, Vt., 620.

38. First Lt. Matthew H. Masterson had just received his commission in October and was killed by guerrillas on November 1. John W. Rabb commanded the Second Indiana Battery that consisted of "four six-pound brass James Rifles and two brass six-pound smoothbores." Rabb's Battery served in the trans-Mississippi until the fall of 1864, when it was transferred to Tennessee. Christ, "*This Day We Marched,*" 44 n. 87; Banasik, *Reluctant Cannoneer,* 30; Dyer, *Compendium,* 2:1111.

39. Thomas Livingston, a prewar Missouri miner, organized the "Cherokee Spikes," a guerrilla band, in February 1862. Livingston's men joined with Stand Watie's in September 1862, but it is unlikely that Livingston's men were responsible for the death described because they operated primarily in southwestern Missouri. In January and February 1863 Ellithorpe and his men engaged in combat several times with Livingston's men. Bruce Nichols, *Guerrilla Warfare in Civil War Missouri,* vol. 1: *1862* (Jefferson, N.C.: McFarland, 2012), 37, 176.

40. Col. Sanford Faulkner, a resident of Little Rock, got lost in the Arkansas countryside about 1840 and stopped at a squatter's cabin to ask directions. Unwilling to offer hospitality at first, the squatter was won over when Faulkner played the next "turn" of the fiddle tune "Arkansas Traveler" that the squatter was performing. Eventually, the Arkansas Traveler became a cultural phenomenon that included sheet music, a painting, and the development of a stereotype. *Encyclopedia of Arkansas History & Culture,* s.v. "Arkansas Traveler," accessed November 17, 2014, www.encyclopediaofarkansas.net/encyclopedia/entry-detail.aspx?search=1&entryID=505.

41. It is clear from Ellithorpe's journal entries that he did not accompany the scout; instead, his description is probably based on verbal accounts from participants.

42. Ellithorpe was referring to Rhea's Mill.

43. Organized in Milwaukee in the fall of 1861, the Ninth Wisconsin Infantry, composed mostly of German immigrants, served in trans-Mississippi throughout the war. Dyer, *Compendium*, 2:1677.

44. A reference to humorist Marcus Lafayette Byrn, *The Life and Adventures of an Arkansaw Doctor by David Rattlehead, M.D.*, published in 1851. *Encyclopedia of Arkansas History & Culture*, s.v. "Arts, Culture, and Entertainment" accessed November 17, 2014, www.encyclopediaofarkansas.net/encyclopedia/entry-detail.aspx?search=1&entryID=386.

45. Capt. Matthew Quigg served as commander of Company B in the Tenth Kansas Infantry. He never became an officer in the First Indian Home Guards but did command the Eighteenth Kansas Militia during Price's Missouri Raid in 1864. Burke, *Official Military History;* Paul Kirkman, *The Battle of Westport: Missouri's Great Confederate Raid* (Charleston, S.C.: History Press, 2011), 146.

46. Capt. J. C. Stanley entered "under a flag of truce to advise Blunt of a problem with some paroled prisoners." When Stanley returned to Brig. Gen. John S. Marmaduke he reported the approximate size and the condition of the Union camp. Shea, *Fields of Blood*, 91.

47. Ellithorpe probably was referring to Dr. Rufus Gilpatrick (or Gillpatrick), an uncle and brother-in-law of Blunt's. Blunt married Nancy G. Putnam in 1850, and Gilpatrick was married to Nancy's sister, Elizabeth. Gilpatrick had been one of Blunt's teachers at the Starling Medical College in Columbus, Ohio. In 1855 Gilpatrick had arrived in Kansas, where he became a stanch Free State advocate. He helped organize the Republican Party in Kansas and was elected to the House of Representatives in 1860. Robert Collins, *General James G. Blunt: Tarnished Glory* (Gretna, La.: Pelican, 2005), 17; W. A. Johnson, *The History of Anderson County, Kansas, from Its First Settlement to the Fourth of July, 1876* (n.p.: Kauffman & Iler, 1877), 205–7; Bryce D. Benedict, *Jayhawkers: The Civil War Brigade of James Henry Lane* (Norman: University of Oklahoma Press, 2009), 54.

48. The Hermann family ran the Dutch Mills, which "changed hands four times during the Prairie Grove campaign." Some of the Union Indian soldiers passed through Dutch Mills on November 14. Hughes, "Wartime Gristmill Destruction," 36–37; Clarence Evans, "Memoirs, Letters, and Diary Entries of German Settlers in Northwest Arkansas, 1853–1863," *Arkansas Historical Quarterly* 6 (Fall 1947): 242.

CHAPTER 4. THE PRAIRIE GROVE CAMPAIGN

1. Shea, *Fields of Blood*, 93.

2. Ibid., 4, 6; *Encyclopedia of Arkansas History & Culture*, s.v. "Prairie Grove Campaign," accessed October 7, 2014, www.encyclopediaofarkansas.net/encyclopedia/entry-detail.aspx?entryID=514&media=print.

3. Col. W. F. Cloud to Maj. A. C. Ellithorpe, December 1, 1862, Ellithorpe Family Papers, Kansas Historical Society; Shea, *Fields of Blood*, 90; Banasik, *Embattled Arkansas*, 262–63, 289.

4. *Encyclopedia of Arkansas History & Culture*, s.v. "Cane Hill (Washington County)," accessed October 7, 2014, www.encyclopediaofarkansas.net/encyclopedia/entry-detail.aspx?entryID=2705.

5. Shea, *Fields of Blood*, 128; *Encyclopedia of Arkansas History & Culture*, s.v. "Prairie Grove Campaign."

6. Zellar, *African Creeks*, 62–63; United States War Department, *War of the Rebellion*, ser. 1, 22,

pt. 1, 92–94, 121; A. C. Ellithorpe to Col. N. P. Chipman, January 7, 1863, Ellithorpe Compiled Service Record, National Archives.

7. *Official Records*, ser. 1, 22, pt. 1, 85, 93–94; Carbutt, *Biographical Sketches*, 257; "Biography," 13; Pension records on Albert C. Ellithorpe, RG T-288, Invalid Record Application 1033517, National Archives.

8. Ellithorpe dated his entry November 29, but the action at Cane Hill occurred on November 28. Shea, *Fields of Blood*, 93.

9. Col. William F. Cloud's Third Brigade, which included the First Indian Home Guards, led the way. Col. William Weer's Second Brigade and Brig. Gen. Frederick Salomon's First Brigade followed. Stockton's Ohio Battery (six guns), Tenney's First Kansas Battery (six guns), Rabb's Second Indiana Battery (six guns), and Hopkins's Kansas Battery (four guns) comprised part of the force, as did the two mountain howitzers of the Third Wisconsin Cavalry's artillery, the two mountain howitzers of the Sixth Kansas Cavalry artillery, the two mountain howitzers of the Ninth Kansas Cavalry artillery, and the two mountain howitzers of the Second Kansas Cavalry artillery. Banasik, *Embattled Arkansas*, 506–7.

10. Actually, only Capt. Joseph Bledsoe's Missouri Battery (two guns) and Capt. John C. Shoup's Arkansas Battery (two guns) participated in the action. Shea, *Fields of Blood*, 94, 96.

11. The Confederate force numbered approximately 1,953, far less than Ellithorpe's estimate, and Union forces totaled about 5,216. Banasik, *Embattled Arkansas*, 498, 506–7.

12. Union losses were less than Ellithorpe stated and totaled "eight killed and thirty-six wounded." Confederate casualties were "ten killed and upward of seventy wounded or missing." Shea, *Fields of Blood*, 104.

13. A. F. Bicking served as a first lieutenant in Company A of the First Indian Home Guards. National Park Service, Soldiers and Sailors Database, accessed November 13, 2014, www.nps.gov/civilwar/search-soldiers-detail.htm?soldierId=C3463082-DC7A-DF11-BF36-B8AC6F5D926A.

14. Frederick Crafts served as a first lieutenant in Company I of the First Indian Home Guards. Soldiers and Sailors Database, accessed November 13, 2014, www.nps.gov/civilwar/search-soldiers-detail.htm?soldierId=BB698291-DC7A-DF11-BF36-B8AC6F5D926A.

15. Francis J. Fox served a first lieutenant in Company E of the First Indian Home Guards. Soldiers and Sailors Database, accessed November 13, 2014, www.nps.gov/civilwar/search-soldiers-detail.htm?-soldierId=6F775E9E-DC7A-DF11-BF36-B8AC6F5D926A.

16. Solomon C. Hall served as a first lieutenant in Company F of the First Indian Home Guards. Soldiers and Sailors Database, accessed November 13, 2014, www.nps.gov/civilwar/search-soldiers-detail.htm?soldierId=CE6474A4-DC7A-DF11-BF36-B8AC6F5D926A.

17. Edwin Cassander Manning served as a first lieutenant in Company C of the First Indian Home Guards. He wrote *Biographical Historical and Miscellaneous Selections*, which contains some information about his military service. Soldiers and Sailors Database, accessed November 13, 2014, www.nps.gov/civilwar/search-soldiers-detail.htm?soldierId=CBBEC4B5-DC7A-DF11-BF36-B8AC6F5D926A.

18. Brig. Gen. John S. Marmaduke, a Missouri native, graduated from the United States Military Academy in 1857. He fought at the battle of Shiloh as colonel of the Third Confederate Infantry in Brig. Gen. Thomas C. Hindman's brigade. Marmaduke achieved fame, though, as a cavalry leader and participated in many cavalry actions until taken prisoner at the battle of Mine Creek, Kans., in October 1864. Warner, *Generals in Gray*, 211–12; O. Edward Cunningham, *Shiloh and the Western Campaign of 1862*, ed. Gary D. Joiner and Timothy B. Smith (New York: Savas Beatie, 2007), 402–3.

19. A native Kentuckian, Col. Joseph Orville Shelby participated in the Missouri-Kansas border war of the 1850s and organized a cavalry company when the war started. A gifted cavalry leader, Shelby campaigned actively throughout the war in the trans-Mississippi. Warner, *Generals in Gray,* 273–74.

20. Col. Emmett MacDonald commanded a cavalry brigade in Marmaduke's division that consisted of Young's Missouri Cavalry, Crump's Texas Cavalry, and West's Arkansas Battery. A Missourian, MacDonald was captured at Camp Jackson, Mo., on May 10, 1861. He served on Maj. Gen. Sterling Price's staff at Wilson's Creek and commanded an artillery battery at Pea Ridge. Shea, *Fields of Blood,* 292; William Garrett Piston and Richard W. Hatcher III, *Wilson's Creek: The Second Battle of the Civil War and the Men Who Fought It,* Civil War America (Chapel Hill: University of North Carolina Press, 2000), 311; Richard C. Peterson et al., *Sterling Price's Lieutenants: A Guide to the Officers and Organization of the Missouri State Guard, 1861–1865,* rev. ed., (Independence, Mo.: Two Trails Publishing, 2007), 41 n. 194.

21. William Clarke Quantrill, a native of Ohio, because one of the most infamous guerrilla leaders of the war. When the war started he joined a Missouri guerrilla band and then created his own band. In November 1862 Quantrill arrived in Hindman's camps, and he mustered the group as an independent cavalry company and put them in Shelby's brigade under the command of Lt. William Gregg. Albert Castel, *Civil War Kansas: Reaping the Whirlwind* (Lawrence: University Press of Kansas, 1997), 102–3; Shea, *Fields of Blood,* 84, 292.

22. Lt. Col. Owen A. Bassett commanded the Second Kansas Cavalry and its battery. Shea, *Fields of Blood,* 290.

23. During the skirmish at Old Fort Wayne, the four guns of Capt. Sylvanus Howell's Texas Battery were captured. Five days after the skirmish, the "Trophy Battery" was organized and given the four captured guns. The battery was composed of the men of the Second Kansas Cavalry's Company B under the command of Capt. Henry Hopkins. Ralph A. Wooster, *Lone Star Regiments in Gray* (Austin: Eakin Press, 2002), 296–97; Burke, *Official Military History,* 37.

24. Capt. John W. Rabb's Indiana Battery suffered one man killed and four wounded during the Cane Hill engagement. During the fight one solid shot from Shoup's Arkansas Battery killed a soldier and two horses belonging to Rabb's Battery. *Official Records,* ser. 1, 22, pt. 1, 48; Shea, *Fields of Blood,* 96.

25. Hindman's army did not retreat to Van Buren until after the battle of Prairie Grove. His army left the battlefield sometime before midnight on December 7 and reached Van Buren, located on the Arkansas River about fifty-two miles south of Prairie Grove, on December 11. Shea, *Fields of Blood,* 242, 247.

26. Ellithorpe was possibly referring to the Pyeatte-Moore Mill (also called the Moore-Buchanan Mill) that was built in the 1830s. The mill was used to grind wheat and corn but also "to saw logs, and even to card wool." The draw wheel has survived and may be seen on Jordan Creek where it was moved to in 1902. *Encyclopedia of Arkansas History & Culture,* s.v. "Cane Hill (Washington County)," accessed October 7, 2014.

27. Only a captain in the First Iowa Infantry when the war started, Francis J. Herron was commissioned as a brigadier general at age twenty-five to date from July 16, 1862. After fighting at the battle of Wilson's Creek, Herron won his promotion by rendering extraordinary service as colonel of the Ninth Iowa Infantry during the battle of Pea Ridge. Warner, *Generals in Blue,* 228–29.

28. Hindman's army numbered about twelve thousand men, far less than Ellithorpe's estimate but still more than the Army of the Frontier's ninety-five hundred men. Banasik, *Embattled Arkansas,* 517, 534.

29. Leaders from both armies met on the morning of December 8, and Blunt granted a six-hour

truce to allow for the gathering of the wounded and the burial of the dead. It was apparent to Blunt at the time that Hindman's army was already retreating from the battlefield. Shea, *Fields of Blood,* 245–46.

30. Blunt and Hindman reported casualties that were nearly equal. The Army of the Frontier suffered losses of 175 killed, 813 wounded, and 263 captured or missing, for a total of 1,251 casualties. Hindman reported losses of 164 killed, 817 wounded, and 336 missing, for a total of 1,317. *Official Records,* ser. 1, 22, pt. 1, 86, 142.

31. Ellithorpe left blank space in his journal after this entry as well as the next one. Regrettably, he never went back to describe the battlefield or to write about his interviews with Confederate officers.

32. Several hospitals were established in Fayetteville, and they were indeed full. Initially, there were many inefficiencies in dealing with the wounded, but these problems were resolved after Union surgeon Ira Russell arrived on December 23 and took charge. Shea, *Fields of Blood,* 258–59.

CHAPTER 5. REGIMENTAL TURMOIL

1. Pension records on Stephen Wattles, RG T-288, Invalid Record Application 765519, National Archives; Wattles Compiled Service Record, National Archives.

2. Grant Foreman, "Fort Davis," *Chronicles of Oklahoma* 17 (June 1939): 148; Shea, *Fields of Blood,* 269, 273.

3. Gary W. Gallagher and Kathryn Shively Meier, "Coming to Terms with Civil War Military History," *Journal of the Civil War Era* 4 (December 2014): 496. Interested readers should examine *Visualizing Emancipation,* a project funded by a National Endowment for the Humanities "We the People" grant and maintained by the University of Richmond. The project's map shows the chronological course of emancipation. The project needs more input from trans-Mississippi sources but is still quite informative. dsl.richmond.edu/emancipation/about/; *Chicago Evening Journal,* January 29, 1863; Nichols, *Lincoln and the Indians,* 60.

4. Abiding by the terms of a truce, Union soldiers "transported Hindman's wounded to Boonsboro. Nearly every building in town was filled with broken humanity." Shea, *Fields of Blood,* 260.

5. Brig. Gen. James G. Blunt praised the services of several of his aide-de-camps during the battle of Prairie Grove, including Lt. H. G. Loring. During the battle of Honey Springs on July 17, 1863, Loring served as Blunt's acting assistant adjutant general. United States War Department, *War of the Rebellion,* ser. 1, 22, pt. 1, 77, 448.

6. This is a reference to Ellithorpe's wife, Maria Louise.

7. Ellithorpe's assessment of the importance of Prairie Grove is accurate. Modern historian William L. Shea refers to the battle as "a resounding strategic victory" for Union forces. Shea, *Fields of Blood,* 265.

8. J. Irvine Dungan, a soldier in the Nineteenth Iowa Infantry, wrote that after Prairie Grove, men in his regiment found "several copies" of Maj. Gen. Thomas C. Hindman's order "printed on poor paper." Blunt sarcastically wrote Hindman: "I avail myself of this opportunity to express to you my thanks for the very flattering description of the troops under my command, as contained in your address of December 4, to your soldiers upon the eve of battle. Your instructions to your soldiers to pick off my officers smacks very strongly of chivalry, and when they are especially directed to pick off mounted officers, I consider them as complimentary to myself." J. Irvine Dungan, *History of the Nine-*

teenth Regiment Iowa Volunteer Infantry (Davenport, Iowa: Publishing House of Luse & Griggs, 1865), 64; *Official Records*, ser. 1, 22, pt. 1, 81.

9. Pin Indians refer to members of the Cherokee's Keetoowah Society. Sometime before the war, members started wearing crossed pins to denote membership. They were full-blood Cherokee who supported Chief John Ross's neutrality stance. Warde, *When the Wolf Came*, 36–37.

10. William Gannaway Brownlow grew up near Knoxville, Tenn., and became a Methodist minister in 1826. His other occupation was as a newspaper editor, and his staunch Unionist viewpoints led to his arrest and later banishment by Confederate officials. "Parson" Brownlow's writings and lectures were popular among many northerners. Faust, *Historical Times Illustrated Encyclopedia*, 85.

11. Brig. Gen. John S. Marmaduke requested permission to send medical supplies to wounded Confederate soldiers under a flag of truce. Hindman indeed asked permission to make a "plat" of the battlefield. Blunt replied to Hindman by writing that his request was "a very modest one, and will be granted, provided you allow me to send an artist to your present camp to sketch it and the approaches leading thereto. Such little courtesies must be reciprocated." Hindman failed to respond. *Official Records*, ser. 1, 22, pt. 1, 81–82.

12. Prices continued to rise in the Confederacy. By early 1863 flour cost "$200 per barrel, boots sold for $106 a pair, and tea cost $10 a pound in Little Rock." A Confederate soldier stationed there reported other prices: "Butter $2.50 per lb., Eggs $2. per dozen, chickens $2. each. Pepper $10.00 per lb., Flour 60 cents per lb. &c &c." Quotes from Mark K. Christ, *Civil War Arkansas, 1863: The Battle for a State* (Norman: University of Oklahoma Press, 2010), 98.

13. Ellithorpe's letter dated December 23, 1862, was published in the *Chicago Evening Journal* on January 8, 1863.

14. The British .577 caliber Enfield rifle was an accurate weapon and comparable to the Springfield rifle. Faust, *Historical Times Illustrated Encyclopedia*, 243–44.

15. The model 1855 Colt Revolving Rifle was not a particularly popular weapon among soldiers because of the dangerous tendency of several or all of the chambers to ignite at once. Part of the Thirty-Seventh Illinois Infantry was armed with the weapon at Prairie Grove. Lord, *Civil War Collector's Encyclopedia*, 251; Michael A. Mullins, *The Fremont Rifles: A History of the 37th Illinois Veteran Volunteer Infantry* (Wilmington, N.C.: Broadfoot Publishing Co., 1990), 16.

The model 1858 Merrill carbine was a breech-loading weapon. William B. Edwards, *Civil War Guns: The Complete Story of Federal and Confederate Small Arms* (Secaucus, N.J.: Castle 1978), 119.

16. The Model 1841 Mississippi Rifle was sometimes referred to as the "Yager," an Americanization of the German word *Jaeger*. Lord, *Civil War Collector's Encyclopedia*, 242–43.

Other Union soldiers also expressed surprise that the Confederates were armed with such good weapons. Thanks to Hindman's diligence and the efforts of officials east of the Mississippi River, most of the Confederate soldiers at Prairie Grove had adequate weapons. Shea, *Fields of Blood*, 260; C. L. Webster III, *Entrepôt: Government Imports into the Confederate States* (Roseville, Minn.: Edinborough Press, 2010), 181–84.

17. None of the Confederate batteries at Prairie Grove were armed with Parrott guns, but the Confederate army had thirty-one artillery pieces at Prairie Grove. Banasik, *Embattled Arkansas*, 512–17.

18. Eighteen infantry regiments, two sharpshooter battalions, thirteen cavalry units, and eight artillery batteries comprised the Confederate army. Shea, *Fields of Blood*, 291–92.

19. Little Rock, the capital of Arkansas, numbered 3,727 residents in 1860. During much of 1862

and until March 1863 the city served as the headquarters for the Confederacy's Trans-Mississippi Department. Richard N. Current, ed., *Encyclopedia of the Confederacy* (New York: Simon & Schuster, 1993), 2:939, 941.

20. Ellithorpe was probably referring to the Creek Agency located just a few miles west of Fort Davis; however, an older location for the agency was north of the Arkansas River and within just a few miles of the Verdigris River. Goins and Goble, *Historical Atlas of Oklahoma*, 49.

21. Four steam transports, the *Frederick Notrebe*, the *Key West*, the *Rose Douglas*, and the *Violet* were captured and burned at Van Buren. Shea, *Fields of Blood*, 274, 280.

22. Two Union soldiers were killed and six were wounded during the raid on Van Buren. Confederate losses are unknown, but William L. Shea estimated that there were twelve killed, twenty-four wounded, and "several hundred" captured or paroled. Ibid., 281.

23. A native of Connecticut, American general Benedict Arnold turned traitor and tried to turn West Point over to the British in exchange for money. That plan failed, but Arnold became a British brigadier general and even launched attacks on his home state. Mark M. Boatner III, *Encyclopedia of the American Revolution* (New York: David McKay Co., 1966), 25, 29, 35–37.

24. Due to poor health, Brig. Gen. John M. Schofield turned command of the Army of the Frontier over to Blunt on November 20 but reclaimed his army command on January 1, 1863. Blunt returned to his command of the District of Kansas at Fort Leavenworth. Vindictive and jealous, Schofield spent a lifetime attempting "to blacken the reputations of Curtis, Blunt, and Herron." Shea, *Fields of Blood*, 71–72, 285–86.

25. Issued on January 1, 1863, by President Abraham Lincoln, the Emancipation Proclamation freed slaves in areas of rebellion. Faust, *Historical Times Illustrated Encyclopedia*, 242.

26. Part of the Compromise of 1850, the Fugitive Slave Act strengthened the ability of slaveholders to retrieve runaway slaves, however, many abolitionists refused to obey it and some northern states passed laws designed to weaken it. Ibid., 294.

27. Both men were "leaders of the loyal Cherokees then staying at Neosho, Missouri." Warde, *When the Wolf Came*, 143.

28. The Army of the Potomac had been defeated at the battle of Fredericksburg on December 13, 1862, and then about five weeks later endured the embarrassing "Mud March." The army then remained fairly static until the beginning of the Chancellorsville campaign in April 1863. Mark M. Boatner III, *The Civil War Dictionary* (New York: David McKay Co., 1959), 136, 313, 573.

CHAPTER 6. GUERRILLA WARFARE

1. Gallagher and Meier, "Coming to Terms with Civil War Military History," 492–93; Daniel E. Sutherland, *A Savage Conflict: The Decisive Role of Guerrillas in the American Civil War* (Chapel Hill: University of North Carolina Press, 2009), 75; Sutherland, "Guerrillas," 133, 135; Michael Fellman, *Inside War: The Guerrilla Conflict in Missouri during the American Civil War* (New York: Oxford University Press, 1989), 98.

2. Sutherland, "Guerrillas," 136–38, 141, 151; Nichols, *Guerrilla Warfare in Civil War Missouri*, 1:39, 49, 212; Matthew M. Stith, "'The Deplorable Condition of the Country': Nature, Society, and War on the Trans-Mississippi Frontier," *Civil War History* 58 (September 2012): 323; Bruce Nichols, *Guerrilla Warfare in Civil War Missouri*, vol. 2: *1863* (Jefferson, N.C.: McFarland, 2012), 18.

3. Nichols, *Guerrilla Warfare,* 1:47–48, 50, 52, 54; Stith, "'Deplorable Condition,'" 324.

4. Nichols, *Guerrilla Warfare,* 1:58–59, 2:11; Fellman, *Inside War,* 87, 92–93.

5. *Chicago Evening Journal,* January 26, February 3, 11, 1863; Fellman, *Inside War,* 168, 178; Sutherland, *Savage Conflict,* 124.

6. Nichols, *Guerrilla Warfare,* 2:37, 161; Nichols, *Guerrilla Warfare,* 1:212.

7. Case MM377—Lt. George W. Dobler, Records of the Army Judge Advocate, Court-Martial Case Files, RG 153, National Archives.

8. Col. William A. Phillips to Maj. Gen. Samuel R. Curtis, February 10, 1863, Ellithorpe Family Papers, Kansas Historical Society; United States War Department, *War of the Rebellion,* ser. 1, 22, pt. 2, 57–58, 69, 163, 169.

9. *Leavenworth Daily Conservative,* December 31, 1862, April 29, 1863; Compiled Service Records of Union Volunteers from the State of Kansas, First Indian Home Guards, RG 94, National Archives; *Chicago Evening Journal,* February 26, 1863; Britton, *Memoirs,* 185; Lause, *Race and Radicalism,* 89.

10. The camp was named for Maj. Gen. Samuel R. Curtis then serving as the commander of the Department of the Missouri. Warner, *Generals in Blue,* 108.

11. Ellithorpe was referring to Col. Stand Watie, the commander of the First Cherokee Mounted Rifles. Ibid., 328.

12. The Sambo image developed in the seventeenth century or possibly earlier. Sambo was a black, comedic figure, a type of "Jester or Fool." Joseph Boskin, *Sambo: The Rise and Demise of an American Jester* (New York: Oxford University Press, 1986), 7–8.

13. There were no soldiers with the surname of McCall in Watie's First Cherokee Mounted Rifles.

14. This is a reference to 1st Lt. Solomon Hall of Company F in the First Indian Home Guards. No documentation of the charges preferred by him could be located. Soldiers and Sailors Database, accessed 11/13/14, www.nps.gov/civilwar/search-soldiers-detail.htm?soldierId=-CE6474A4-DC7A-DF11-BF36-B8AC6F5D926A.

15. The deadliness of pneumonia is an accurate assessment by Ellithorpe. The disease was "one of the most feared," and approximately 24 percent of white soldiers that contracted pneumonia died of the disease; the mortality rate was probably just as high among Indian soldiers. Alfred Jay Bollet, *Civil War Medicine: Challenges and Triumphs* (Tucson: Galen Press, 2002), 271.

16. Elizabeth Betsey Chapman was born in Connecticut in 1783 and died in Chicago in 1874 at the age of ninety. The *Los Angeles Daily Herald* reported that she had borne twelve children and "was the grandmother of 84 children, and the great grandmother of over 100 children" (March 21, 1874).

17. James G. Blunt was promoted to major general on March 16, 1863. Warner, *Generals in Blue,* 38.

18. Col. William A. Phillips detailed Maj. Moses B. Wright of the Second Indian Home Guards to serve as the president of the court-martial board. Case MM377—Lt. George W. Dobler, Court-Martial Case Files.

19. Majors and lieutenant colonels generally oversaw grand guards that were "the advanced posts of a camp or cantonment." Regulations, however, did allow for captains to perform this duty. United States Army Department, *Regulations for the Army of the United States* (New York: Harper & Brothers, 1861), 78–79.

20. First Lt. George W. Dobler served in Company G of the First Indian Home Guards. Soldiers and Sailors Database, accessed November 14, 2014, www.nps.gov/civilwar/search-soldiers-detail.htm?-soldierId=ECF2C696-DC7A-DF11-BF36-B8AC6F5D926A.

21. "The cold in clime are cold in blood, / Their love can scarce deserve the name" is a quote from Lord Byron's poem "The Giaour," written in 1813 (accessed December 11, 2014, www.bartleby.com/205/72.html).

22. Lt. Col. Lewis Downing of the Third Indian Home Guards was one of the founding members of the Keetoowah Society, an organization for full-blood Cherokee. In January 1863 Downing led a scout into the Indian Territory, where he distributed "flour and meal . . . to the most needy." Trevor Jones, "In Defense of Sovereignty: Cherokee Soldiers, White Officers, and Discipline in the Third Indian Home Guard," *Chronicles of Oklahoma* 82 (December 2004): 414; *Official Records*, ser. 1, 22, pt. 2, 85.

23. Sometime in early 1863 a group of Keechis and Tawakonies raided into the Muscogee Creek and Cherokee nations. At the same time Osage Indians resided in their own reservation in southeastern Kansas, and members of various other tribes, including the Kickapoo, were in refugee camps in Kansas and Missouri. Warde, *When the Wolf Came*, 139, 142.

24. The battle of Murfreesboro (Stones River) occurred on December 31, 1862, and January 2, 1863, resulting in 24,645 combined casualties. E. B. Long, *The Civil War Day by Day* (1971; repr., New York: Da Capo Press, 1985), 302–3, 307.

25. On January 23, 1863, Lt. Col. James Stuart took 150 men and two howitzers from the First Arkansas Cavalry plus his own regiment, the Tenth Illinois Cavalry, on a scout to Van Buren. Stuart and his men captured and paroled 249 men from the steamer *Julia Roan*. The Union force suffered no casualties but reported that it had killed 6 enemy soldiers. *Official Records*, ser. 1, 22, pt. 1, 220–21.

26. Several regiments consisting of Arkansas unionists and other disaffected men were raised in Arkansas. Men from northwestern Arkansas comprised the First Arkansas Cavalry, which had been in service since August 1862. When Ellithorpe wrote this article, authorities were organizing the First Arkansas Light Artillery in Fayetteville and in Springfield, Mo., and in March 1863 the First Arkansas Infantry was mustered in Fayetteville. Dyer, *Compendium*, 2:997–99.

27. The Cherokee Council convened on February 4, 1863, reasserted its loyalty to the United States, and emancipated slaves in the Cherokee Nation. Abel, *American Indian in the Civil War*, 255–57.

28. Thomas Pegg served as a major in John Drew's Confederate but defected and became captain of Company E of the Third Indian Home Guards. Pegg served as the acting principal chief at the meeting of the Cherokee Council. Lt. Col. Lewis Downing served as the president pro-tempore. Warde, *When the Wolf Came*, 75, 137; Soldiers and Sailors Database, accessed November 14, 2014, www.nps.gov/civilwar/search-soldiers-detail.htm?soldierId=402B1FC2-DC7A-DF11-BF36-B8AC6F5D926A.

29. Second Lt. Avery T. Spencer served in Company D of the Ninth Kansas Cavalry. Soldiers and Sailors Database, accessed November 18, 2014, www.nps.gov/civilwar/search-soldiers-detail.htm?soldierId=E10EC8D3-DC7A-DF11-BF36-B8AC6F5D926A.

The scouting party consisted of thirty-eight men from the Ninth Kansas Cavalry, and guerrillas killed five men from the Ninth Kansas, including Lieutenant Spencer. Nichols, *Guerrilla Warfare*, 2:18.

CHAPTER 7. CLOSING WAR SCENES

1. Pension records on Albert C. Ellithorpe, RG T-288, Invalid Record Application 1033517, National Archives.

2. Lause, *Race and Radicalism*, 89; Warde, *When the Wolf Came*, 145; *Chicago Evening Journal*, May 20, 1863; United States War Department, *War of the Rebellion*, ser. 1, 22, pt. 2, 6; Shea, *Fields of Blood*,

286–87, 334 n. 8; Kip Lindberg and Matt Matthews, "'To Play a Bold Game': The Battle of Honey Springs," *North & South* 6, no. 1 (December 2002): 59.

3. Lindberg and Matthews, "'To Play a Bold Game,'" 60, 68; Spurgeon, *Soldiers in the Army of Freedom*, 166.

4. *Chicago Evening Journal*, March 18, 1864; Warde, *When the Wolf Came*, 200–201; Whit Edwards, *"The Prairie Was on Fire": Eyewitness Accounts of the Civil War in the Indian Territory* (Oklahoma City: Oklahoma Historical Society, 2001), 90.

5. Richard J. Hinton, *Rebel Invasion of Missouri and Kansas and the Campaign of the Army of the Border against General Sterling Price in October and November 1864* (1865; repr., Ottawa: Kansas Heritage Press, 1994), 255; *Leavenworth Daily Conservative*, November 29, 1864; Carbutt, *Biographical Sketches*, 257; Albert Castel, *Civil War Kansas: Reaping the Whirlwind* (Lawrence: University Press of Kansas, 1997), 177; Richard N. Current, ed., *Encyclopedia of the Confederacy* (New York: Simon & Schuster, 1993), 3:1252–54.

6. Kyle S. Sinisi, *The Last Hurrah: Sterling Price's Missouri Expedition of 1864* (Lanham, Md.: Rowman & Littlefield, 2015), 230–31; Current, *Encyclopedia of the Confederacy*, 3:1254–55; *Official Records*, ser. 1, 41, pt. 1, 547–48; Hinton, *Rebel Invasion*, xii–xiii, 255–56; Warner, *Generals in Blue*, 410–11.

7. Faust, *Historical Times Illustrated Encyclopedia*, 474; Larry Wood, *The Two Civil War Battles of Newtonia* (Charleston, S.C.: History Press, 2010), 131; Current, *Encyclopedia of the Confederacy*, 3:1253; *Leavenworth Daily Conservative*, November 26, November 29, 1864; Castel, *Civil War Kansas*, 199, 202; Carbutt, *Biographical Sketches*, 257.

8. Abel, *American Indian in the Civil War*, 219 n. 618; E. B. French to Hon. Sidney Clark, February 14, 1865, Ellithorpe Family Papers, Kansas Historical Society.

9. According to William L. Shea: "The Prairie Grove campaign was the last significant Confederate offensive west of the Mississippi River. . . . The Confederates abandoned nearly everything north of the Arkansas River, and the Federals shifted their attention and their resources to other theaters." Shea, *Fields of Blood*, 287.

10. Following the defeat at Prairie Grove, morale dropped in Maj. Gen. Thomas C. Hindman's army resulting in heavy desertions by Arkansas conscripts and significant desertions from some of the Texas regiments. Ibid., 250–51.

11. A Mexican War veteran and former governor of Missouri, Maj. Gen. Sterling Price had fought at Wilson's Creek and Pea Ridge in the trans-Mississippi as well as Iuka and Corinth in Mississippi. The popular Price returned to Arkansas in March 1863 and was warmly welcomed by his new command, an infantry division comprising Brig. Gen. Mosby M. Parsons's Missouri brigade and Brig. Gen. Dandridge McRae's Arkansas brigade. Mark K. Christ, *Civil War Arkansas, 1863: The Battle for a State* (Norman: University of Oklahoma Press, 2010), 101–2.

12. Soon after Col. William A. Phillips Indian brigade arrived at Fort Blunt (Gibson) on April 13, the men started constructing earthworks and additional buildings. Warde, *When the Wolf Came*, 145.

13. Colonel Phillips's force attacked Col. Stand Watie's First Cherokee Mounted Rifles at Webber's Falls in a dawn assault on April 25, 1863. The Confederates were routed and much of their equipment seized. The attack was timed to occur on the day that Watie was to preside at a meeting of the Cherokee Council. The Confederates lost at least three killed and an unreported number were captured. Phillips's command lost one killed and ten wounded. *Official Records*, ser. 1, 22, pt. 1, 314–15; Edwards, *"The Prairie Was on Fire,"* 41–42; Britton, *Memoirs*, 226.

14. Dr. Rufus Gillpatrick was indeed summoned to aid a wounded Confederate soldier. Wiley Britton, a soldier that participated in the skirmish as part of the Sixth Kansas Cavalry, wrote in his memoirs, "After the skirmish was over, he [Dr. Gillpatrick] was called upon by a rebel woman to dress the wound of a rebel soldier, who had fallen a hundred yards of so from where we halted." Gillpatrick "was basely slain by a small force of the dispersed rebels that came out of the cane." According to a postwar account, Gillpatrick was "a secret detective on the border (a most difficult and hazardous service)." Britton, *Memoirs*, 226; *Official Records*, ser. 1, 22, pt. 1, 315; W. A. Johnson, *The History of Anderson County, Kansas, from Its First Settlement to the Fourth of July, 1876* (Kauffman & Iler, 1877), 205–7.

15. Ellithorpe was not exaggerating the dangers for Unionists who publically expressed their loyalties, but eventually it became dangerous for Confederate supporters to express their sympathies. A well-written and absorbing trans-Mississippi classic by William Baxter, a resident of Fayetteville, illustrates the perils of being a Unionist. Baxter, *Pea Ridge and Prairie Grove; Or, Scenes and Incidents of the War in Arkansas* (1864; repr., Fayetteville: University of Arkansas Press, 2000).

16. In his February 11, 1863, *Chicago Evening Journal* article, Ellithorpe wrote, "He is here—famine is sitting upon the thresholds of almost every cabin in the country." It is highly unlikely that there were as many provisions available in northwestern Arkansas, as Ellithorpe suggested, but perhaps he was referring to potentially greater agricultural production if the Union army permanently occupied the region.

17. Maj. Gen. Samuel R. Curtis, an abolitionist Republican based in St. Louis as commander of the Department of the Missouri, tangled too often with "conservative, proslavery Democrats" such as Missouri governor Hamilton R. Gamble. President Abraham Lincoln removed Curtis from command of the Department in May and appointed the newly promoted Maj. Gen. John M. Schofield in his place. Curtis eventually commanded the Department of Kansas and helped repulse Price's expedition in the fall of 1864. Schofield remained in command of the department until January 1864. Warner, *Generals in Blue*, 108, 426; Shea, *Fields of Blood*, 286.

18. Maj. Gen. James G. Blunt reported that he had "less than 3,000 men" when he left Fort Blunt on July 15 to attack the Confederate army camped near Elk Creek. *Official Records*, ser. 1, 22, pt. 1, 447.

19. Located about forty miles north of Fort Blunt (Gibson), the crossing of Cabin Creek was on the Texas Road. In the prewar period, "Greenbriar" Joe Martin built a two-story brick house near the Cabin Creek crossing and owned as many as 103 slaves; the house was destroyed during the war. The First Cabin Creek skirmish occurred on July 1–2, 1863, when Confederate troops made an unsuccessful attempt to capture a Federal wagon train. Steven L. Warren, *Brilliant Victory: The Second Civil War Battle of Cabin Creek, Indian Territory, September 19, 1864* (Wyandotte, Okla.: Gregath Publishing Co., 2002), 7–8; *Encyclopedia of Oklahoma History & Culture*, s.v. "Battles of Cabin Creek," accessed November 24, 2014, digital.library.okstate.edu/encyclopedia/entries/C/CA001.html.

20. Confederates actively campaigned in the Indian Territory in the spring of 1863 and threatened the supply lines leading to Fort Blunt (Gibson) so effectively that the fort was in effect besieged. Edwards, *"Prairie Was on Fire,"* 44.

21. There were no Arkansas units present at the battle of Honey Springs, but there were Chickasaw, Cherokee, Choctaw, Muscogee Creeks, and Texas soldiers in Brig. Gen. Douglas H. Cooper's Confederate force. Lindberg and Matthews, "'To Play a Bold Game,'" 61.

22. Tennessee native David Crockett played up his frontier background and common man origins while he served in the U.S. House of Representatives. Following a failed reelection bid, he migrated to Texas in 1835 where he was executed as a prisoner following the battle of the Alamo in March 1836.

Stephen L. Hardin, *Texian Iliad: A Military History of the Texas Revolution, 1835–1836* (Austin: University of Texas Press, 1994), 117–18, 148–49.

23. Much of the battle of Honey Springs occurred along Elk Creek. Blunt was ill that day and suffered from chills and a fever, possibly a result of malaria. He collapsed on the morning of the battle but recovered sufficiently to actively deploy troops during the battle. Lindberg and Matthews, "'To Play a Bold Game,'" 61–62, 65.

24. The First Kansas Colored Infantry was not a part of the expedition into the Choctaw and Chickasaw Nations. Col. William A. Phillips commanded a force comprising "450 mounted men" made up of parts of the First Indian Home Guards, the Third Indian Home Guards, one battalion of the Fourteenth Kansas Cavalry, and "a section of Kaufman's howitzers." *Official Records*, ser. 1, 34, pt. 1, 107, 111.

25. Colonel Phillips estimated that 250 enemy soldiers were killed and twenty were captured during the expedition. Ibid., 108.

26. An outbreak of smallpox occurred in the spring of 1863 at Fort Blunt (Gibson) resulting in deaths among the Indian refugees and Indian soldiers. In the fall of 1863, smallpox claimed the lives of several men from the First Kansas Colored Infantry stationed at Fort Smith, Arkansas. Britton, *Memoirs*, 367; Spurgeon, *Soldiers in the Army of Freedom*, 180–81.

27. Holata Micco (Billy Bowlegs), the principal chief of the Seminoles died of smallpox sometime between September 1863 and March 1864. Kenneth W. Porter, "Billy Bowlegs (Holuta Micco) in the Civil War, Pt. II," *Florida Historical Quarterly* 45 (April 1967): 400.

28. In 1866 the Reconstruction Treaties were negotiated between the federal government and each of the Five Civilized Tribes (the Cherokee, Chickasaw, Choctaw, Muscogee Creeks, and Seminoles). The treaties all contained provisions for granting freedom to slaves owned by tribal members, however, the tribes differed on how the freedmen were to be treated. A variety of ideas were considered with one being to provide land allotments from the "Unassigned Lands" (present-day central Oklahoma) for the freedmen from these tribes. Warde, *When the Wolf Came*, 274–75.

29. On October 10, 1864, Maj. Gen. George Sykes was relieved of command of the District of South Kansas and replaced by Blunt. Sykes, an 1842 United State Military Academy graduate, served in several eastern campaigns before being relieved in December 1863 and transferred to Kansas. *Official Records*, ser. 1, 41, pt. 1, 572; Warner, *Generals in Blue*, 492–93.

30. The vote was not quite unanimous, but Republican president Abraham Lincoln and his running mate, Andrew Johnson, carried all but six counties in Kansas. Democratic presidential candidate, George B. McClellan, won 3,794 civilian votes in Kansas compared to 14,200 for Lincoln. Samuel J. Crawford, *Kansas in the Sixties* (1911; repr., Ottawa: Kansas Heritage Press, 1994), 203; Castel, *Civil War Kansas*, 201.

31. Canadian-born John McNeil, a former Missouri state legislator and president of a St. Louis insurance company, served in Missouri throughout the Civil War. Commissioned as a brigadier general in the fall of 1862, he held a variety of commands in Missouri during the war. McNeil and his men participated in the running fight after the victory at Mine Creek described in Ellithorpe's article. Warner, *Generals in Blue*, 306.

Maj. Gen. Andrew Jackson Smith commanded two divisions of the Sixteenth Army Corps during Price's expedition. His men marched hundreds of miles in Missouri during the expedition but experienced little fighting. Warner, *Generals in Blue*, 454; *Official Records*, ser. 1, 41, pt. 1, 320–23.

Col. Samuel J. Crawford served as an aide to Maj. General Curtis and was present at the battle of Mine Creek. Two weeks after the battle, Crawford was elected governor of Kansas. Lumir F. Buresh, *October 25th and the Battle of Mine Creek* (Kansas City, Mo.: Lowell Press, 1977), 108, 128.

32. Trading Post was located about seven miles north of Mine Creek. Ibid., 60.

33. Men from the Third Iowa Cavalry captured Brig. Gen. John S. Marmaduke and Brig. Gen. William L. Cabell at the battle of Mine Creek. Warner, *Generals in Blue,* 41, 212; Buresh, *October 25th,* 133–34.

34. Lt. Col. Charles W. Blair, an aide of Curtis, commanded the Third Brigade in Blunt's division. He fought at the battle of Mine Creek and presented Marmaduke to Curtis. *Official Records,* ser. 1, 41, pt. 1, 596, 601, 604.

35. The battle at Mine Creek on October 25, 1864, and the fighting later that day along Little Osage Creek was a disaster for the Confederate army. Altogether about 300 or more Confederates were killed, about 250 were wounded, and 686 or more were captured. The Confederates lost eight artillery pieces at the battle. A number of Confederate soldiers were probably "killed while trying to surrender." Buresh, *October 25th,* 136, 179, 233; Sinisi, *Last Hurrah,* 289.

36. Maj. Gen. Alfred Pleasonton, an 1844 U.S. Military Academy graduate, served in the eastern theater until he was sent to Missouri in March 1864. He served fairly well during Price's expedition but informed Curtis that he was ill on October 26. Although misspelled, the town of Pleasanton near the Mine Creek battlefield, was named in honor of the general. Ibid., 185–86, 201.

37. Senator James H. Lane was traveling with McNeil, and during the fighting along Little Osage Creek, he carried a verbal message from McNeil to Pleasonton. Ibid., 177.

CHAPTER 8. LIFE AFTER THE WAR

1. During the short life of his *Chicago Evening Star,* Ellithorpe sniped at Joseph Medill for his opposition to John C. Fremont's proclamation that freed slaves in Missouri and his criticism of Col. James A. Mulligan at the Lexington, Mo., siege in September 1861. Of the Mulligan matter Ellithorpe wrote sarcastically that Medill "could have planned the whole affair, and brought off the troops without the loss of a single man." *Chicago Evening Star,* October 2, 1861; *Proceedings of the Common Council of the City of Chicago* (Chicago: The Council, 1865–66), 289; *Chicago Tribune,* October 2, 1867, December 23 and 24, 1868, Fold3.com.

2. Eleven years later John Lyle King published *Trouting on the Brule River, or Lawyers' Summer-Wayfaring in the Northern Wilderness* (Chicago: Chicago Legal News Co., 1879), a regional classic. Pierce, *History of Chicago,* 2:447; Pierce, *History of Chicago,* 3:8, 360, 395; *Chicago Tribune,* December 23, 1868, Fold3.com; King, *Trouting on the Brule River,* iv–v.

3. *Chicago Tribune,* December 24, 25, 29, 1868, Fold3.com.

4. *Chicago Tribune,* December 25, December 30, 1868, January 1, 1879, March 29, 1891, Fold3.com; A. C. Ellithorpe, *The Chicago Tribune as a Libeler of Men, a Defamer of Women and a Menacer of Courts and Juries* ([Chicago?], 1869 [?]), 1; *Edwards' Sixteenth Annual Directory of the Inhabitants, Manufacturing Establishments and Incorporated Companies of the City of Chicago: Embracing a Complete Business Directory for 1873* (Chicago: Richard Edwards, 1873), 1214; *Cook County, Illinois Marriage and Death Indexes, 1833–1889* (Provo, Utah: Ancestry.com Operations, 2011), Ancestry.com.

5. *The Lakeside Annual Directory of the City of Chicago, Embracing a Complete General and Business*

Directory: 1875–6 (Chicago: Donnelley, Loyd & Co., 1875), 1230; *The Lakeside Annual Directory of the City of Chicago* (Chicago: Donnelley, Loyd & Co., 1878–79), 363; *Chicago Tribune,* September 30, November 3, 1875, September 15, September 28, 1876, May 28, 1879, Fold3.com.

6. Miller, *City of the Century,* 143–44, 159, 178, 302, 304, 314; *Map Showing the Burnt District in Chicago,* 3rd ed., ([Chicago?]: R. P. Studley Co., 1871), accessed September 22, 2014, www.greatchicagofire.org/ruined-city/burnt-district.

7. A. C. Ellithorpe, Improvement in dredging scoops, U.S. Patent 116171, issued June 20, 1871; A. C. Ellithorpe, Improvement in mortar mixing machines, U.S. Patent 116172, issued June 20, 1871; A. C. Ellithorpe and C. Haas, Fire extinguisher and escape tower, U.S. Patent 202009, issued April 2, 1878, *U.S. Patent and Trademark Office Patents, 1790–1909* (Provo, Utah: Ancestry.com Operations, 2008), Ancestry.com; W. Sloane Kennedy, "The Vertical Railway," *Harper's New Monthly Magazine* 65 (November 1882): 888.

8. A. C. Ellithorpe, Improvement in elevators, U.S. Patent 218119, issued August 5, 1879; Improvements in elevators, U.S. Patent 229982, issued July 13, 1880; Safety devise for elevators, U.S. Patent 248150, issued October 11, 1881; Safety devise for hoisting apparatus, U.S. Patent 255956, issued April 4, 1882; Fire escape, U.S. Patent 277891, issued May 22, 1883; Safety devise for elevators, U.S. Patent 376374, issued January 10, 1888; Valve controlling devise for elevator mechanism, U.S. Patent 391597, issued October 23, 1888; Improvements in elevator mechanisms, U.S. Patent 391598, issued October 23, 1888; Piston packing, U.S. Patent 451209, issued April 28, 1891; Lubricator, U.S. Patent 452101, issued May 12, 1891; Safety devise for elevators, U.S. Patent 557117, issued March 31, 1896, *U.S. Patent and Trademark Office Patents, 1790–1909;* A. T. Andreas, *History of Chicago,* vol. 3: *From the Fire of 1871 until 1885* (Chicago: A. T. Andreas Co., 1886), 498–99.

9. Albert Betteley, Air reservoir in elevator shafts, U.S. Patent 23818, issued May 3, 1859, *U.S. Patent and Trademark Office Patents, 1790–1909;* Kennedy, "Vertical Railway," 890, 894.

10. *Chicago Tribune,* October 8, 19, 30, 1879, January 11, 1880, Fold3.com; Kennedy, "Vertical Railway," 894; Andreas, *History of Chicago,* 498–99.

11. *Chicago Tribune,* December 22, 1883, June 11, 1886, November 20, 1887, February 16, 1889, Fold3.com; *Washington (D.C.) Evening Star,* February 26, 1889, April 24, 1901.

12. Warner, *Generals in Blue,* 37–38; Shea, *Fields of Blood,* 287; *Tenth Census of the United States,* 1880, Leavenworth County, Kans., 286; Kip Lindberg and Matt Matthews, "'It Haunts Me Night and Day': The Baxter Springs Massacre," *North & South* 4, no. 5 (June 2001): 42, 44, 48, 50–52.

13. This typed letter possesses many handwritten changes in Ellithorpe's hand. In the interest of readability the version presented in this chapter incorporates his changes but excludes most of the editorial markings denoting deletions, additions, and such.

14. Most editorial markings have also been excised from Gillpatrick's letter.

15. *Chicago Tribune,* March 29, April 17, 1891, Fold3.com; obituary for Mrs. Mariah L. Ellithorpe, undated newspaper clipping, Ellithorpe Family Papers, Kansas Historical Society.

16. *Chicago Tribune,* August 9, 1896, Fold3.com; "Biography," 1–2, 12–13; Pension records on Albert C. Ellithorpe, RG T-288, Invalid Record Application 1033517, National Archives.

17. *Twelfth Census of the United* States, 1900, Cook County, Ill., 13B; Pension records on Albert C. Ellithorpe; Philip Knopf, *Official Proceedings of the Board of Commissioners of Cook County, Illinois for the Year 1899–1900* (Chicago: J.M.W. Jones Stationery & Printing Co., 1900), 858–59; *Chicago Tribune,* January 15, 1901, Fold3.com.

18. *Chicago Tribune*, September 8 and 24, 1901, Fold3.com.

19. Obituary for Albert Chapman Ellithorpe, *Chicago Chronicle*, February 20, 1907, Ellithorpe Family Papers; Carbutt, *Biographical Sketches*, 257. His son, Frederick, moved to Newark, N.J., sometime near the turn of the century and was president of the Ellithorpe Safety Air Cushion Company. He also participated in dramatic elevator tests and received several patents for elevator safety devises. Mitchell C. Harrison, comp., *New York State's Prominent and Progressive Men: An Encyclopedia of Contemporaneous Biography* (New York: New York Tribune, 1902), 3:111; F. T. Ellithorpe, Safety device for elevators, U.S. Patent 527171, issued October 9, 1894, *U.S. Patent and Trademark Office Patents, 1790–1909*.

SELECTED BIBLIOGRAPHY

MANUSCRIPTS

Kansas Historical Society, Topeka

Ellithorpe Family Papers

Nebraska State Historical Society, Lincoln

Robert Furnas Papers

NEWSPAPERS

California

Los Angeles Daily Herald (1874)

Colorado

Daily Rocky Mountain News (1860–61)

Rocky Mountain News (1860–61)

Rocky Mountain News Weekly (1860–61)

Western Mountaineer (1860–61)

District of Columbia

Evening Star (1889, 1901)

Illinois

Chicago Evening Journal (1862–65)

Chicago Evening Star (1861)

Chicago Tribune (1860–1901)

Kansas

Leavenworth Daily Conservative (1861–65)

SELECTED BIBLIOGRAPHY

PUBLIC DOCUMENTS

Hewett, Janet B., Noah Andre Trudeau, and Bryce A. Suderow, eds. *Supplement to the Official Records of the Union and Confederate Armies.* 100 vols. Wilmington, N.C.: Broadfoot Publishing Co., 1994.

National Archives and Records Administration. RG94. Compiled Service Records of Union Volunteers from the State of Kansas, First Indian Home Guards.

———. M234. Letters Received by the Office of Indian Affairs, 1824–81, Southern Superintendency. Reel 834.

———. Pension Records on Albert C. Ellithorpe, RG T-288, Invalid Record Application 1033517.

———. Pension Records on Stephen Wattles, RG T-288, Invalid Record Application 765519.

———. Records of the Army Judge Advocate, Court-Martial Case Files. RG 153. Case MM377—Lt. George W. Dobler.

———. RG94. United States War Department. Records of the Adjutant General's Office. Muster Rolls. First Indian Home Guards.

Official Register of the Volunteer Force of the United States Army for the Years 1861, '62, '63, '64, '65. Pt. 7. Washington, D.C.: Adjutant Generals Office, 1867.

United States Army Department. *Regulations for the Army of the United States.* New York: Harper & Brothers, 1861.

United States Census Bureau. *Eighth Census of the United* States, 1860. Provo, Utah: Ancestry.com Operations, 2005.

———. *Seventh Census of the United* States, 1850. Provo, Utah: Ancestry.com Operations, 2005.

———. *Tenth Census of the United* States, 1880. Provo, Utah: Ancestry.com Operations, 2005.

———. *Twelfth Census of the United* States, 1900. Provo, Utah: Ancestry.com Operations, 2005.

United States Office of Indian Affairs. *Report of the Commissioner of Indian Affairs for the Year 1862.* Washington, D.C.: Government Printing Office, 1863.

United States Patent and Trademark Office. *Patents, 1790–1909.* Provo, Utah: Ancestry.com Operations, 2008.

United States War Department. *War of the Rebellion: A Compilation of the Official Records of the Union and Confederate Armies.* 128 vols. 1880–1901. Reprint, Harrisburg, Pa.: National Historical Society, 1971.

BOOKS

Abel, Annie Heloise. *The American Indian and the End of the Confederacy, 1863–1866.* 1925. Reprint, Lincoln: University of Nebraska Press, 1993.

———. *The American Indian in the Civil War, 1862–1865*. 1919. Reprint, Lincoln: University of Nebraska Press, 1992.

Allardice, Bruce S. *More Generals in Gray*. Baton Rouge: Louisiana State University Press, 1995.

Andreas, A. T. *History of Chicago*. Vol. 3: *From the Fire of 1871 until 1885*. Chicago: A. T. Andreas Co., 1886.

Bailey, Anne J., and Daniel E. Sutherland, eds. *Civil War Arkansas: Beyond Battles and Leaders*. Fayetteville: University of Arkansas Press, 2000.

Banasik, Michael E. *Embattled Arkansas: The Prairie Grove Campaign of 1862*. Wilmington, N.C.: Broadfoot Publishing Co., 1996.

———, ed. *Reluctant Cannoneer: The Diary of Robert T. McMahan of the Twenty-Fifth Independent Ohio Light Artillery*. Unwritten Chapters of the Civil War West of the River. Iowa City: Camp Pope Bookshop, 2000.

Baxter, William. *Pea Ridge and Prairie Grove; Or, Scenes and Incidents of the War in Arkansas*. 1864. Reprint, Fayetteville: University of Arkansas Press, 2000.

Benedict, Bryce D. *Jayhawkers: The Civil War Brigade of James Henry Lane*. Norman: University of Oklahoma Press, 2009.

Berry, Stephen, ed. *Weirding the War: Stories from the Civil War's Ragged Edges*. UnCivil War Series. Athens: University of Georgia Press, 2011.

Boatner, Mark M., III. *The Civil War Dictionary*. New York: David McKay Co., 1959.

———. *Encyclopedia of the American Revolution*. New York: David McKay Co., 1966.

Bollet, Alfred Jay. *Civil War Medicine: Challenges and Triumphs*. Tucson, Ariz.: Galen Press, 2002.

Boskin, Joseph. *Sambo: The Rise and Demise of an American Jester*. New York: Oxford University Press, 1986.

Britton, Wiley. *Memoirs of the Rebellion on the Border, 1863*. 1882. Reprint, Lincoln: University of Nebraska Press, 1993.

Buresh, Lumir F. *October 25th and the Battle of Mine Creek*. Kansas City, Mo.: Lowell Press, 1977.

Burke, W. S. *Official Military History of Kansas Regiments during the War for the Suppression of the Great Rebellion*. 1870. Reprint, Ottawa: Kansas Heritage Press, 1995.

Carbutt, John. *Biographical Sketches of the Leading Men of Chicago*. Chicago: Wilson, Peirce, & Co., 1876.

Castel, Albert. *Civil War Kansas: Reaping the Whirlwind*. Lawrence: University Press of Kansas, 1997.

Christ, Mark K. *Civil War Arkansas, 1863: The Battle for a State*. Norman: University of Oklahoma Press, 2010.

———, ed. *"This Day We Marched Again": A Union Soldier's Account of War in Arkansas and the Trans-Mississippi*. Little Rock: Butler Center for Arkansas Studies, 2014.

Christ, Mark K., and Patrick G. Williams, eds. *I Do Wish This Cruel War Was Over: First-Person Accounts of Civil War Arkansas from the Arkansas Historical Quarterly.* Fayetteville: University of Arkansas Press, 2014.Collins, Robert. *General James G. Blunt: Tarnished Glory.* Gretna, La.: Pelican, 2005.

Crawford, Samuel J. *Kansas in the Sixties.* 1911. Reprint, Ottawa: Kansas Heritage Press, 1994.

Cunningham, O. Edward. *Shiloh and the Western Campaign of 1862.* Edited by Gary D. Joiner and Timothy B. Smith. New York: Savas Beatie, 2007.

Current, Richard N., ed. *Encyclopedia of the Confederacy.* 4 vols. New York: Simon & Schuster, 1993.

Danziger, Edmund Jefferson, Jr. *Indians and Bureaucrats: Administering the Reservation Policy during the Civil War.* Urbana: University of Illinois Press, 1974.

Dungan, J. Irvine. *History of the Nineteenth Regiment Iowa Volunteer Infantry.* Davenport, Iowa: Publishing House of Luse & Griggs, 1865.

Dyer, Frederick H., comp. *A Compendium of the War of the Rebellion.* 2 vols. 1908. Reprint, Dayton, Ohio: Press of Morningside Bookshop, 1979.

Edwards, Whit. *"The Prairie Was on Fire": Eyewitness Accounts of the Civil War in the Indian Territory.* Oklahoma City: Oklahoma Historical Society, 2001.

Edwards, William B. *Civil War Guns: The Complete Story of Federal and Confederate Small Arms.* Secaucus, N.J.: Castle Books, 1978.

Faust, Patricia L. *Historical Times Illustrated Encyclopedia of the Civil War.* New York: Harper & Row, 1986.

Fellman, Michael. *Inside War: The Guerrilla Conflict in Missouri during the American Civil War.* New York: Oxford University Press, 1989.

Fergus, Robert, comp. *Fergus' Directory of the City of Chicago, 1839.* Chicago: Fergus Printing Co., 1876.

Foreman, Grant, ed. *A Traveler in Indian Territory: The Journal of Ethan Allen Hitchcock, Late Major-General in the United States Army.* 1930. Reprint, Norman: University of Oklahoma Press, 1996.

Gaines, W. Craig. *The Confederate Cherokees: John Drew's Regiment of Mounted Rifles.* Baton Rouge: Louisiana State University Press, 1989.

Gause, Isaac. *Four Years with Five Armies: Army of the Frontier, Army of the Potomac, Army of the Missouri, Army of the Ohio, Army of the Shenandoah.* New York: Neale Publishing Co., 1908.

Goins, Charles Robert, and Danney Goble. *Historical Atlas of Oklahoma.* 4th ed. Norman: University of Oklahoma Press, 2006.

Halaas, David Fridtjof. *Boom Town Newspapers: Journalism on the Rocky Mountain Mining Frontier, 1859–1881.* Albuquerque: University of New Mexico Press, 1981.

Hardin, Stephen L. *Texian Iliad: A Military History of the Texas Revolution, 1835–1836.* Austin: University of Texas Press, 1994.

Harrison, Mitchell C., comp. *New York State's Prominent and Progressive Men: An Encyclopedia of Contemporaneous Biography.* New York: New York Tribune, 1902.

Hewitt, Lawrence L., Arthur W. Bergeron Jr., and Thomas E. Schott, eds. *Confederate Generals in the Trans-Mississippi.* Vol. 1: *Essays on America's Civil War.* Knoxville: University of Tennessee Press, 2013.

Hinton, Richard J. *Rebel Invasion of Missouri and Kansas and the Campaign of the Army of the Border against General Sterling Price in October and November 1864.* 1865. Reprint, Ottawa: Kansas Heritage Press, 1994.

History of Tioga, Chemung, Tompkins, and Schuyler Counties, New York with Illustrations and Biographical Sketches of Some of Its Prominent Men and Pioneers. Philadelphia: Everts & Ensign, 1879.

Johnson, W. A. *The History of Anderson County, Kansas, from Its First Settlement to the Fourth of July, 1876.* N.p.: Kauffman & Iler, 1877.

King, John Lyle. *Trouting on the Brule River, Or Lawyers' Summer-Wayfaring in the Northern Wilderness.* Chicago: Chicago Legal News Co., 1879.

Kirkman, Paul. *The Battle of Westport: Missouri's Great Confederate Raid.* Charleston, S.C.: History Press, 2011.

Knopf, Philip. *Official Proceedings of The Board of Commissioners Of Cook County, Illinois for the Year 1899–1900.* Chicago: J.M.W. Jones Stationery and Printing Co., 1900.

Lause, Mark A. *Race and Radicalism in the Union Army.* Urbana: University of Illinois Press, 2009.

Long, E. B. *The Civil War Day by Day.* 1971. Reprint, New York: DaCapo Press, 1985.

Lord, Francis A. *Civil War Collector's Encyclopedia: Arms, Uniforms, and Equipment of the Union and Confederacy.* Secaucus, N.J.: Castle, 1982.

Lowry, Thomas P. *Tarnished Eagles: The Courts-Martial of Fifty Union Colonels and Lieutenant Colonels.* Mechanicsburg, Pa.: Stackpole Books, 1997.

Manning, Edwin Cassander. *Biographical Historical and Miscellaneous.* Cedar Rapids, Iowa: privately printed, 1911.

McGhee, James E. *Guide to Missouri Confederate Units, 1861–1865.* Fayetteville: University of Arkansas Press, 2008.

Miller, Donald L. *City of the Century: The Epic of Chicago and the Making of America.* New York: Simon & Schuster, 1996.

Mullins, Michael A. *The Fremont Rifles: A History of the 37th Illinois Veteran Volunteer Infantry.* Wilmington, N.C.: Broadfoot Publishing Co., 1990.

Nichols, Bruce. *Guerrilla Warfare in Civil War Missouri.* Vol. 1: *1862.* Jefferson, N.C.: McFarland and Co., 2012.

———. *Guerrilla Warfare in Civil War Missouri.* Vol. 2: *1863.* Jefferson, N.C.: McFarland and Co., 2012.

Nichols, David A. *Lincoln and the Indians: Civil War Policy and Politics.* 1978. Reprint, St. Paul: Minnesota Historical Society Press, 2012.

Oliva, Leo E. *Fort Scott: Courage and Conflict on the Border.* Topeka: Kansas State Historical Society, 2008.

Peterson, Richard C., et al. *Sterling Price's Lieutenants: A Guide to the Officers and Organization of the Missouri State Guard, 1861–1865.* Rev. ed. Independence, Mo.: Two Trails Publishing, 2007.

Pierce, Bessie Louise. *A History of Chicago.* Vol. 1: *The Beginning of a City, 1673–1848.* New York: Knopf, 1937.

———. *A History of Chicago.* Vol. 2: *From Town to City, 1848–1871.* New York: Knopf, 1940.

———. *A History of Chicago.* Vol. 3: *The Rise of a Modern City, 1871–1893.* New York: Knopf, 1957.

Piston, William Garrett, and Richard W. Hatcher III. *Wilson's Creek: The Second Battle of the Civil War and the Men Who Fought It.* Civil War America. Chapel Hill: University of North Carolina Press, 2000.

Piston, William Garrett, and Thomas P. Sweeney, M.D. *Portraits of Conflict: A Photographic History of Missouri in the Civil War.* Fayetteville: University of Arkansas Press, 2009.

Proceedings of the Common Council of the City of Chicago. Chicago: Council, 1865–66.

The Rail-Roads, History and Commerce of Chicago. Chicago: Democratic Press Job & Book Steam Printing Office, 1854.

Shea, William L. *Fields of Blood: The Prairie Grove Campaign.* Chapel Hill: University of North Carolina Press, 2009.

Shea, William L., and Earl J. Hess. *Pea Ridge: Civil War Campaign in the West.* Chapel Hill: University of North Carolina Press, 1992.

Sinisi, Kyle S. *The Last Hurrah: Sterling Price's Missouri Expedition of 1864.* Lanham, Md.: Rowman & Littlefield, 2015.

Spencer, John D. *The American Civil War in the Indian Territory.* Long Island, N.Y.: Osprey Publishing, 2009.

Spurgeon, Ian Michael. *Soldiers in the Army of Freedom: The 1st Kansas Colored, the Civil War's First African American Combat Unit.* Norman: University of Oklahoma Press, 2014.

Sutherland, Daniel E. *A Savage Conflict: The Decisive Role of Guerrillas in the American Civil War.* Chapel Hill: University of North Carolina Press, 2009.

Warde, Mary Jane. *When the Wolf Came: The Civil War and the Indian Territory.* Fayetteville: University of Arkansas Press, 2013.

Warner, Ezra J. *Generals in Blue: Lives of the Union Commanders.* Baton Rouge: Louisiana State University Press, 1992.

———. *Generals in Gray: Lives of the Confederate Commanders.* Baton Rouge: Louisiana State University Press, 1999.

Warren, Steven L. *Brilliant Victory: The Second Civil War Battle of Cabin Creek, Indian Territory, September 19, 1864.* Wyandotte, Okla.: Gregath Publishing Co., 2002.

Webster, C. L., III. *Entrepôt: Government Imports into the Confederate States.* Roseville, Minn.: Edinborough Press, 2010.

Winkle, Kenneth J. *The Young Eagle: The Rise of Abraham Lincoln.* Dallas: Taylor Trade Publishing, 2001.

Wood, Larry. *The Two Civil War Battles of Newtonia.* Charleston, S.C.: History Press, 2010.

Woods, James M. *Rebellion and Realignment: Arkansas' Road to Secession.* Fayetteville: University of Arkansas Press, 1987.

Wooster, Ralph A. *Lone Star Regiments in Gray.* Austin: Eakin Press, 2002.

Zellar, Gary. *African Creeks: Estelvste and the Creek Nation.* Norman: University of Oklahoma Press, 2007.

ARTICLES, CITY DIRECTORIES, PAMPHLETS, AND ESSAYS

"13th Illinois Cavalry Regiment." *Illinois in the Civil War.* civilwarillinoisgenweb.org/reg_html/cav_013.html.

Blunt, James G. "General Blunt's Account of His Civil War Experiences." *Kansas Historical Quarterly* 1 (May 1932): 211–65.

Bowen, Nancy Bunker. "An Uncivil Warrior: Missouri's Col. James J. Clarkson." www.chrisanddavid.com/wilsonscreek/JamesClarkson.htm.

Catalogue of the Corporation, Officers and Students of Knox Manual Labor College, Galesburg, Knox County, Ill., for the Year Ending July 2, 1845. Peoria, Ill.: S. H. Davis, Printer, 1845.

Catalogue of the Corporation, Officers and Students of Knox College, Galesburg, Ill., for the Year Ending June 24th, 1846. Peoria, Ill.: S. H. Davis, Printer, 1846.

Danziger, Edmund J., Jr. "The Office of Indian Affairs and the Problem of Civil War Indian Refugees in Kansas." *Kansas Historical Quarterly* 35, no. 3 (1969): 257–75.

Edwards' Sixteenth Annual Directory of the Inhabitants, Manufacturing Establishments and Incorporated Companies of the City of Chicago: Embracing a Complete Business Directory for 1873. Chicago: Richard Edwards, 1873.

Ellithorpe, A. C. *The Chicago Tribune as a Libeler of Men, a Defamer of Women and a Menacer of Courts and Juries.* [Chicago?], 1869 [?].

Evans, Clarence. "Memoirs, Letters, and Diary Entries of German Settlers in Northwest Arkansas, 1853–1863." *Arkansas Historical Quarterly* 6 (Fall 1947): 225–49.

Farb, Robert C. "The Military Career of Robert W. Furnas." *Nebraska History* 32 (March 1951): 18–41.

Foreman, Grant. "Fort Davis." *Chronicles of Oklahoma* 17 (June 1939): 147–50.

Gallagher, Gary W., and Kathryn Shively Meier. "Coming to Terms with Civil War Military History." *Journal of the Civil War Era* 4 (December 2014): 487–508.

Garfield, Marvin H. "The Military Post as a Factor in the Frontier Defense of Kansas, 1865–1869." *Kansas Historical Quarterly* 1 (November 1931): 50–62.

Halpin's Eighth Annual Edition Chicago City Directory, 1865–66. Chicago: T. M. Halpin, Compiler and Publisher, 1865.

Heath, Gary N. "The First Federal Invasion of Indian Territory." *Chronicles of Oklahoma* 44 (Winter 1966–67): 409–19.

Jones, Trevor. "In Defense of Sovereignty: Cherokee Soldiers, White Officers, and Discipline in the Third Indian Home Guard." *Chronicles of Oklahoma* 82 (December 2004): 412–27.

Kennedy, W. Sloane. "The Vertical Railway." *Harper's New Monthly Magazine* 65 (November 1882): 888–94.

Kerber, Linda A. "The Abolitionist Perception of the Indian." *Journal of American History* 62 (September 1975): 271–95.

The Lakeside Annual Directory of the City of Chicago, Embracing a Complete General and Business Directory: 1875–6. Chicago: Donnelley, Loyd & Co., 1875.

The Lakeside Annual Directory of the City of Chicago. Chicago: Donnelley, Loyd & Co., 1878–79.

Lindberg, Kip, and Matt Matthews. "'It Haunts Me Night and Day': The Baxter Springs Massacre." *North & South* 4, no. 5 (June 2001): 42–53.

———. "'To Play a Bold Game': The Battle of Honey Springs." *North & South* 6, no. 1 (December 2002): 56–69.

Palmer, Richard. "Remember the Old Fanning Mill?" www.crookedlakereview.com/articles/101_135/126winter2003/126palmer3.html.

Porter, Kenneth W. "Billy Bowlegs (Holuta Micco) in the Civil War, pt. II." *Florida Historical Quarterly* 45 (April 1967): 391–401.

Rein, Chris. "The U.S. Army, Indian Agency, and the Path to Assimilation: The First Indian Home Guards in the American Civil War." *Kansas History: A Journal of the Central Plains* 36 (Spring 2013): 2–21.

Spence, Clark C., and Robin W. Winks. "William 'Colorado' Jewett of the Niagara Falls Conference." *Historian: A Journal of History* 23, no. 1 (1960): 23–53.

Stith, Matthew M. "'The Deplorable Condition of the Country': Nature, Society, and War on the Trans-Mississippi Frontier." *Civil War History* 58 (September 2012): 322–47.

Zellar, Gary. "First to Fight for Freedom: African Creek Soldiers Enter the Civil War." *Journal of the Indian Wars* 1, no. 4 (2000): 1–20.

———. "Occupying the Middle Ground: African Creeks in the First Indian Home Guard, 1862–1865." *Chronicles of Oklahoma* 76, no. 1 (1998): 48–71.

ELECTRONIC DATABASES

Cook County, Illinois Marriage and Death Indexes, 1833–1889. Provo, Utah: Ancestry.com Operations, 2011.

"Jo Minert's Family Tree." trees.ancestry.com/tree/23988265/person/1528091690?ssrc=.

National Park Service. *Soldiers and Sailors Database.* www.nps.gov/civilwar/soldiers-and-sailors-database.htm.

New Orleans, Passenger Lists, 1813–1945. Provo, Utah: Ancestry.com Operations, 2006.

Springfield-Greene County Library District. *Community & Conflict: The Impact of the Civil War in the Ozarks.* www.ozarkscivilwar.org.

INDEX